STANDING I

THE KATRINA BOOKSHELF

Kai Erikson, Series Editor

In 2005 Hurricane Katrina crashed into the Gulf Coast and precipitated the flooding of New Orleans. It was a towering catastrophe by any standard. Some 1,800 persons were killed outright. More than a million were forced to relocate, many for the remainder of their lives. A city of five hundred thousand was nearly emptied of life. The storm stripped away the surface of our social structure and showed us what lies beneath—a grim picture of race, class, and gender in these United States.

It is crucial to get this story straight so that we may learn from it and be ready for that stark inevitability, *the next time*. When seen through a social science lens, Katrina informs us of the real human costs of a disaster and helps prepare us for the events that we know are lurking just over the horizon. The Katrina Bookshelf is the result of a national effort to bring experts together in a collaborative program of research on the human costs of the disaster. The program was supported by the Ford, Gates, MacArthur, Rockefeller, and Russell Sage Foundations and sponsored by the Social Science Research Council. This is the most comprehensive social science coverage of a disaster to be found anywhere in the literature. It is also a deeply human story.

STANDING IN THE NEED

CULTURE, COMFORT, AND
COMING HOME AFTER KATRINA

KATHERINE E. BROWNE

University of Texas Press

AUSTIN

Requests for permission to reproduce material from this work should be sent to:
Permissions
University of Texas Press
P.O. Box 7819
Austin, TX 78713-7819
http://utpress.utexas.edu/index.php/rp-form

♾ The paper used in this book meets the minimum requirements of
ANSI/NISO Z39.48-1992 (R1997) (Permanence of Paper).

LIBRARY OF CONGRESS CATALOGING-IN-PUBLICATION DATA

Browne, Katherine E., 1953– author.
Standing in the need : culture, comfort, and coming home after Katrina /
Katherine E. Browne. — First edition.
pages cm. — (The Katrina bookshelf)
Includes bibliographical references and index.
ISBN 978-1-4773-0728-1 (cloth : alk. paper)
ISBN 978-1-4773-0737-3 (pbk. : alk. paper)
ISBN 978-1-4773-0738-0 (library e-book)
ISBN 978-1-4773-0739-7 (non-library e-book)
1. Hurricane Katrina, 2005—Social aspects.   2. Disaster victims—
Louisiana—New Orleans—Biography.   3. Refugees—Louisiana—New Orleans—
Social conditions.   I. Title.   II. Series: Katrina bookshelf.
HV636 2005 .N4 B76 2015
976'.0440922—dc23
2015000672
doi:10.7560/307281

*Dedicated to the Peachy Gang and the
entire Johnson-Fernandez family*

It's me, it's me, it's me, O Lord,
Standing in the need of prayer.
It's me, it's me, it's me, O Lord,
Standing in the need of prayer.

—REFRAIN OF AFRICAN AMERICAN
SPIRITUAL OF UNKNOWN ORIGIN

CONTENTS

PREFACE

Working in the aftermath of disaster cuts to the core of what it means to be human. The family I came to know through my eight years of research after Hurricane Katrina taught me precious lessons about life, theirs and mine. Their stamina and courage helped me consider weighty questions about loss, change, belonging, purpose, meaning, well-being, and human nature:

- How do human communities adapt to sweeping, sudden change?
- How do people restitch a ripped social fabric and thread their sense of life's purpose and meaning through the process of recovery?
- What helps people flourish and feel a sense of well-being, and how can that knowledge be integrated into the work of disaster recovery?

Within each of these questions lies a hidden dimension of life that needs fuller excavating: conscious and unconscious cultural commitments. Human nature, in all these regards, cannot be separated from cultural life any more than it can be separated from the natural world. The work of this book is my attempt to demonstrate that idea.

New Orleans is the only American city with a distinctive French Caribbean culture and ethos, and for that reason alone, it always felt to me like an emotional home base. For nearly fifteen years, I had focused my studies in Martinique, French West Indies, an overseas department of France in the eastern Caribbean. When Katrina ripped at the heart of New Orleans and its surrounding parishes, I decided to shift my focus and learn about disaster from African Americans with a similar heritage of plantation slavery and Latin (French and Spanish) colonization.

My research after Katrina began as a film documentary project, one I recruited filmmaker Ginny Martin to help me produce with a grant I had been awarded by the National Science Foundation. *Still Waiting: Life After Katrina* tracks a large African American family that had evacuated from St. Bernard Parish, just southeast of New Orleans, to Dallas, before the storm in late August 2005. Over twenty months, we followed the 155 members of the family to their bayou environment and documented the beginnings of their recovery. The film was first broadcast on PBS stations across the country during the second anniversary of Katrina, August 2007. My research with the family continued for another six years and now, in summer 2014, I have written this book as a witness to the recovery process, from my perspective as an anthropologist.

This story belongs to the family alone, but it is far from unique. Family patterns that cohere with those in the New Orleans area include large kin networks; gatherings centered on homemade Creole and Cajun dishes that feature fresh seafood; personal connections to water (lakes, bayous, the Mississippi River, the Gulf of Mexico); conversation-heavy interaction, even with strangers; a slow pace of life; interest in music; a vital connection to ancestors; and the frequent celebration of holidays that summon involvement in costuming festivity, parades, and/or preparation of specialty foods. The vitality of the natural and cultural environment of the entire New Orleans area holds people together in this place, and—as Katrina demonstrated—they will do their level best to remain there against all odds. Statistics also tell us that more than anywhere else in the United States, people who are born here are likely to die here.

In the bayou family I studied, this attachment to place is nurtured by additional forces that reinscribe a powerful sense of belonging on the bayou—deep family history, loyalty to one's church, easy access to affordable and fresh seafood, and a small-town atmosphere with its relative safety for raising children. Moreover, having so many kin nearby offers the assurance of help with family matters like babysitting and care for the sick. Everyday conversation on ample front porches keeps information flowing. Staying put, however, effectively reduces the possibilities for upward mobility, in part because there are few jobs other than in parish administration or with the oil or gas refineries. It is for this reason that today, most parents encourage their children to get a college education.

This book is intended for interested general readers, for agents of recovery, and for students of disaster. Moreover, students of family may also find this study intriguing. Beyond the inherent value of the story itself, I hope the book might offer three other kinds of value to readers.

LONG-TERM STUDY OF RECOVERY TELLS A MORE COMPLETE PICTURE

My research suggests that by studying the full life cycle of recovery, it is possible to spot unpredictable patterns and uneven tracks of progress. I learned firsthand that recovery is not a linear process but rather a lurching process, sometimes involving major setbacks or complete stalls. As the demands of recovery shift over time, different emotional and material challenges come into view. If I had stopped researching at the end of Year One, for example, I would have written about the strength of collective resolve. If

I had stopped researching at Year Two, I might have written about the vulnerability of a historically resilient kin group when all members experience disaster. If I had stopped researching at the end of Year Three, I would have written about survivors' lives as hostages to bureaucracies. At the end of Year Four, I would likely have written about the individualization of the collective group. At the end of Year Five, I might have written about the shock of a double dunk of grief with the BP oil spill and its impact on the family's bayou environment. And so on. As it is, I am writing about eight years and all of the above. The process has helped clarify for me how, irrespective of the ultimate recovery of routine life, there is no lessening of the struggle it takes to reach that point, or the costs endured along the way.

CULTURAL VALUES AND PRACTICES ARE THE SITE OF COLLECTIVE COMFORT

Academic attempts to understand the human impacts of disaster and the capacities for recovery are not often channeled into analyses of cultural life. Studies of what it takes for a community to demonstrate resilience after disaster have instead remained focused on other qualities: the psychological characteristics of individuals, the composition of their social networks, the local institutions and resources available to communities, the will and work of political leaders. None of these lenses of analysis look to cultural patterns.[1] Studies of community resilience following disaster draw scholars from across the social sciences, yet the work of anthropologists concerned specifically about the role of culture in recovery has struggled to find its voice. By contrast, one of the newest frameworks of disaster studies, known as social vulnerability, has benefited from the ethnographic approach of anthropologists and sociologists alike. Anthropologists such as Tony Oliver-Smith, Susanna Hoffman, Gregory Button, and Melissa Checker have helped advance our understanding of the interaction of cultural norms and structured systems of inequality and the ways these play out in disaster. As these and other vulnerability scholars have made clear, marginalized populations are likely to get disproportionately walloped by a disaster, just as they are disproportionately disadvantaged in the social structure generally.

In the best of times, culture is an elusive concept to get hold of. That is probably why many people pluck out the visible workings of culture and ignore the circulation of meaning (see Figure 21). It is easier to think of the expressions of culture as something concrete, like artifacts that could be displayed in a museum, or costumes people wear on festive occasions. Such common ideas about culture make it hard to imagine why culture should factor into a plan for disaster recovery. Needs following catastrophic loss are universal—food, water, shelter. When people's homes and neighborhoods have been badly damaged or destroyed, who is worried about re-enacting rituals or preparing special food? But as anthropologists point out, "The essence of a culture is not its artifacts, tools, or other tangible cultural elements but how the members of the group interpret, use, and perceive them. It is the values, symbols, interpretations, and perspectives that distinguish one people from another in modernized societies."[2]

THE ORGANIZATION OF RECOVERY FROM DISASTERS COULD BENEFIT FROM CULTURAL KNOWLEDGE

In this book, I hope to demonstrate how anthropological knowledge about cultural needs can offer an essential companion to insights about human vulnerability and collective resilience. Cultural awareness can provide clues about collective comfort, and in this way, provide a clearer path to improving the speed and wholeness of recovery itself.

This is a story shared with me by people I have come to love and respect. For sheer lack of space, it leaves out many voices and many developments and is based purely on what I saw from where I stood. Two implications of my stance as a researcher deserve early mention.

First, a methodological point: an anthropologist undertaking ethnographic research *is* the research instrument by which information is collected, in which it is stored, and through which it is processed. Thus, my own feelings and life experiences, my own class position, family background, education, race, gender, profession, and personal sensibilities all impact the research process and shape my lens of interpretation.

A second, related point concerns my literary style: the closer you get to people in this kind of research, and the longer you spend trying to understand something, the easier it becomes to feel absorbed in their world. Indeed, participant-observation is the central ethnographic method of anthropology. What I experienced in the field became personal, as you will see in my use of the first-person singular. If that adds to this scholarly endeavor a touch of ethnographic memoir, so be it.

ACKNOWLEDGMENTS

For an anthropologist, undertaking a book manuscript typically begins years before the first paragraph materializes on the page. It starts with a research question and a desire to learn from others through long-term field research. There is little about that entire process—from initiating the project to completing the manuscript—that one does without help. As a result, my set of acknowledgments is necessarily long. Even so, I cannot name all the people I feel grateful to. During long days of research in the field, there were people who made my everyday tasks easier—librarians, bookstore clerks, government agents, yoga teachers, musicians. All of them did their work with splendid care, making it possible for me to sustain a positive momentum, freshened by the goodwill and competence of complete strangers.

My biggest debt is to the Johnson-Fernandez family, and especially to the Peachy Gang. They put up with my never-ending questions, probes, phone calls, and evolving kin charts long after the novelty of an interested outsider had passed. Family members indulged these questions, if sometimes with bemusement. The elder sisters, their children and grandchildren, and their nieces and nephews brought me into their conversations and homes. They insisted I eat the delicious food that always seemed to be ready and treated me as a member of the family who did not need an invitation to show up. Their steadfast helpfulness and embrace over these many years have allowed our relationships and affection to blossom in ways I could not have anticipated. I will forever hold this extraordinary family in my heart with love, gratitude, and respect.

I owe special thanks to Connie Tipado for opening her Dallas home to us, for helping secure permission to conduct a study with her large family, and for enthusiastically facilitating the research process in the Dallas phase of this work.

Outside the family, I want to thank several people in the parish who were especially helpful: Junior Rodriguez kept an open door for me, both during the time he was parish president and as a former president busy with many other projects; Father Luke and Trudy Mackles at Our Lady of Lourdes; Cynthia and Scott Giroir; Sylvia Guillot; and Tony and Roselyn Fernandez provided help and hospitality. Bill Hyland, parish historian, provided historical details and context. Sister Frances Duos offered me lodging, friendship, and insights from her years with St. Bernard Project.

Every professor has special students who reinforce the pleasure of an academic path. Many gifted graduate students helped me in critical ways through this process, and I want to thank them for their superb work and support. John McGreevy conducted a month of parish fieldwork, did GIS mapping, and helped code interviews; Aziza Bayou helped in the field with kin-chart revisions and photo collection; Maureen McNamara conducted comprehensive secondary research about FEMA; Anne Reeder built skillfully on Maureen's work; Kristy Glenn helped me locate answers from institutional authorities in the Gulf Coast area; Emily Thorn helped code interviews; and Trevor Even offered insights from his own thesis studies in disaster. I also want to thank the undergraduate students who contributed to this work: Cathy Smith helped input kinship data into mapping software; Heather Baily conducted parish-level archival research; Leigha Bohn helped format photographs and text; and many students transcribed my interviews, including Kate Girdler, Heather Baily, Jessica Lenderts, Crystal Antonio, Cathy Smith, and Brittany Holzworth.

My research was star-kissed to have a particular person enter my life at just the right time: Martha Ward, a fellow anthropologist and longtime professor at the University of New Orleans, was someone I met soon after Katrina. Martha's knowledge and practical wisdom pierced layers of local complexity and contradiction, and it seemed fated that she became my intellectual spirit guide through the messy, exuberant world of New Orleans. No one could have mentored me better. She also became a dear friend. Her contributions to my life and my work belong to a unique category.

Other scholars in New Orleans provided valuable assistance: Zarus Watson, mental health counseling professor at the University of New Orleans; Raphael Cassimere, UNO historian of black studies; Shirley Laska, emeritus professor of sociology at UNO, and Pam Jenkins, professor of sociology at UNO. I thank each of them for their rich insights that helped expand my understanding of the local social and physical environment, and post-Katrina realities.

I also want to thank a number of technical scholars and librarians from the New Orleans region who provided superb assistance with imagery and maps, including Brady Couvillion and Holly Beck from the US Geological Survey (USGS) National Wetlands Research Center; Steven Darwin and Anne Bradburn at the Tulane University Herbarium; Lowell Urbatsch, professor of biology and Herbarium director at Louisiana State University; and Jessica Lacher-Feldman and Judy Bolton, in Special Collections at LSU Libraries.

On several occasions I had the good fortune to meet with Carol Stack, anthropologist, whose work about African American families inspired my own. Her advice and encouragement are embedded in this work. I also want to thank Julia Offen, whose narrative ethnography workshop at the annual anthropology meetings helped launch me on the storytelling approach to this study.

During the writing phase, a critical source of help came from novelist and creative-writing professor Charlie Smith, to whom I extend heartfelt thanks. Charlie's patient reading of chapters in development and his keen sense of character and flow helped me shape and sharpen the story line of the book. In addition, I am immensely grateful to each of the readers of the full manuscript who saw some version of this work. Their insightful comments provided vital feedback for improving the manuscript: Ellen Durkee, Rachel Gwin, Louis Gwin, Lori Peek, Martha Ward, Susanna Hoffman, and Kate Hawthorne. I also thank the outside reviewers I do not know for their very helpful comments.

I thank Chris Richardson for his brilliant work to help me produce graphics that enhance the value of the text. In the category of professional support, I also wish to thank Dave Hamrick's outstanding team at the University of Texas Press: Robert Devens shepherded this book with expert care and aplomb; Robert Kimzey brought calm and immense skill to managing this project; Sarah Rosen and Kaila Wyllys provided vital and timely professional support; Michele Wynn handled copyediting with exquisite care and precision; Sandra Spicher redefined the art of creating an index; Lindsay Starr brought creative excellence to the book's layout and cover design; and Ellen McKie's entire design and production team helped assure a top-quality publication. A dream team I had. I also thank Ginny Martin, gifted filmmaker, with whom I produced the documentary film about this family, *Still Waiting: Life After Katrina*.

Not long after Katrina devastated the Gulf Coast, Professor Kai Erikson envisioned the Katrina Bookshelf. He rounded up grants to enable the authors of his vision to come together a number of times to update each other on their research. Now, he has brought this outrageously ambitious vision to fruition. It is fitting that someone of Kai's stature and reputation for disaster scholarship has led this effort, and I am grateful to him for inviting me to be part of this stellar group of scholars. Kai has pored over each of our manuscripts and shared with each author a set of comments that reflect his inimitable clarity, humor, wisdom, and practicality.

My research has been supported by two grants from the National Science Foundation, (Awards No. 0555146 and No. 1049048), and I thank Cultural Anthropology Program officers Deb Winslow and Jeff Mantz for their ongoing encouragement and support. I also thank Colorado State University for numerous small grants that helped support portions of the research. My department of anthropology has provided a collegial environment, and our chair, Mica Glantz, has been an inspired and supportive leader.

Finally, to the personal support team around me, I owe unimaginable thanks. My parents, Donna and Leland Browne, have always been and remain my hearty cheerleaders. My siblings and larger family live at the ready with support and help. I am especially grateful to my sister, Becky Browne, who has not only kept abreast of this work all along but also, without blinking, set aside her own career demands to make two critical trips to help me capture photos and video of the family. At home, Karen Dickey has helped take charge of Louie Peppercorn on countless occasions, and her willing, gracious nature has been instrumental in my ability to complete this book. I also want to give special thanks to Carla Rudiger, an extraordinary teacher whose body-mind centering approach to yoga has deeply enhanced my life and influenced the heart-forward nature of my work. Lori Peek has been a treasured friend and steady support through the years of this project, from the first post-Katrina National Science Foundation grant we got shortly after meeting in 2005. Lori's friendship and her scholarly contributions to my thinking always come delivered with joy and a brightness of spirit that enrich my work and my life immeasurably.

The most special person in my life has also provided constant and important help during this project. My life partner, Jane DeHart Albritton, is my biggest champion. For decades and in the long course of this latest project, she has helped me slow down, remember to breathe, and think with all my senses. She has shared her agile intellect to help me make good decisions that honor the family and the interests of this research. And if all that weren't enough, she has been my editor-in-residence, helping bring this work to a level I could not have achieved without her.

FIGURES

IMAGE CREDITS

All graphic materials are original and copyrighted by Katherine Browne unless otherwise specified.

1. Katherine Browne took all photographs unless otherwise noted.
2. Additional photo credits:
   a. Julian Gothard (Figure 13): gator; bayou (Figure 33): turtle
   b. Chuck Rhode (Figure 13): cypress swamp
   c. Christian Åslund (Figure 17): devastation
   d. Ginny Martin (Figure 18): Connie's back; paperwork
   e. FEMA Trailer floor plan (Figure 25): redrawn to scale from the plans for a Gulf Stream Cavalier, a typical FEMA travel trailer model
   f. Faces of family (Figure 35): family members provided a number of the small photos used on this final page.
3. Iris watercolor (Figure 34): Iris fulva Ker-Gawl by Margaret Stones, *Native Flora of Louisiana Watercolor Drawings*, E. A. McIlhenny Natural History Collection, LSU Libraries Special Collections.

STANDING IN THE NEED

People

Women in the Family

"Peachy" Johnson James	(1909-1984), Alma, mother of the Peachy Gang
Cynthia Winesbury	Peachy's eldest daughter, mother of three
Katie Williams	Peachy's third daughter, mother of five
Roseana Maurice	Peachy's fourth daughter, mother of four
Audrey Brown	Peachy's youngest daughter, mother of four
Roz King	Katie's oldest daughter
Nell Rosebud	Katie's second daughter
Janice Tambrella	Cynthia's daughter
Melanie Bienemy	Audrey's third daughter
Connie Tipado	Peachy's granddaughter (Sherman's daughter) who lives in Dallas
Robin James	Peachy's granddaughter (Sherman's daughter) who lives in Violet, La.

Fig. 01   xx

Men in the Family

Gray Eye (Leroy Sr.) Williams — Katie's husband

Buffy (Gregory) James — Peachy's grandson (Raymond's son) who stayed during the storm

Potchie Smith — Peachy's grandnephew (Davis's grandson)

Earl Rosebud — married to Nell, Katie's daughter

Turb (Leroy Jr.) Williams — Katie's firstborn son

Mr T (Terrance) Maurice — second son of Roseana, local party DJ

Parish Notables

Pastor Raymond Smith — pastor of First Baptist Church in Verret

Junior Rodriguez — parish president (2004–2008), Isleño descent, family friend and neighbor in Verret

Outside the Parish

Martha Ward, Ph.D. — anthropologist and professor at University of New Orleans

Zarus Watson, Ph.D. — mental health counseling professor at University of New Orleans

Lolis Elie — journalist and filmmaker based in New Orleans

The Johnson-Fernandez Family
(Simplified)

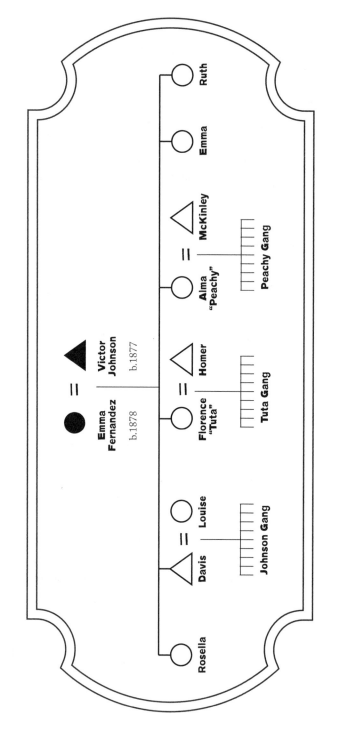

Fig. 02

xxii

The **Peachy** Gang
(Simplified)

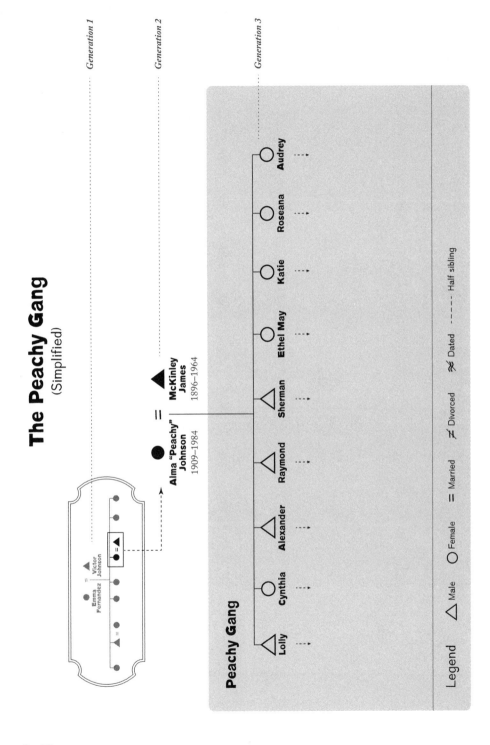

Fig. 03

xxiii

Lolly's Branch
(Simplified)

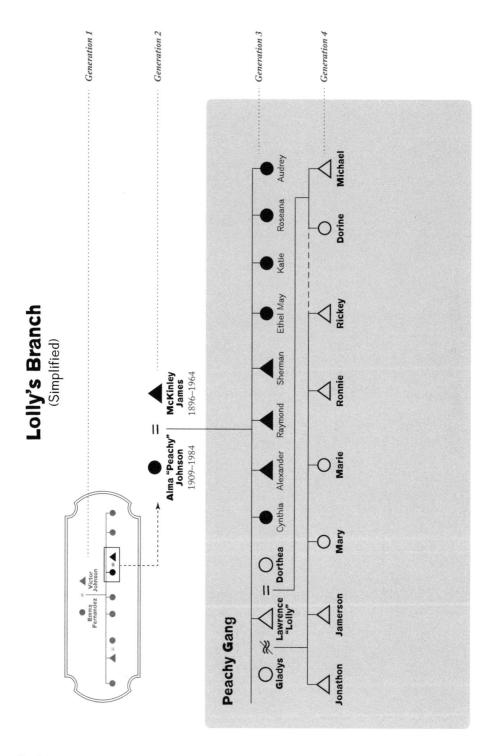

Fig. 04

xxiv

Cynthia's Branch

(Simplified)

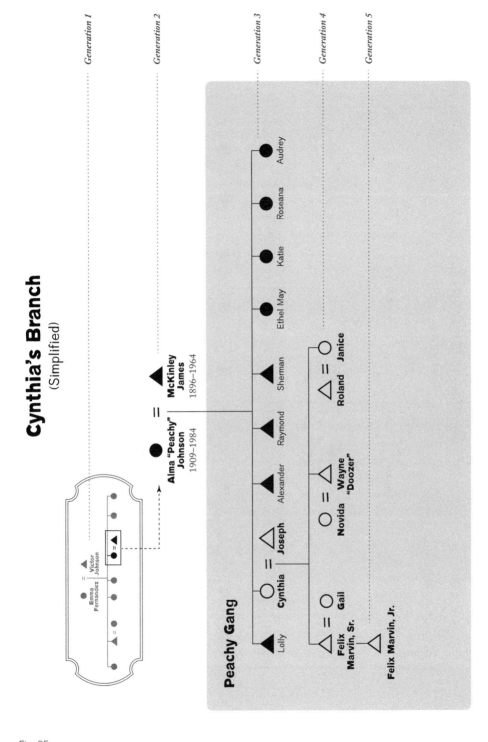

Fig. 05

xxv

Raymond's Branch
(Simplified)

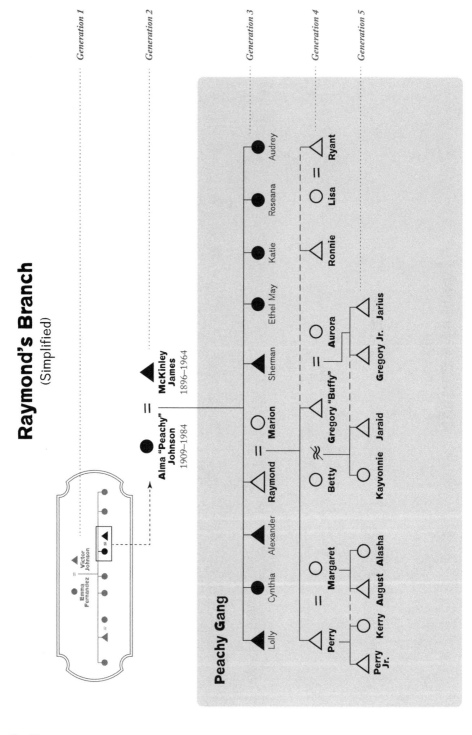

Fig. 06

xxvi

Sherman's Branch

(Simplified)

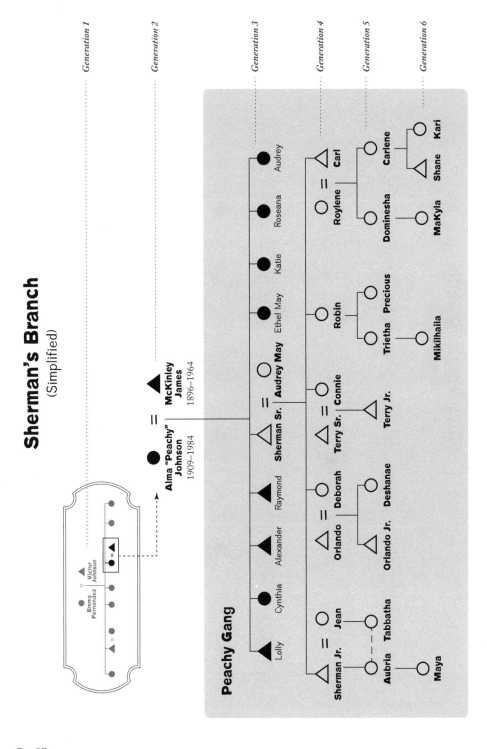

Fig. 07

Ethel May's Branch
(Simplified)

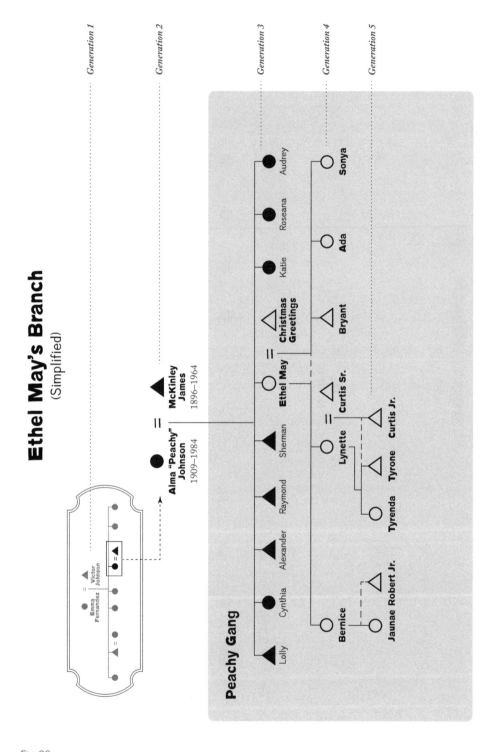

Fig. 08

xxviii

Katie's Branch

(Simplified)

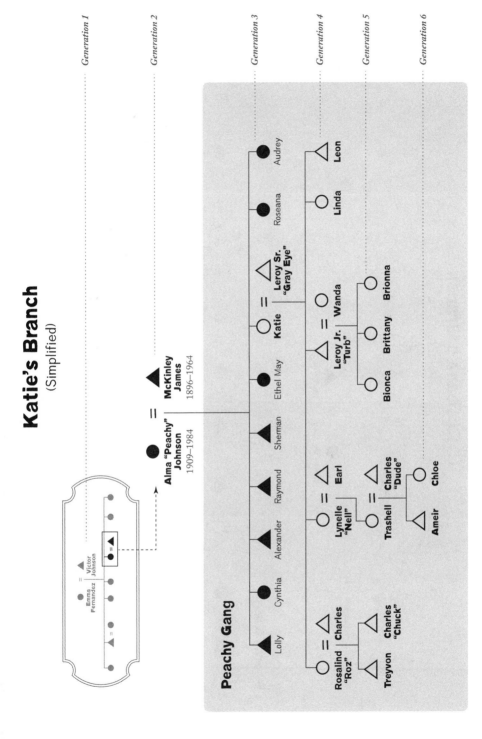

Fig. 09

xxix

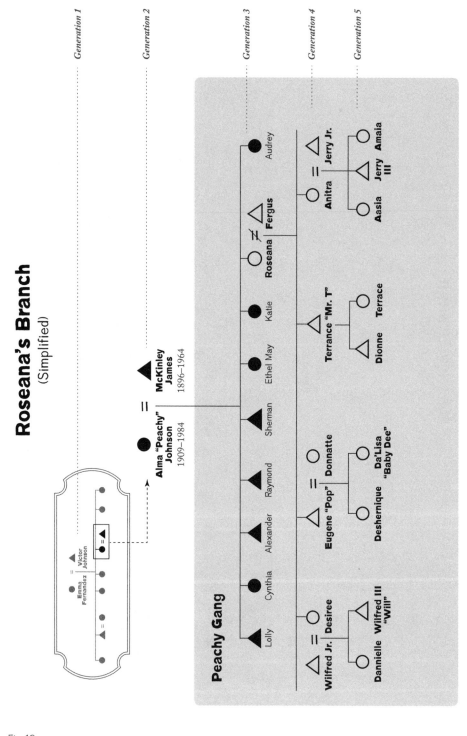

Roseana's Branch
(Simplified)

Fig. 10

xxx

Audrey's Branch
(Simplified)

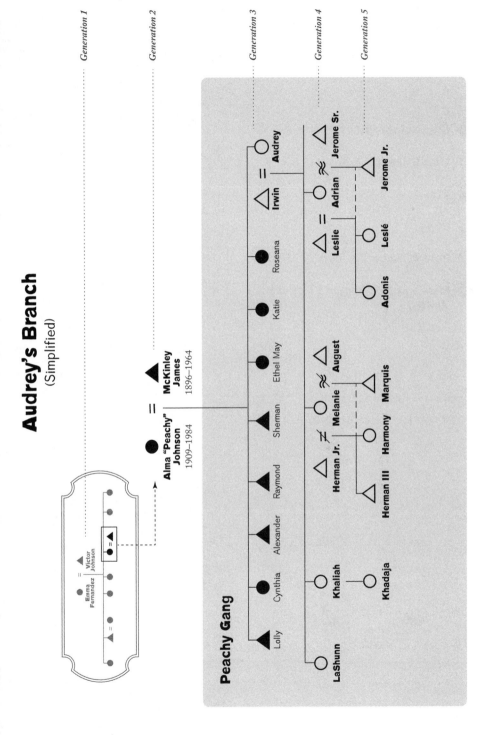

Fig. 11

Places

The most watery parish in Louisiana, St. Bernard was the only parish to have been completely drowned by Katrina.

① **Mississippi River**

② **New Orleans**

③ **Violet**

④ **Verret**

⑤ **Boundaries of St. Bernard Parish**

⑥ **Mississippi River Gulf Outlet (MRGO)**

Lake Ponchartrain

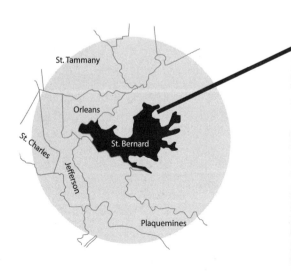

St. Tammany

Orleans

St. Charles

Jefferson

St. Bernard

Plaquemines

Fig. 12

Source: USGS LandSAT for Lousianna
Image taken 2011

Lake
Borgne

Gulf of Mexico

The brown pelican, state bird of Louisiana, makes its home on the bayou.

The environment of lower St. Bernard Parish

Gators glide through the bayous and swamps and sometimes end up as dinner.

Cypress swamps once dominated the landscape, providing refuge for slaves and trees for the timber industry.

Great blue herons live off the bounty of the bayou.

Fig. 13

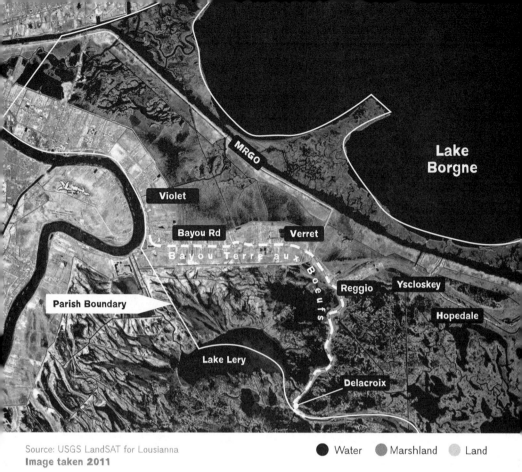

Violet

MRGO

Lake Borgne

Bayou Rd

Verret

Bayou Terre aux

Boeufs

Reggio

Yscloskey

Hopedale

Parish Boundary

Lake Lery

Delacroix

Source: USGS LandSAT for Lousianna
Image taken 2011

● Water ● Marshland ● Land

The historic lower parish and disappearing land

At the time the family rhizome took root on slave plantations near Verret on Bayou Terre aux Boeufs, a substantial hurricane buffer stood between them and the open waters of the Gulf.

Since 1930, Louisiana has lost 1,883 square miles of coastal lands, including protective wetlands and swamps.

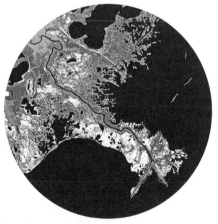

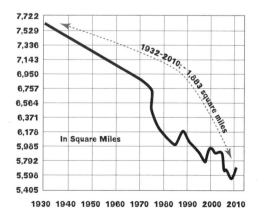

1932-2010: -1,883 square miles

In Square Miles

7,722
7,529
7,336
7,143
6,950
6,757
6,564
6,371
6,178
5,985
5,792
5,598
5,405

1930 1940 1950 1960 1970 1980 1990 2000 2010

Fig. 14   White areas indicate land lost between 1932 and 2010

Source of landloss map and chart data: USGS

INTRODUCTION

Scattered across hundreds of miles of coastal and wetland areas of southeast Louisiana, the wild red iris bows gently with the coastal breezes. Its coppery blooms with lush red inner margins and tall green stalks are right at home in this environment of grasses, shrubs, and cypress trees with knees that spike up out of the water. Long before people arrived, iris plants of many hues spread their rootstock in all directions. Like other native rhizome plants, their growth habit helps bind the soil and protect the wetlands from erosion. The rhizome requires no pollination or germination; it is self-sustaining, hardy, and enduring.

The story that unfolds here involves a human rhizome, a large family rooted to the same bayou in southeast Louisiana. The family shares a life source, has endured the greatest tribulations, and brings beauty and stability to the environment. In August 2005, members of the family faced violent change, and despite the strength of their rhizome and its rootedness to place, it wasn't clear for years whether their special lives in the bayou environment would recover.

Hurricane Katrina tore into the Gulf Coast, bringing fright and ruin and heartbreak. It ripped open the collective American psyche and, for a brief moment, left a void. That space within fresh disaster is quiet and terrifying, and in the stillness we glimpse the human condition of impermanence.

Those people enduring the shock and grief of the disaster needed every possible comfort. They needed every shred of understanding about what would help restore their lives. Instead, the system deployed to secure their recovery and help them heal piled on new hardships and, in the years to come, increased the suffering of survivors and prolonged the time it took them to get their lives back in order.

The chapters that follow chronicle the lives of this family and the shifting terms of their ordeal over the course of eight years. From them, I learned how material loss merges into the pain of the heart. I learned about their sense of belonging and comfort, where these come from, how they matter in wretched situations, and how living without them created a social pain that was largely unnecessary. The time required to move from ruins to a rebuilt community took more years than anyone expected, and the recovery cost more lives and created more hurt than anyone imagined possible. But the people whose story I tell do not think of themselves as victims. However mistreated they were, they maintained a sense of dignity and humanity.

That dignity is conveyed in the book's title, drawn from the African American spiritual "Standing in the Need of Prayer." The lyrics evoke circumstances that are beyond any individual's ability to overcome: precisely the situation this family encountered during the recovery. The deepest hurts of human life, it seems to say, can only be lifted by giving in to the vulnerability of being human and reaching out to a higher power for relief. As with the family's own communal form of life, this individual articulation of need occurs in the midst of a black congregation in which the collection of voices rises to create a whole, unified plea for help.

This story takes shape in three waves. "Part I: Shock Wave" follows the family members' evacuation to Dallas and the adaptations they made to life away from home. Connie Tipado, the Dallas relative, becomes a critical intermediary and a model for what I came to see as the key to recovery success.

"Part II: Wave of Trouble" begins as family members return to their home environment, where the brief honeymoon period transitions into months and then years of hardship caused by institutional approaches to recovery. In the absence of an advocate, cultural divides between the family's way of life and the demands imposed by outsiders in charge become the real source of heartache.

"Part III: Wave of Reckoning" identifies the terms of resolution, and its costs.

I

SHOCK WAVE

1

WHEN THEY SAY GO

"They kept coming. They just kept coming," Connie Tipado said with a worried giggle as she summoned us to enter her home in early October 2005, a few weeks after the storm. Barely through the door, I got a glimpse of my future. Filmmaker Ginny Martin and I became part of a noisy living room animated by dozens of conversations and children dashing about. The names Cynthia, Katie, Roseana, and Audrey echoed through a rush of introductions and then dissolved back into a universe of voices and faces. I had high hopes that many of Connie's relatives would want to participate in our film documentary project.[1] She had already gotten their approval, but which ones would want to talk with us? What would our story be? I had no idea what to expect that day when we pulled up to Connie's house in a semirural area about thirty minutes from downtown Dallas. The two-story powder-blue residence with fresh white trim was a storybook home in Folk Victorian style, with a covered second-story balcony and an optimistic bearing. Only later, on our first trip to St. Bernard Parish, would I realize how strikingly different this Texas home was from family homes on the bayou.

Before I even knew Connie existed, my National Science Foundation grant proposal to research post-Katrina impacts had focused on a single question: how does a large black family from New Orleans recover from disaster? That question took up three angles of interest: African American families, disaster, and culture. I had not plucked this question out of thin air. From fifteen years of research in the French Caribbean, I knew that large Afro-Creole families were the norm, irrespective of their socioeconomic resources. The same rooted families were commonplace in an area scholars recognize as the northern outpost of the French Caribbean—New Orleans. Moreover, in the 1970s, anthropologist Carol Stack had documented how African Americans used their kin networks to help them absorb economic risk and instability by spreading out modest resources across the entire group.[2] Stack's groundbreaking work had inspired me to wonder how a large African American family with modest resources would manage in the face of a catastrophe.

Then there was the fact that Katrina and the storm's conspirators had drowned a city I loved. Hurricane Katrina introduced a research urgency to grasp the scale of hurt unknown in the modern history of the United States. At first, I wasn't sure how I could contribute, but the more I paged through existing studies of disaster impacts, the more I could see that the cultural dimensions of recovery had gone insufficiently recognized. The role of culture in recovery would be my lens, and the documentary film provided an ideal chance to capture these ideas and share them with a broad audience.

Our search for an African American family impacted by Katrina led us to Connie in Dallas and the 155 members of her family who had evacuated there.[3] Meeting them raised more research questions: Did the family's dense relationships to each other buffer the blow, or did the blow hurt them worse? How could their story help explain other stories of disaster?

By the time we arrived at Connie's home, everyone we met there knew the unthinkable had happened: the storm had wrecked the homes and swept away the belongings of every single member of the family living in the parish.

Here is how it all began.

THE STORM ARISES

Katrina formed quietly enough as Tropical Depression Twelve close to the Bahamas on Tuesday, August 23, 2005. By Wednesday morning, August 24, Tropical Depression Twelve had gotten stronger, strong enough to qualify as a tropical storm and get a name instead of a number.

By early Thursday evening, August 25, Tropical Storm Katrina had centralized in the Atlantic Ocean, gathering enough power to earn a new title: Hurricane Katrina. Wielding Category 1 winds of 80 m.p.h., Hurricane Katrina smashed into South Florida, snapping tree limbs, ripping off shingles and gutters, dismantling power systems, and killing six people. Florida returned the favor by sapping Katrina's strength and demoting the hurricane back to a tropical storm.

Then Katrina veered west, into the warm waters of the Gulf of Mexico. The storm refueled and reclaimed its status as Hurricane Katrina. By 2:00 p.m. Friday, August 26, the National Hurricane Center identified the hurricane as a new Category 2 storm with 96–110 m.p.h. winds. Meteorologists revised their projections for the path of the hurricane: it was now headed straight for the Gulf Coast of Louisiana and Mississippi. Both Governor Kathleen Blanco of Louisiana and Governor Hayley Barbour of Mississippi immediately declared states of emergency.

By 11:00 p.m. that Friday, energized by Gulf water heat, Hurricane Katrina had intensified. The National Hurricane Center reported that by the time Hurricane Katrina reached the central area of the Gulf, it would likely form a "major" hurricane—a Category 3, 4, or 5.

By 8:00 a.m. on Saturday, August 27, while twenty members of Connie's bayou family were enjoying a regular Saturday breakfast of fish and grits in lower St. Bernard Parish, Hurricane Katrina was churning into a more powerful, Category 3 storm just 435 miles southeast of the mouth of the Mississippi River, five hundred miles from family homes in the parish. Forecasters began to express concern about the storm's potential to cause grave damage to southeast Louisiana.

RUNNING BEFORE THE STORM

Katie Williams recalled that she was spooning up her second helping of sister Audrey Brown's buttered grits. As was their custom, family members had gathered that Saturday morning at the home of their sister Cynthia Winesbury.

"Hmmm," Katie said, registering the rising winds on such a clear day. It wasn't time to make a move just yet, but Katie and her sisters were cautious. Their parish was vulnerable, jutting out into Gulf waters on two sides and flanked by the Mississippi on another. When it came to hurricanes, holing up at home on the bayou wasn't the kind of risk that members of the family were willing to take. If Henry "Junior" Rodriguez, the president of St. Bernard Parish, called people to evacuate, that's just what they'd do. It didn't matter that the drill took time and cost money, or that abruptly leaving town upset the rhythm of everyday life. It's what they did.

In recent years, though, there had been a higher than usual number of warnings. False alarms carried a kind of good news, but evacuation had started to feel like an exercise that left everyone weary. The Gulf Coast hurricane season is long—spanning half the year, from June 1 through November 30. In a typical season, one hundred or so disturbances in the Gulf of Mexico, Atlantic Ocean, and Caribbean Sea carry hurricane potential. But on average, only ten become tropical storms, and only two churn into hurricanes that strike the United States. Usually the odds seemed in their favor, but this time there had been talk in the news about "the big one," the possibility of a hurricane that could destroy the whole region. So as the days turned into late August, closer to the peak hurricane month of September, the family kept an ear to the news and an eye to the sky.

Cynthia's house, just down the street from the home of her sister Roseana Maurice, was located in the lower-parish village of Verret. It was always open for company, but Saturdays were reserved for a breakfast of speckled trout and grits, sausage, biscuits, and eggs. For years, Katie's daughter Nell had taken the lead in cooking, but all the sisters of Katie's generation helped, and they prepared enough for dozens. Most of the time, you'd find a line of cars and thirty or forty people enjoying the morning together. The family ritual had been in place for so many years, no one remembered when it began.

The four sisters—Cynthia, Katie, Roseana, Audrey—sat together on the front porch, waiting for everyone to serve themselves before they fixed their own plates. Soon, the front porch rockers and every plastic chair dotting the side yard had been claimed; some people preferred eating inside in the small, but air-conditioned, living and dining rooms. Inside and out, three generations of family balanced the bounty of a fresh bayou breakfast on their laps, circulating stories and talk of weather. Like almost every other family gathering except holidays and special occasions, women outnumbered men, and children animated the action.

Not so long ago, Verret had been the place that everyone in the family recognized as home. Alma "Peachy" Johnson James—the woman whose descendants called themselves the "Peachy Gang"—had raised nine children there,[4] most of whom had also grown up in the tiny village, no more than a mile long and half a mile wide. But today, there were only a few dozen homes, the historic Baptist church, and the small fire station left to define the village. The three sisters who lived there helped keep Verret alive with all the gatherings they hosted, and the church had locked in long-standing and widespread loyalty among the lower parish's black population. Though less than a hundred residents, Verret remained a vital place.

Verret was the last village inside the levee system, the other side of which led quickly to the vast expanse of wetlands and marshes, mostly uninhabited, that constituted the "lowest" part of the lower one-third of the parish. These watery lands ultimately opened into the Gulf of Mexico. From Cynthia's house, it was only a fifteen-minute drive through rural bayou country to the few small settlements that lay outside the levees: to the south, there was Delacroix Island, long known as "the end of the road"; to

Sisters

In 2005, the four sisters, members of the oldest generation of the Peachy Gang, evacuated to Dallas.

Cynthia Winesbury

Katie Williams

Roseana Maurice

Audrey Brown

Fig. 15

the east, Yscloskey and Hopedale, located near the shores of Lake Borgne (see Figure 14).

Residents of these unprotected villages were almost all white and Catholic, and some still spoke Spanish like their ancestors. These Isleños had settled here about 230 years earlier, having come from the Canary Islands at the invitation of the Spanish colonists who needed more Spanish speakers to populate the area. A few had married Indians, and some had mixed with French-speaking Cajuns. Isleños had shaped their livelihoods around fishing and trapping and had over time become suppliers for New Orleans fish markets and the city's restaurants. Fresh crab and shrimp, oysters and crawfish, and dozens of varieties of fresh fish came off their boats. Many in the lower parish who didn't fish for a living bought their seafood directly from the docks and trucks of these same fishers.

That August 27, the sisters stayed for more conversation after the other family members had headed back up the road to Violet, a fifteen-minute drive toward the city of New Orleans, where most of the family lived. Compared to the rural flavor of areas like Verret farther down the road, Violet offered more housing and suburban-style neighborhoods, more choices of black churches, a ball field where black baseball leagues played weekly, and closer proximity to nearby schools and to better jobs in the upper parish and the city beyond. Violet's population before the storm numbered 8,555 residents, 39 percent of whom were black, 58 percent of whom were white. Violet's black residents constituted two-thirds of all blacks in the parish.[5]

"We knew the storm was getting bad after we got home from my nanny's house that Saturday morning," said Nell Rosebud, Katie's daughter. Cynthia was Nell's aunt and her "nanny," her godmother. "So we were looking at the news and calling each other. Everybody said, 'OK, we need to get together and figure out what we're going to do.'"

TV news announced that at 10:00 that morning, the entire metropolitan area of New Orleans had been placed under a hurricane warning. A "warning" was much more serious than a "watch": it meant something was expected to happen within twenty-four hours. The city of New Orleans had not issued an order to evacuate, but the warning prompted three of the surrounding parishes—St. Charles, St. Tammany, and Plaquemines—to announce mandatory evacuations for their residents. St. Bernard Parish issued a voluntary evacuation, but its lower-parish residents were urged to leave.[6] At the same time, Ray Nagin, mayor of New Orleans, spoke at a news conference indicating that in the interest of allowing people from low-lying areas to evacuate first, he would call for an evacuation of city residents later, once the expected landfall was within thirty hours. "This is not a test," said

Nagin. "This is the real deal. Things could change, but as of right now, New Orleans is definitely the target for this hurricane."[7]

Nell and her daughter, Trashell, used the Internet to figure out what direction they should go if they had to leave: Dallas with higher ground to the west. Family there. Done.

It's quick work to spread news in a big family accustomed to living connected lives. Barely having digested their fish-and-grits breakfast, Trashell and her mother began calling, and within minutes, calls between cousins and aunts and uncles buzzed in every direction. The buzz was not about whether to leave, but about which way to go.

"Where you going? You want to follow us? We going for Dallas." Before this hurricane named Katrina could make landfall, the four sisters and almost all their kids and grandkids had a plan. Cousin Connie lived in a big house just outside the city of Dallas, and she encouraged them to come.

In Katie's caravan, there were eight vehicles packed to capacity with people and a couple of days' worth of provisions. These vehicles included three SUVs and a seventeen-passenger van that Katie's youngest sister, Audrey, drove for her job with the Area Council on Aging, as well as passenger cars. Everybody else would meet up in Dallas.

But while each group was getting its vehicles and passengers assembled, Nell's husband, Earl, announced he saw no point in leaving and retreated to the bathroom for an unhurried shower. As the designated driver of his in-laws' SUV, he got to decide. Everyone knew about his lackadaisical attitude toward hurricanes. Earl wasn't from the parish. He had married Nell some ten years earlier, and he wasn't so sure he wanted to just fall in line with the decision of others. He preferred to think things over for himself. But he was up against a collective habit that would not yield to one individual's need for control. Katie's brothers and sisters had socialized the younger set with the family mantra, "When they say go, we go."[8]

"C'mon, Earl," Katie said, exasperated. "We got to go, everybody waiting on you."

Katie knew who the white parish politicians were, and Lynn Dean, former parish president,[9] was one of the few who had earned her trust. "Look," Katie told Earl, "when I turned on the TV, Lynn Dean was saying, 'Get out of town, get out of town.' And gosh, if Lynn Dean says get out of town, baby, it's time to go."

Hours later, Earl relented. They would drive all night and get to Dallas by Sunday morning.

There was a reason the family didn't mess around when it came to hurricanes. Katie and her sisters had run from some bad storms when they were younger, and now that they were the elders, their views prevailed. The hurricane they remembered best was Betsy, forty years before. In September 1965, when Katie was twenty-three years old, Hurricane Betsy slammed the New Orleans area. Cynthia, the oldest living member of the Peachy Gang, then thirty-three, described the damage Betsy did to the lower-parish areas of Verret. In the house she and her husband had been building, "the water came up to the windows," she said. The house nearby where Peachy, Cynthia's mother, lived was ruined. Yet, ironically, Verret was not hit as hard as some areas farther inland from the Gulf. Parts of both the upper parish and the city of New Orleans got hammered because of the ten-foot surges that shoved their way up both the Mississippi River and the brand-new shipping canal that ran parallel to it, the Mississippi River Gulf Outlet (MRGO, known as "Mister GO"). The damage exceeded $1 billion for the first time in the history of any US disaster, earning the storm a memorable nickname: Billion Dollar Betsy. Betsy roused action for a more comprehensive system of levees, including flood protection for the lower parish.[10]

By late afternoon that Saturday, August 27, virtually every member of the family was en route to higher ground. They had plenty of company on the road. Traffic analyses showed that the highest volume of vehicles leaving the city left that same day and early on Sunday. But if the roadways were clogged, there were no major accidents, and getting out of town had been smoother than anyone expected. Traffic engineers credited the success of new transportation planning strategies begun because of evacuation problems during Hurricane Georges in 1998, the first major evacuation in the area in the preceding twenty years. Six years after Georges, in 2004, warnings about Hurricane Ivan brought the next major evacuation. Planners tried out a contraflow, lane-reversal traffic idea, and that experience then got folded into a revised plan that was ready by summer 2005. These new strategies included staged evacuations, beginning with residents from the lowest-lying areas; designating portions of roadways for contraflow to increase outbound capacity; and routing traffic onto lesser arteries so that the freeways were not overwhelmed. During Katrina, those strategies worked, making the evacuation of the area the most successful in US history.[11]

Family members evacuated to different destinations, but they all kept tabs on each other's plans. A handful headed east to stay with close relatives in Atlanta, a 470-mile drive. The rest went west, joining more than 250,000 other evacuees on the road to Texas. From Violet, some chose a longer route out of town to avoid the worst evacuation traffic clogging Interstate 10. Others took I-10 west because they were headed to Baton Rouge or Houston. By far the largest group of family headed northwest to Dallas, about

550 miles from Violet. Given the seriousness of the storm and Connie's emphatic invitation, more than 150 family members had decided Dallas was the place to go.

For anyone raised in this big family, evacuating was a familiar ritual. People had gotten casual, not about leaving but about what they packed. There was never much room for personal belongings, and besides, people always squeezed in and rode together. This time, Katie and her husband, Leroy, known as Gray Eye, left their papers and only took a little cash. Nell and Earl brought their papers, but left their brand-new black SUV in the driveway.

Family members grabbed what seemed essential. Robin James, Connie's sister, helped their mother load up her piggy banks, papers, clothes, a bag of medicine, and all her wigs. Trietha, called "Tri," Robin's older daughter, took three sets of clothes, her DVDs, and her laptop. Robin was so busy trying to make sure that her mother and her younger daughter, Precious, were ready, she left her own bag by the front door. Tri left her binder of clippings and photos she had collected every year of high school. She also left a thick binder of all the poetry she had written. All those things would be lost.

By 9:30 a.m. on Sunday, August 28, Katrina had grown huge in the Gulf and was spinning her winds to a roaring 173 m.p.h. Mayor Ray Nagin held a news conference to issue a mandatory evacuation for Orleans Parish, stating, "We're facing the storm most of us have feared."[12] In total, 1.5 million people evacuated their homes and communities along the Gulf Coast to escape Hurricane Katrina. In New Orleans proper, the only major city in the path of the storm, 80 percent of the five hundred thousand residents left. The one hundred thousand remaining were either unable to leave for lack of transport or funds, or they had chosen to ride out the storm against the odds. The structure Mayor Nagin termed the "shelter of last resort"—the Superdome—drew some twenty thousand people, who later learned that they had made a bad bet on getting help. Katrina evacuees scattered to each of the forty-eight lower states.

That Sunday morning, Connie had left for early church, and when she returned, she was astonished at the numbers of people arriving at her doorstep, 550 miles from home ground in St. Bernard Parish.

"When I got home from church, I had a bunch a people . . . everybody was coming up to me, to Texas. And more family kept calling me . . . I called my girlfriend, Sharon," Connie said, explaining her panic. "'Sharon, I have forty-eight people in my house, and I'm wondering what to do next, and I have more on their way,' and I just kept praying, and boy I'm telling you, it was a lot of people to care for and a lot to do."

Dallas

One hundred fifty-five family members evacuated on Saturday and began arriving at Connie's home in Dallas on Sunday. Other family members went to Houston and Atlanta.

SUN

"WHEN THEY SAY GO, WE GO."

- KATIE

Fig. 16

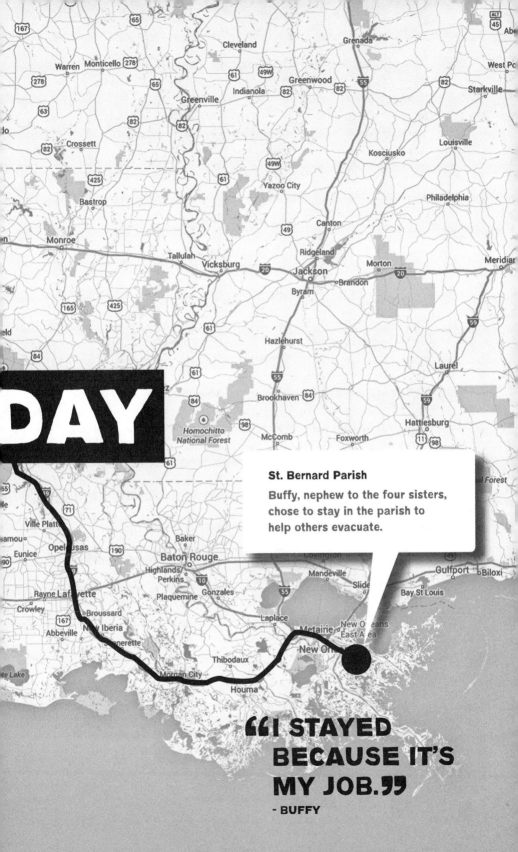

DAY

St. Bernard Parish
Buffy, nephew to the four sisters, chose to stay in the parish to help others evacuate.

"I STAYED BECAUSE IT'S MY JOB."
– BUFFY

In my first interview with Connie a few weeks after that day, she struggled for words to describe her own mental state. "We all was in the house that Sunday night, and we kept looking at TV to see what the media would tell us, what was going to happen. I'll never forget that night, when a hurricane was going on. We all just sit upstairs, crowded around the TV all night. My Aunt Katie was cooking, making sure we had food to feed everybody . . . We waited, and waited. Everybody kept looking and waiting to see."

KATRINA ARRIVES

Just after midnight on August 28, early Sunday morning, while family members were still on the road, Hurricane Katrina was cranking up more power than most storms ever achieve, becoming a Category 4 monster with counterclockwise winds reaching 145 m.p.h. By 7:00 a.m. Sunday morning, whipping furious circles in the Gulf less than three hundred miles from family homes in St. Bernard Parish, the hurricane intensified as the pressure dropped, accelerating wind speeds to 167 m.p.h. Hurricane Katrina had become the deadliest of storms, a Category 5.

If Hurricane Katrina had been a military commander bent on destruction, she would have known that in 2005 in southeast Louisiana, a Category 3 storm would actually produce damage consistent with a much worse Category 4 storm. She would have known that in this area of the Gulf, she had collaborators who had been at work for decades on the ground, chipping away at the natural defenses of the area and rendering it more vulnerable to an outside attack. The agents at work to weaken area defenses, however unwittingly, did not appear to act in concert with each other, thus blinding the local population to their cumulative, devastating impact. Their work targeted two critical lines of defense that might otherwise have abated Hurricane Katrina's force: the wetlands and the levees.

The collaborators didn't have to organize themselves. Their separate efforts converged in a shared commitment to a belief system, an allegiance to an ethic of growth. The loyalists to this urban ethic promoted its benefits—jobs, opportunity, even safety. Left unchecked, however, this ethic would produce staggering public harm. And even though the "growth machine's" systemic nature made it hard to see, Katrina's collaborators eased the way for destruction.[13]

The first line of defense against Katrina and her storm surges should have been the land itself. But the collaborators had been busy destroying coastal land for fifty years. It took the Mississippi River seven thousand years to deposit the sand, clay, and silt that produced the 3 million acres of Louisiana's wetlands, marshlands, and barrier islands.[14] The consequences of a voracious growth machine have included a staggering loss of land, amounting to one-fourth of all deposits laid in the last thousand years.[15] Scientists from the US Geological Survey (USGS) have found that in the last twenty-five years alone, from 1985 to 2010, the rate of land loss in coastal Louisiana averaged the size of a football field every hour (see Figure 14 map and chart).[16]

In the name of growth, city planners in New Orleans worked through the twentieth century to reclaim floodplains by building higher earthen dams and concrete supports and more concrete flood walls along the riverbanks of the Mississippi. By 2005, nearly 3,600 miles of levees lined the Mississippi, making it the most extensively controlled river in the world. These human interventions in the flow of the river preempted the annual sediment deposits from spring flooding. Without replenishment of soil, the land gradually sank, contributing to land loss and making coastal areas more vulnerable to flooding.

Growth also preoccupied many business interests that exploited the wetlands through decades of merciless cuts in the intricate wetland system. Most prominent among these business interests were (and remain) the oil and gas companies, whose formidable economic presence in southeast Louisiana has brought an unhampered death by a thousand cuts to the coastal lands. Since the 1950s, these companies have dug 8,600 miles of canals to lay their pipelines, etching out a latticework welcome mat for the Gulf saltwater to wash in and gobble the organic matter that holds this marshy land together. When Katrina shoved into coastal Louisiana, the buffer that had always tempered such invading forces had been significantly dismantled.

Other business interests loyal to the growth machine cooked up an economic rationale for a shipping canal in St. Bernard Parish that would give oceangoing vessels in the Gulf a shortcut to the port of New Orleans. Despite strong opposition by residents of the parish, powerful local promoters pushed the construction of the Mississippi River Gulf Outlet. The US Army Corps of Engineers began to dig in 1958. The excavation of land required to make way for this massive, seventy-five-mile-long navigation canal through bayou wetlands heaved up more dirt than was displaced to build the entire Panama Canal.[17] The MRGO channel, barely used by the ships and barges it was intended to serve in a larger, ambitious shipping plan, quickly became obsolete as interest in the bigger scheme evaporated just as the canal was finished in 1968. But the damage was done: saltwater intrusions into the canal from the Gulf destroyed forever twenty-three thousand acres of surrounding cypress swamps and wetlands.[18]

Katrina's other significant collaborator was the designated defender of the Crescent City: the US Army Corps of Engineers, builder of levees designed to protect the city and its outlying areas so the city could expand and the population could grow. The Corps surely intended no harm, but during Katrina, their levees breached in fifty-two places. The unnecessary and catastrophic flooding that ensued became known as "the worst civil engineering disaster in US history." Design flaws and bad decisions produced an astonishing 75–80 percent of the flooding in New Orleans from Katrina, flooding that would not have otherwise occurred.[19]

Further south, in St. Bernard Parish, both the levees and the natural defenses of the wetlands buffer failed before the howling force of the storm. Scientists and independent engineers had predicted all these failures.

At 6:10 a.m. in New Orleans, on Monday, August 29, when dozens of exhausted family members were trying to sleep in Connie's Dallas home, Hurricane Katrina ripped into Louisiana near the mouth of the Mississippi River in Buras-Triumph at wind speeds of 125 m.p.h., a Category 3 level. The storm smashed into St. Bernard Parish and surged on to drown major portions of St. Tammany Parish. For a Category 3 hurricane, the storm surges were historic: surges from twenty to twenty-two feet flooded most of St. Bernard Parish. The surges were made worse by the funneling impact of the MRGO, the sides of which had eroded to leave a channel two and one-half times its original width. The seventeen-foot levees along the MRGO were breached in twenty places, and when the levee walls failed on the Industrial Canal, the flooding engulfed the rest of the parish. By mid-morning on Monday, St. Bernard Parish had earned the distinction of being the sole parish to have been completely inundated.[20]

BUFFY STAYS

As carloads of family left for Dallas or Houston or Atlanta on Saturday, Buffy James, nephew to Katie and her sisters and cousin to Connie and dozens of others, stayed behind. He never even thought about evacuating. It wasn't out of stubbornness or naïve resistance. It wasn't because he was a thrill seeker or because he didn't believe the danger was real. Buffy had other priorities.

"I stayed because it's my job. We don't have that many people in the parish that work for the city that chose to stay, you know, but I love my job, I love helping out people and I think that's what I'm here for."

Even during the worst storms he had known, he had always stayed put to help those left behind—the elderly, the disabled, or those without transportation. Somebody needed to stay for people like this, and Buffy didn't give it a second thought.

Buffy James is a lean man, about five feet nine. But his stature and soft-spoken manner belie the force of his resolve. In August 2005, he was forty-five years old. Buffy lives in Violet, across the street from family, down the street from other family, and a short two-minute drive from scores of nearly all his family members in St. Bernard Parish. He is hardworking and, as a black man in a mostly white parish, has become experienced at taking things in stride. Buffy's cousins and aunts and uncles respect his carpentry skills and his role as a head cook at large family gatherings. He is one of the few family members with a parish government job, a job with the road crew that he had been promoted to supervise not long before the storm.

Buffy also stayed out of loyalty to the parish president, Junior Rodriguez. Junior was a longtime friend of Buffy's family. He had Isleño heritage and was as white as a cumulus cloud. Whites and blacks may not visit each other's homes much, but they often share a bayou culture. Junior and Buffy's father fished and trapped together as young men. Both families lived in Verret. As Buffy was growing up, it was Junior who taught him to fish in the open sea and to trap muskrat. Years later, when Junior got elected president of the parish, he promoted Buffy to supervisor of the road crew, heading up about forty-five workers. "Buffy's such a good worker," Junior said, "he was a natural to head up the crew."

That Sunday, the day after almost everyone Buffy knew had arrived somewhere on higher ground, he and a small brigade of other parish employees who had chosen to stay worked far into the night. Their mission was to secure their beloved parish, exposed to the Gulf, and in the apparent path of the storm. Through high winds and heavy rains, hour after hour, they sandbagged levees, cleared trees off the road, and barricaded roads to keep looters out. Finally, at 3:00 a.m., Junior's lead man ordered Buffy and the others to stop work and get to safety. They made it to the government building in Chalmette, the parish seat, where a few managed to sleep from sheer exhaustion.

Hurricane Katrina made landfall in southeast Louisiana early Monday morning, August 29, but it was hard to get news of its impact. It wasn't clear what had happened, but there were newscasters saying that the New Orleans area had "dodged the big one."

By 8:00 a.m. Monday, a member of the NBC crew covering the storm looked at the dry streets of the city outside the Superdome and said to anchor Brian Williams, "Looks like we dodged the bullet!" And seven miles southeast, at the government building in St. Bernard Parish, Buffy's boss roused the men with his relief at what he saw out the window, "Looks like we dodged another one." That very phrase got repeated over and over, on the news and in homes across the country. At Connie's, the watch team said it, too, and their assessment got out to others quickly—we're okay, everybody's okay.

But it wasn't true.

Buffy's boss had just finished laying out the plan for the morning, telling the crew that after a few hours of rest, they would load up all the chain saws on trucks and get busy clearing trees off the roads. "So everybody go get some rest," he said.

"And," Buffy recalled, "a little after 9:00 a.m., maybe 9:30 a.m., we're looking out the window and we say, 'The water's to the top of the tie.' And that's when one of my co-workers come running from the back telling us to, 'Come on, get out, get out, the water's coming! It's like a tidal surge.' We ran downstairs to see what he was talking about, and by the time we got downstairs, we couldn't even get out the door because the water had done blocked us in, closed the door up. We had, like, two foot of water, two, three foot of water where we couldn't open the door. And so we all ran upstairs and one of them say, 'Don't run upstairs because we gonna get trapped up here, so do not run up here.'

"So we ran back downstairs, and it had got to about four foot of water, and we couldn't open the door at all, so we had to break the door to get out. There were fourteen or fifteen of us there in the building and some on the second floor trying to get out. But then the roof came down on the third floor. So we had no choice but to go out through all this water. We also had one guy, he was about sixty-five or seventy years old. He just came back to work with a triple bypass, and he was with us. And it looked like everybody for theirself at first, and then we realized he was still in there, so we had to go back and get him. And we got him and he came into a shock because, you know, he just was, like, shaking, and so we had to lead him, like a blind person lead a blind person. And by that time the water had got about six foot high when we went back to get him. And we got him to safety, and the supervisor said, 'We gonna need chain saws.'

"We figured the water not going to get higher. And so, I went with four other employees and the supervisor to get chain saws and stuff, and equipment to use after it all over. And by the time we got everything collected,

MONDAY

Everyone thought they had dodged the bullet, but they were wrong.

Fig. 17

the water is fourteen feet high. So we had to swim out from there. The force of the water pinned me up against a building—I was the smallest one out of the crew that left to go get supplies. They thought I had done drowned, washed away, because they had made it back to the building, inside. They said they were looking around hollering for me. So they had to come back, and they saw I couldn't make it. But we got out.

"That was the scariest moment. And finally the Fire Department, the first responder team came and rescued us and brought us to a high school, Chalmette High School. And they had three or four thousand people there, in the gym, and, like, ten thousand animals. The water inside was about five feet high, and the building is, like, six feet off the ground. I don't know how can I describe it—you had feces just floating in front of you like it was—it just wasn't right, you know. And we stood there for about forty-five minutes until the first responders came and took us, the crew, to the culture center. The parish president had called and told them to get us and take us over there. So we got there and that's where we stood—top of the building. That was another scary moment.

"It was a flat roof made of pea gravel—it's like shells up there. So we took sheetrock off the wall to sleep on because it was better than sleeping directly on rocks, on gravel. Never thought I'd taste so much Spam. That's what we was eating, fried Spam."

It took more than a week for help to arrive to get Buffy and the rest of the men off the roof and to safe quarters where they could access provisions and get back to work helping others. The rest of Buffy's family was considerably more comfortable, but the news that came to them was devastating. Huddled around Connie's TV, family members learned that St. Bernard Parish had taken the brunt of the storm.

"It was unbelievable to see what was going on," Connie said. "The devastation, and to hear that my parish, where we live, where I was raised, where I went to school, where we went to church, where I dated guys, where I was a cheerleader, where we got married, it was a different kind of beauty, all those little things. And that whole parish was devastated. Gone."

2

THE CULTURE BROKER

By the time Ginny and I first met Connie in October 2005, she had already helped her family find temporary housing, and many were able to locate together in a Dallas apartment complex. She had begun to leverage her twenty years of experience with a big city and big institutions to negotiate the wilderness between her deeply wounded family and the alien cultures of the Federal Emergency Management Agency (FEMA), the Red Cross, middle-class churches, and landlords.[1] As I listened to accounts of family members and then watched her manage these separate cultural worlds, I realized Connie had stepped quite naturally into a role that anthropologists call a "culture broker." She called it a calling.

"They didn't have nobody but me, nobody but me," she said, recounting how she had come to see her responsibility as a gift. "I said, 'God, I see now why you sent me here twenty years ago, you had a purpose for me to be here in Texas, in north Texas,' and He blessed me with a big home. And I always wondered the blessing, but I see why. I always used to say, 'It's only me, my husband, and my son and the dog, Bourbon, that lived in Texas.'"

Connie's religious framework for embracing the colossal job with which she had suddenly been charged made her an enthusiastic and tireless culture broker: one who bridges cultural divides and smooths communication between groups that don't quite "get" each other. Culture brokers use their ears and their voices. They listen and then communicate their insights, back and forth, back and forth, helping both parties make sense of each other. Invisible cultural divides reside everywhere, quietly separating people by region, class, race, language, power, gender, ethnicity, education. But because cultural values and practices rarely get a hearing in disaster scholarship, the value that culture brokers could bring to efforts focused on recovery has been left unexplored.[2] Connie opened my eyes to that value.

Connie had grown up on the bayou, in the family system, but since leaving her home for Dallas with her engineer husband, Terry, she had acquired experience dealing with medical and educational institutions. That know-how endowed her with the skills to navigate the divide between the worlds of the institutional "recovery culture" and the "wounded culture" of the family. For the many months that family members were stuck in Dallas, Connie found ways to connect the worlds and keep help coming to those she loved.

"They don't have nothing," Connie said tearfully on that first visit. "Everything been pulled away from them, taken from them. Everything—their homes, their church, their community, everything."

When she had first moved to Dallas as a young woman from the bayou with no sense of how to live in a big city, Connie, too, had felt bereft of everything familiar. Based on her own experience, she rightly assumed that her mother and sisters and aunts and uncles and cousins would not be able to work comfortably with large institutions like FEMA. Not only were they grieving and consumed with the news of their devastated homes and communities, they had almost no experience dealing with government agencies. But Connie had plenty. And so, Connie made calls every day on behalf of her family members to FEMA and the Red Cross.

"I always wondered why I had gotten the business management degree, but it came in handy," Connie said. "I could ask the pertinent questions. Never been in this situation. I had to keep calling Junior Rodriguez, the parish president: 'Will we be able to come back? When will we get lighting and water?'"

SANCTUARY

Inside Connie's home that first day, we entered a healing universe—full of animation and love. Connie introduced us to every person, starting with her beloved godmother and aunt, Katie Williams. We shook hands with adults and smiled as they called out the names of the children and young people we were passing. One precocious boy of about six years old did whole-body sways this way and that, and with a twirl and a jump, arrived squarely in front of us. He thrust out his arm and flashed a sly grin. He wanted a shake, too. This buoyant youngster was the son of one of the dozens of Connie's cousins now gathered in her home. She toured us around the house, silently reinforcing the point about just how many people were there. In the kitchen, women were crowded around the table, and others were tending to things in the oven or on the stove. We also visited the back porch, where a group

Backyard briefing with Connie on the phone to authorities

Connie, culture broker

Junior Rodriguez, parish president and family friend from Verret

Lots of paperwork!

Men keeping the grills going

Safe Haven

More than 150 family members spent months marooned in Dallas. Connie helped them stay connected to the keepers of their fate, and gave them a place to enjoy cooking and gathering.

Fig. 18

of men sat talking around a table and children played in the spacious yard beyond.

Over the next hours we must have met one hundred people, many of whom we would come to know better over time: Katie's husband, Gray Eye; Katie's son, Leroy Jr. (Turb), and her daughter Nell; Nell's daughter, Trashell; and Nell's husband, Earl. We met Connie's other aunts, Cynthia, Roseana, and Audrey, and their grown children, their spouses, and their young children, now the youngest generation of the three. We met Connie's sister Robin and Robin's daughters, Trietha and Precious. We met Connie and Robin's other sister, Deborah Green; their mother, Audrey May James; and Audrey May's mother, Gladys.

Entering Connie's ample kitchen felt like crossing a sacred threshold. Women huddled around the stove and at the counters, putting the final touches on dishes they had prepared earlier that day from ingredients the men had shuttled back from Louisiana. Katie stirred her giant pot of gumbo, a concoction that looked brown as the swamp itself but would deliver the taste buds a complex array of flavors made from seafood, sausage, and chicken, all folded into a special gravy. Nell tossed her store-bought dressing with the mixed salad greens she had brought and placed in Connie's large wooden bowl. Cousin Janie peeked into her Dutch oven, filled to the brim with the tomato-reddened jambalaya, made with shrimp and spicy smoked sausage, green bell peppers, celery, tomatoes, and lots of spices. Everyone moved with fluid precision, clear about what they were doing, as if they had all shared the same kitchen for years. On a countertop sat a proud triple-layer white cake with coconut frosting. Three pies coming out of the oven were destined to sit beside it—a pecan pie, and two sweet-potato pies.

Connie cried, "Everybody, we ready to eat!" calling as she moved from room to room, to the back porch and the yard beyond. It was no accident that Connie had invited us to come at a time when her family had gathered from around the area to share a meal that felt like home. We could see what made them special, and they could meet us under the best possible circumstances. The busy rooms emptied toward the kitchen and backyard, where there were more offerings from the grill. Food in this family was a self-serve affair. No one fixed a plate or set a table for anyone else. The labor was strictly confined to making food delicious.

The exodus from the living area to the kitchen gave us the chance to sit down with Connie, and with Katie. While others ate, each of them talked to us.

Katie's shock about the news of the disaster came in terms of her expectations about the evacuation and how these had always worked in the past: "You know, I am so used to going right back home. Because last year for Ivan we went to Houston, and we was home in three days. And that is all we took with us, like, three days of clothes, three days of medication, you know. I was busy thinking we going right back home."

"They thought they were coming for one or two days," Connie said. "But it didn't happen like that."

"It was devastating when they showed us the pictures," Katie said. "My nephew, Doozer (Cynthia's son), went back and took video of the whole parish. He works down there at a gas plant, and they called him to come back. When I saw it, I couldn't believe it."

"PEOPLE WERE IN SHOCK," CONNIE SAID

"There's no more St. Bernard Parish" Katie said, shaking her head. "It's wiped off the map. Never had a storm like this one before."

"I had to see my seventy-three-year-old aunt Cynthia sad for her house, wondering what to do," said Connie. "My mother was sick and wondering what was going on, and we was all worrying about her home that she raised us in. And she was so worried about my father's grave."

"Doozer told us some of the tombs broke up," Katie said, "And they floated away." Her lowered eyes and tilt of her head told me not to probe. The distress was still too intense, even weeks after they learned this news. The final resting place for ancestors in this family and in other families in the region clearly held an important, present-day role.

The toppled tombs had stood above ground, as all tombs do in southeast Louisiana, in a modest, unnamed cemetery, one belonging to the Baptist church that the family had attended for generations.[3] Many maintained an everyday relationship with the cemetery and visited there whenever the mood struck, especially if a close relative had recently died. Others came on holidays with offerings of fresh flowers. When one of the young people wanted to learn who was where, Katie or a sister strolled the scruffy grounds to identify people and recount stories about this or that relative. Once a year, every November 1 for All Saint's Day, a core group of elders and younger members of the family held an all-day ritual in the graveyard. Like the honoring-the-dead rituals common on this day all over New Orleans, and seen in Day of the Dead ceremonies in communities throughout Latin America, the group showed up with provisions for sprucing up the grounds

Wrecked home with
remnants of bayou life

Devastation

Poorly built levees and wetland loss opened the door
to Katrina's breathtaking destruction.

Fig. 19

Century-old live oak
yanked up like a weed

Bayou shrimp boat,
grounded and out of
business

"St. Bernard, I'll be back!"

and painting the tombs. They arranged fresh flowers from their gardens and fried up fish they brought for lunch. The occasion called for stories and laughter—there were no tears at such times.

Months later, I learned from her daughter Nell that Katie had a habit of sitting out in back of her house, facing the graveyard. Her son was entombed there. He had died in a car accident in 1993 while driving on Bayou Road, just blocks from their home. He was only twenty, and Katie missed him. He was her artist. Katie's mother, the "big mama" everyone knew as Peachy, was also laid to rest there, as well as her father, her brothers, a sister, and dozens of others, some of whom were not family. The cemetery was a place where people kept connected to their past. Learning that the resting place of ancestors had been disturbed, that some of the tombs had broken apart, releasing caskets to float away, and that there was an open coffin in Katie's front yard was especially distressing news.

That single first day in Connie's full house set the course for the next eight years of research. Here, collected in one place, were 155 members of a family willing to share their stories. The affection, the pleasure in cooking and eating special bayou foods were clear. So was the worry about the ruin back home, the broken-up tombs, and the unclear next steps. I had also learned something useful from a blunder, as anthropologists often do. I had asked Katie what it was like to miss New Orleans. She glanced up from her backyard chair and responded firmly, but with a smile, "We not from New Orleans, we from St. Bernard Parish." With charm and her deep, musical voice, Katie had asserted the family's cultural difference from New Orleans. The point was important enough to establish immediately, even in the middle of her grief and uncertainty about the future. I heard and jotted down what she said; but it took a trip to the bayou for me to understand what she meant.

After reviewing my notes from that first day, I began the task of sorting out the names and faces and family branches, adding bits of information about this person or that, this relationship or that. A few weeks later, in November, the shock and rawness of the horrific news had begun to give way to conversations about practical worries like how to get back, when the electricity and gas would be available, and how to inventory losses. I then began drawing anthropological kinship charts for the family. People enjoyed the exercise. It provided a different way to talk about themselves and served as a small distraction from their losses and hurt.

These rough kinship maps began to reveal a pattern: almost all the people we had met over the preceding weeks, except for Connie's mother and grandmother, belonged to the "Peachy Gang." The Peachy Gang represented all the descendants of "Peachy," Alma Johnson (1909–1984), and her husband, McKinley James (1896–1964). There were nine children: five daughters and four sons. Only one of the sons (Lawrence, nicknamed "Lolly") was living, as were four of the five daughters: Cynthia, Katie, Roseana, and Audrey. Lolly and his four sisters represented the oldest living generation. Lolly was a father figure to many, but he wasn't here in Dallas. He had evacuated to Baton Rouge where he had other family. All the sisters (then aged fifty-nine to seventy-three) and most of their children (aged thirty-five to fifty-five) had evacuated to Dallas. Most middle-aged adults had children of their own (aged fifteen to thirty-four), and most of them were here as well. A few of them had children, too, making it four living generations of family. However, as big as the Peachy Gang was, with approximately 150 members, it was just the beginning of family as the group defined it. Cousins and aunts and uncles also included the siblings of Peachy, all of whom had descended from Emma Fernandez and Victor Johnson. The Peachy Gang became the core group for our documentary, with the four sisters at the center.[4]

CULTURE BROKER IN MOTION

The terrible news of the disaster had created more than shock and grief. It had also left family leaders—the very people others depended on for clarity and direction in a crisis—uncertain. "I was looking at these ladies that I looked up to—all my aunts. They were just wondering what's next. What's next? What they going to do?"

Connie had had no time to absorb her own shock. "When we found out that everything was flooded and realized this was a full-scale disaster for everyone here, I had to put on another thinking gear. Every day I had to see the next step, what to do, what to do. All these people were my family. They were all my family. So I had to become the mother for everybody, you know. My husband and I, we had to be the mother and father for everyone. We had to take everybody in. And shelter them. And provide for them."

For the family, there would be no returning home anytime soon. That meant Connie's relatives needed everything basic to living: clothing, medical supplies, prescription glasses, and lodging for the months to come. There were special needs as well, for tending the sick, the elderly, the children, the new babies. There would be a process to register with FEMA, to get a victim ID number, to contact insurance companies, to get on a waiting list for a trailer, to check for supplies from the Red Cross and the Salvation Army. So much to do, but no one knew how to begin. Except Connie. She could and did help her family with all of these jobs. She was one of them and recognized their needs. She tried to be methodical, just like her management courses had taught her—stay focused, make lists, keep records, get names.

Without fanfare, Connie moved back and forth from the outer world of bureaucratic institutions to the inner world of her family. She offered what she knew of that bigger world in ways that were sometimes subtle. "At night when we would all settle, I had everybody write down things, what they need me to do for them and their expressions. A lot of them was—some of the moods were angry. 'Why did this happen?' They were angry that they were displaced. I had one cousin she was just, was so sad and so upset, and I sat down with her and I say: 'I understand you angry and upset. But we have to try to make the best of the situation.' She could see, it wasn't just her going through this. Hundreds and thousands of people were going through this, it wasn't just her."[5]

Connie reached out to everyone she knew for help, and fortunately, her social network spanned a wide variety of environments and included good friends and casual acquaintances. Many of her contacts roused the friends of their friends into action, too. Connie contacted churches in the area, housing authorities, and private landlords. Simple acts of kindness multiplied, and soon there were offers of all kinds coming in—food, supplies, clothing, and even lodging.

"People that I had met, people that I had just seen, people that I knew in the community was there, they all helped me and everything just fell in place, it just fell in place."

She depended on help from a large variety of "weak ties," people she knew as colleagues or acquaintances who were not close friends. Weak ties do not require a lot of time or labor to sustain, but they can offer links to key resources at critical moments. In contrast to weak ties, strong ties are those we nurture with close friends and family, and they require work and time to sustain.[6] Someone whose social network consists primarily of strong ties is at a big disadvantage when needs surpass the resources of the people within it.

When people with a lot of weak ties need something, the possibilities provided by their networks can quickly multiply, as each weak tie connects to other weak ties, making information, new contacts, and resources available that weren't there before. Connie explained, "Lynda call me, and she say, 'Connie, we got some mattresses' or 'We got some clothes.' Like right now the back of my trunk of my car is full up with things that I've got and people donating, giving me clothes, giving me canned goods. Giving me whatever, so I load that up, and I'll make that delivery in the morning.

Diapers, to make sure they got diapers for the little kids, formulas for the babies."

Connie's sister Deborah and their mother, Audrey May, later bragged on her. "Connie was talking for the people, you know, from the parish and from New Orleans," Audrey May said. "She was talking for all the people, and telling them what to do and talking to the big people for them. And she had this senator to come. . . ."

"Yeah," said Deborah, filling in the blank. "Duplessis. She came to Connie's house—came in on the airplane and they went and got her."

Connie leveraged every weak tie she could. Ann Duplessis was a black Louisiana state senator and a distant relative. Connie reached out to her for help so her family could feel like they had a hearing with someone they could trust who had some power.

Connie learned what agencies kept track of what information, where to file what paperwork, how to get the right people on the phone. "My brother, we didn't know where he was for a few weeks until we found that him and his family was in another location. We found my uncle. We was writing a list, I was e-mailing Missing Katrina Victims. I would just get on the Internet and e-mail, to see if we could find certain family members."

Connie listened with the ear of family and tried to soothe her godchild who wasn't eating and missed her teddy bear, her little cousin afraid to sleep for fear a hurricane might come and take him away, the teenager who had left her dog behind.

"My mother's still upset because she left her church dress," Connie explained. "She bought her a brand-new suit because they was going to open up our brand-new church and march into the brand-new church that Sunday. And she was happy because they all was going to wear blue suits, the whole church. And they been planning this grand opening of the new church. But they never got to march into their new church. She had her suit, and she had it all laid out to wear that Sunday of Katrina. And she said it's probably got wet, and I said, 'Mother, it's probably done float away!'"

A PLACE TO GATHER

Connie's kitchen became the place where family gathered regularly to experience the closeness they had lost and to talk about losses that few outsiders could understand.

"Girl, I pick crab meat all summer," said Katie, talking to a longtime friend from church, Linda Sanchez, who had joined the family in Dallas.

Linda knew just what she was talking about. "All my seafood," Linda said shaking her head. She had stored one thousand pounds of shrimp in the freezer. That was just the shrimp.

"Yeah," said Katie. "We lost all our shrimp, all the crabs, ten pounds of okra, too, all cut up." It wasn't just the freezers full of raw seafood lost, it was what people had done to it before packing it away. "All summer long every time the man come with crabs I was buying them. I cleaned up my crabs with soap, and I picked them all! I had boxes of that sitting up in the back by the bar. I say, Lord, I ain't got nothing."

Shrimp and crab don't stay in season year round, and so when seafood is at the center of every celebratory event, you store it up so you can continue the traditional form of eating through the off-season. Losing seafood from freezers was not just about the loss of a material item or the money used to purchase it. It was about the loss of cultural continuity. Most households in the family had at least one full freezer in addition to the freezer compartment of the fridge. Food stashed away in freezers was like an insurance policy—you always had what you needed for the next time, and holidays weren't as much work if you collected your primary foods in advance. Now everyone had lost their backup supply and their investment in future meals. They would all have to start over. Maybe in the big picture, the food lost in freezers was a small thing, but it seemed to symbolize everything about their lives—the assurance they thought they had in the levees also didn't hold up, and now they were starting over, from the beginning, no reserve to lean on and nothing to leverage into the future.

One day in early November, we entered Connie's kitchen, redolent with the spicy smells of the bayou. There we found Katie, her daughter, Nell, and Cousin Janie, married to a grandson of Peachy's brother, Davis. Cynthia, Roseana, and Audrey were there, too. Nell had made a big pot of jambalaya and a tossed green salad. Roseana had made red beans. Katie's rice would go with the red beans and with Janie's gumbo that she had prepared that morning in her own apartment kitchen. Audrey was frying chicken; the grease popping and crisping batter filled the air with sounds and aromas of life before Katrina. Earl and Gray Eye had brought in a tray of sizzling hot sausage, fresh off the backyard grill.

"Who made all the table tops for your backyard furniture?" Katie asked, peering out at the backyard from the kitchen door.

"Terry did them all," Connie said. "He used to ask me, 'Why you have all these tables?'"

Katie supplied a rapid answer, turning back to the women in the kitchen, "He'll see now." The women laughed. "I'm tellin' ya," replied Cynthia.

THE IRIS AND THE OAK

Family interdependence showed up in the details of life, from cooking to grieving. Heavy as their hearts were, and personal as their losses were, family members did not spend time mourning in private. Instead, the comfort they sought depended on daily rituals of connection to each other. These everyday interactions mimicked life at home and included spending time in each other's apartments, checking in by phone with family members marooned in other locations, sharing meals, venturing out together to visit donation centers to shop for the basics that had been blown away in the storm. Everyone had to restock personal items, big and small: clothing and shoes for church and everyday; toiletries, eyeglasses, prescriptions. And they had to outfit their temporary apartment homes with furniture and furnishings, kitchenware, and staples.

The tasks of locating, assembling, and getting things installed took time. Children needed special attention, so finding activities and games to keep them occupied became an ongoing and consuming job for many. Although FEMA initially covered the cost of rent and hotel payments, some of the men and a few women got jobs to help offset living expenses. Those who didn't earn money helped by setting up households, shopping for groceries, and cooking meals. They kept each other up to date about the news back home. The interdependence they had long practiced served the family well in the weeks after the storm. They knew how to work together, and doing it in this strained new context gave them a way to focus their time and energy. Through exchanges of information, food, stories, and group outings, the family could sustain and reinvigorate different aspects of cultural life that brought comfort.

All that Connie understood about her family remained opaque to FEMA and disaster-recovery agencies. No official seemed to understand the unusual size of her family's group, nor did anyone realize that to recover from a disaster, a big family like Connie's needed to be treated as a single living thing. This family group was, in fact, irreducible, not the sum of discrete nuclear-family households that, on special occasions like weddings or funerals, recognized their relation to each other. That's why Connie's work had to take place on two separate tracks: one track led her out beyond the group to a style of language and a set of weak ties that could help her negotiate for the family's provisioning, housing, and aid. Connie's advocacy with the recovery culture freed her family members from having to interact with outsiders whose ways they didn't understand.

The second track of Connie's work led her straight inside the family, to the heart of what her relatives needed most—a way to feel like themselves. What Connie knew about the people in her family was that they thrived on interaction. By turning over her home, her spacious kitchen, porch, and yard, Connie made space for the activation of their connections. Every one of her family members had experienced near-total loss from the storm. And because the Peachy Gang functioned as a collective, individual grief and collective grief came bundled together, intensifying the loss and the sorrow.[7] Connie knew instinctively that the more her relatives could live their displaced life in ways that made sense and kept them connected to each other, the more they could avoid additional suffering.

The stakes of different forms of family are not trivial. In a typical Anglo-American family, parents and children constitute the functioning unit, often separated by some distance from grandparents, cousins, and other relatives. As individuals become adults, they exit the nest, arrange their own livelihoods, and form their own families. In this scenario, geographic mobility enables upward mobility. People crisscross the country for opportunities that will enhance their lives and careers (as Connie's husband had). Our society presses these values of "individual growth" into an unspoken ideology that upholds minimal, nuclear-family units as "normal" because small families can more easily relocate for financial or other reasons.

However, choosing to follow individual desires and ambitions comes at a cost that rarely gets accounted for because such choices are supported by social norms and made to seem healthy and inevitable. This bayou family had made a different set of choices—privileging family togetherness. The large family provided benefits of lifelong friendship and belonging. Of course, choosing to maintain the bonds of large, interdependent families comes with its own costs. Staying put in St. Bernard Parish generation after generation had made social life beautiful but had compromised economic life and upward mobility.

These distinct forms of family matter greatly when those wounded by a disaster are required to interact with institutions of the recovery culture that act as if the dominant nuclear-family model were the only one. Institutional forms and documents, for example, assumed that the functioning unit of family coincided with individual households. The people in any family whose reality did not fit the boxes on the paperwork resulting from these assumptions had to explain themselves over and over again. They continually risked being misunderstood or completely ignored. Over the course of eight years of study, I observed the toll of these misunderstandings.

If the default American assumption about the shape of families is "oakish" in nature, Katie's big family more closely resembled a spreading rootstock—a rhizome.[8] Afro-Creole poet and social theorist Edouard Glissant used the rhizome as a metaphor for Creole identity in the French Caribbean and traced his inspiration back to the idea's French source, philosophers Gilles Deleuze and Félix Guattari, who describe rhizomes as communal, resilient, and multiplying. In the Caribbean, the iconic rhizome is the mangrove. In lower St. Bernard Parish, it is the beautiful red iris.

"There's too many of us to count!" said Buffy when I asked him how big his family was.

"And you really know all these people?" I asked.

"Oh, yes, we all know each other. Keeping track is easy because we see each other a lot."

Connie recognized the rhizome-like connectedness of her family. "If one person gets sick, the whole community know about it. If someone dies, everybody know. That's what love is. That's what family is. That's what home is. We go out of our way to show respect and love for each other. People here in Texas are not the same."

Connie's family has always been its own "emotional ecosystem,"[9] binding its members to each other in a single life-support system of nonhierarchical relations. And like a rhizome, the individuals of the family form a dense tangle of interconnections that feed off a shared life source, the "rootstock." Nothing like the rhizome tangle holds true for mighty oaks with roots: root-based specimens are discrete individuals with singular growth capacities. The sprawling, interdependent nature of a rhizome's rootstock is only at risk when the entire organism is threatened by exceptional circumstances such as poisoning or infestation: or a storm and its aftermath.

RHIZOME RECALLED

When Connie moved to Dallas, it was the hardest thing she had ever done. Her husband, Terry, had gotten an irresistible job offer as an engineer at a company in Dallas. She felt terrible grief about leaving, and for a while, it only got worse. She couldn't stretch the rhizome that had given her a sense of identity. No one in Texas knew anything about her or her husband, or their backgrounds. No one knew anything about St. Bernard Parish. No one had ever been crabbing or shrimping on the bayou. It was like being reborn

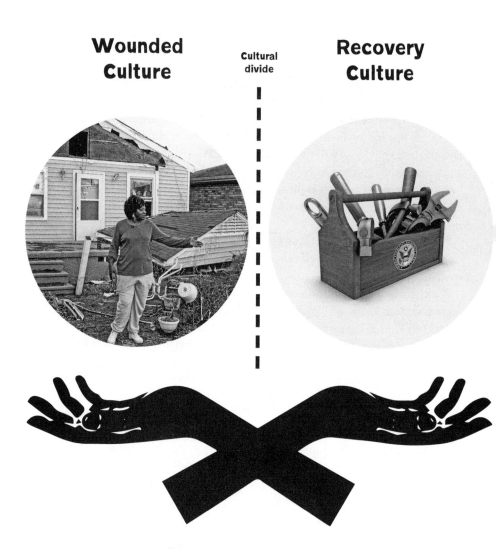

Wounded
Culture

Cultural
divide

Recovery
Culture

Culture Broker

A culture broker understands enough about two
worlds to translate essential information across the
divide. When successful, this translation fosters
both the trust and the communication necessary for
recovery to take place.

Fig. 20

into a new world with a new landscape and unfamiliar faces. Yet over time, she got better about reaching out to complete strangers, someone she met in church, a workmate from her nursing job, a colleague or two from her management studies program, and several women from her breast-cancer survivor group. With few exceptions, the people she brought into her life bore no connection to each other, but they offered friendship and conversation and provided her with a different kind of belonging.

Ironically, Connie's painful adaptation to living in Dallas laid the foundation for her capacity to help her family. She was perfectly positioned to act as an intermediary between the helper agencies and her hurt relatives. She had become educated in the language and skills of the world beyond the bayou. She knew how to communicate with bureaucrats. She understood from years of practice with institutions that there is a way to talk to such people, to ask the right questions, to know when to press.

"Oh Lord, a blessing," Katie said, nodding. "I mean, I don't know how she makes it. She halfway sick and she never stop. And she helping everybody. It doesn't have to be family. Long as you know the family, she find you a place to stay. She go to these different apartments, and if they not up to par she won't get them. Because she'll tell you, you don't want that one, the carpet was dirty. I say, 'You sick, why don't you rest yourself?' She don't have time."

In a post-disaster moment no one ever imagined possible, Connie emerged as a high-profile and potent member of her family. By helping the family meet its cultural needs, she gave them comfort. She knew where to locate key points of entry into that culture that she could support, like a place to gather and talk, and a place to cook big meals. And all the friends she had made since moving to Dallas helped her help them. Beyond that, in the process of summoning the strength she needed for the monumental job, Connie healed an old emotional wound, one left tender from the loss of her rhizome connections twenty years before.

3

NOT JUST ANY RED BEANS

"Couldn't find those red beans," Katie said softly. "Camellia red beans." I'd overheard women in the kitchen and backyard making jokes about what they'd found and not found at the local grocery stores. So when I asked Katie what was hard about living in Dallas, I expected something more profound than a certain brand of beans. But she didn't stop there.

"Couldn't find no kind of—I don't what they use for their meat out here for beans and then greens and things. Couldn't find hot sauces out here either. Louisiana Hot Sauce. I had a time finding crab and shrimp. Because you know they sell those snow crabs. I had never seen those until the first time that I came out by Connie, so I was wondering what they was. Snow crabs. You know, we used to blue paw crabs." Katie's voice made clear that blue paw crabs were an entirely different category of food from snow crabs. What she said was about more than ingredients.

Hearing Katie name the important foods that were out of reach was like hearing an injured person recite all the routine activities that had suddenly been removed from everyday life. Like the mental stress of that incapacitation, missing the foods that made life good carried an emotional weight. Living without the right beans, the right crab, the right hot sauce further estranged family members from their everyday bayou environment. The wrong food created a sensory deficit and became a daily reminder of the family's sorrow, a reminder that something significant was wrong with life.

Anthropologists recognize the cultural value of food in almost every society they study. We all need to eat, but nourishing our bodies is more than just a way to keep us alive. What we eat, what we crave, and what brings satisfaction is culturally learned. As Marshall Sahlins pointed out, most Americans are beef eaters, not because beef is the most logical way to get the calories and protein we need. We reject equally good sources of animal protein such as horse or dog because these animals occupy the status of pets in our culture, making them inappropriate food items.¹ The point is that food choices are not reducible to meeting biological needs. Instead, our taste preferences emerge from historical and place-based realities that, in turn, shape culinary inventions that saturate food traditions with meaning.

Food traditions pump vitality into cultural commitments. In Katie's family, eating food that qualifies as a meal begins and ends very close to home—procuring bayou ingredients, preparing them in a dish, and serving the result. The family's homemade food was not just what you ate; the entire unbroken process reenacted a relationship between people and their environment. Everything about the family's food tradition, from bayou to bowl, reasserted the group's interdependence with the environment and, at the same time, provided the savory context to refresh social bonds that grew denser with each shared meal and conversation. When the family evacuated, people got removed from the source of everyday food traditions and lost all that went with the tradition—not just the food, but the ties to the bayou and to each other.

That's why the family's longing for missing food in Dallas was about much more than food. It was also about the place of belonging, the inseparable relationship to the environment. Unlike home, in Dallas, as in most urban areas, food is separated from its source by many discrete steps and processes of production and commodification. And although Texans traveling beyond the reach of their regional cuisine are quick to pine for Tex-Mex and barbecue, the food traditions of bayou people reflect a need that is different in kind—premised on the uninterrupted nature of food procurement, preparation, and serving.

Since at least the 1870s (and no doubt earlier), an unbroken line of family members had been born and raised into a lifeworld² that they learned to interact with and depend upon. Children learned from parents, aunts, and uncles about the riches of their environment—the seafood and game and long fingers of bayou water that share a habitat with marshlands and cypress swamps and brackish Lake Borgne. Tied to that knowledge of their surroundings came the cultivated love of certain foods, such as turtle and gumbo, crab and shrimp, crawfish and greens. Eating specific foods in large groups came as the culmination of a sequence of practices: there was harvesting the raw ingredients—the seafood (shrimp, crab, crawfish, oysters, speckled trout, drum, redfish), game (wild hog, turtle, coon, rabbit, gator), and vegetables from home gardens (okra, squash, peppers, collards, mustard greens). A whole sequence of steps followed as these ingredients got shaped into a meal. The labor and interaction with the environment tied to these acts of doing made it possible to produce high-quality meals that threaded their connection to the local environment and to each other. In this way, cultural meaning saturated food preferences.

"We always went to the bayous for crab and shrimp," Connie recalled. "My nanny had the nets. They would come and get the crabs out of the net, right on the banks of the bayou . . . Everything we had was shared. It's still like that at home. 'I'm gonna cook a pot of gumbo, you got any crabs?' We shared. We had a lot of food all the time. My uncles would catch the seafood, grow their own okras, fruit like tangerines, and sugar cane. They made candy, praline candy.

"Everything we did centered around food. And you never knew of going to a restaurant. Because you always cooked. I remember I couldn't wait to be a young adult to go and have a boyfriend to take me on a date to go to a restaurant."

Gradually, as wage work became a needed source of income, family members transitioned to buying their seafood from nearby marinas or from the back of an Isleño fisherman's truck. But that was only a slight remove. No one rooted to bayou country could mistake the seamless relation between bayou and human life.

One marker of that seamless relationship belongs to the world of smells. Bayou seafood has a full-bodied aroma, and the rural environment of the lower parish can smell musty and damp. Dallas air by contrast seemed to offer no clues about the surrounding environment, even in the countryside where Connie lived. In the city and suburbs, there were sometimes hints of fragrant trees or diesel engines or industrial chemicals, but nothing resembling uncultivated land or natural bodies of water. The bayous and swamp areas of the lower parish filled the air with a complicated, wild fragrance brought forward by the humidity. The scent was tangy with salt and old water, and with the earthy aroma of natural decay amid profuse, untended growth. It was routine work to clean shrimp and crab, crawfish and oysters, and the pungent smells of the bayou lingered on the skin.

I asked Katie if there was a centerpiece of food that her bayou family liked best. "Gumbo is the main dish," she said, without hesitation. Katie was an expert gumbo maker, as were Cynthia and Connie's mother, Audrey May.

Deborah chuckled when she echoed the place of gumbo in her family: "Oh, my goodness! It's competition! My aunts, my mom, everybody cooks. There is no one person, and you have to eat some of everybody's food or they are highly upset with you. You have to eat. Now if I go to my aunt's house, she's going to say, 'Oh! You ain't tasted any gumbo 'til you taste mine.' Then I go to my grandmother's, 'Oh, you ain't tasted any gumbo 'til you taste mine.' You cannot say 'Well, I've had some.' You cannot say you've had any-body else's. It's like her bowl is your first bowl." Her mother and her aunts were the queens of gumbo, and their scepters were long-handled spoons.

By the time Connie had gotten temporary apartments and furniture for everyone in her care, the gumbo queens had already experimented with new, Dallas versions, made without the bayou crab and shrimp and special sausages from home, but with substitutes people might find worthy. Katie tried a pot with snow crabs, crustaceans with long legs and no flavor. People joked that they looked ridiculous in the pot; no one even wanted to taste them. The bland shrimp imports from Southeast Asia provided no substi-tute for Gulf shrimp. Another cousin tried a version with oxtail but, by all accounts, it too was a culinary flop.

THE TENACITY OF CULTURE SHOCK

Missing familiar food was just the most noticeable source of strain that family members felt living in Dallas: their black bayou dialect was typically recognized as coming from Louisiana, and many in the family complained that locals found their speech hard to follow. Another strain came from the different experience of church. "Why they don't sing out here?" Katie asked. "No one look like they want to be there." Despite the kindness that Connie's friends and many strangers showed the family, the bayou evacu-ees were not prepared for feeling stresses no kind stranger could calm: the loss of familiar food, the hardship of not being understood, and the lack of enthusiastic church services. The longings collided into a whole new source of anxiety: culture shock.

Connie knew that making her family comfortable in the wake of their catastrophic losses and their displacement in Dallas would require more than meeting their material needs for temporary shelter and provisions. "Life here is not like Louisiana," Connie said in late October 2005, about two months after the storm. "It's different. The society of people are differ-ent. Culture is different. It's a culture shock for them. It's a culture shock. The people are not the same. My family, my aunts, they like to sit out on the porch and drink their coffee, and visit. People don't do that here."

In addition to translating her family's needs to the officials in charge of recovery, Connie gave her family a way to understand the culture shock they were going through. She had been there herself.

"Dallas food was so different," Connie told Katie and others. "I was upset because I couldn't get the kind of crabs and shrimp we had at home. That was my biggest thing—not having our food. Never could find good French bread. No red velvet cake, or beignets [French doughnuts]. Everything was chips and salsa and beans—not red beans, but refried beans. All my girlfriends here wanted to eat Mexican. I thought it was a snack. Not real food."

Her own culture shock from twenty years prior was as fresh to her as yesterday. "I remember going into the supermarket and, you know, we so used to seeing people and talking about the produce, 'Oh, these tomatoes are very high,' or talking about if the meat looked good, or ask, 'What you going to cook Sunday?' That's what we would say. But here you would just get what you need, put it in you basket and go to the checkout line. Whereas if I was back home, even if I didn't know them, we would still communicate about what we buying or if something is too expensive, or whatever the situation may be. You would have some form of communication.

"Back home, if they weren't your family, you felt that they were family. People would call you 'cuz' and you wasn't their cousin, but that's the way it is. That's the way our community is. We felt—everybody felt loved. Everybody knew everybody. And when you would come visit, they say, 'Who's your mother?' Like if we would bring someone over or people would be new in our area, people would say, 'Well, who's you mother, where are you from?' People didn't communicate like that when I moved to Texas. It was hard, it was really hard to find people to even bond with."

Like food preferences, dialects of language and styles of interaction are culturally conditioned, but for people who rarely travel or who aren't accustomed to navigating other kinds of English-language dialects, differences from what is familiar can be disorienting. The Peachy Gang had evacuated to the next state over. Yet by leaving the boundaries of their cultural universe, where their own patterns of eating, talking, and gathering were the only ones they knew, unexpected difficulties bubbled to the surface and undermined the comfort they needed.

One afternoon in mid-October 2005 when I was visiting some of the family at Connie's house, she and a group of aunts, nieces, and uncles were sitting in the backyard. There was laughter, but something deeper was going on. Nell said, "When me and Paulette walked in the store and said, 'How you doin'?' he said, 'I know where you're from. Louisiana.' Man, all we had to say was, 'How you doin'!'"

Connie nodded her head slowly, smiling. "I get it a lot," she said, "and they always say we have an accent. 'Ya'll are different,' or 'Where ya'll come from—the islands or whatever?' and that's what we get a lot." Connie knew it was a painful subject, but she wanted them to know it was normal. "I know I did, and I know you guys going to be getting that, too."

"We already are," Katie blurted out before Connie had even finished her sentence. 'Where you from, Louisiana?' I say, 'Yep.'" Katie's way of handling announcements about her different-sounding speech glided right through any chance of insult.

"Some kinda way they know it," said Katie's friend, Linda, genuinely perplexed.

"Well, to be honest with you," Connie said, "the people in St. Bernard Parish even speak totally different than the people of New Orleans—the dialect, the words that they use is totally different, our demeanor, the way we act is totally different, we a little bit more outgoing, social like."

"Friendly," said Connie's husband, Terry.

"Yes, friendly," Nell agreed. "That's what it is."

"But since Katrina," Connie said, "everybody going to understand the way we are and the way we talk and what we're about. And you know, we have been sheltered way down in the bayous for a long time. But now everybody going to get a little flair of us," she said with a giggle.

Terry laughed. "Because Katrina has pushed us all across the United States, even to Colorado," he said, glancing over to me with a wink.

Listening to the exchange, I was struck by the way that Connie and her husband had aligned themselves fully with the bayou culture of Connie's relatives in crisis. It was a kindness, a way to soften the hurt of the family's culture shock and help everyone feel a sense of solidarity.

On the subject of church and churchgoing, Connie conveyed more about her own experience with culture shock. "The first time I went to a church here in Texas, my husband and I went to a Baptist church, and it was totally different. Totally different. Maybe it was the church I went to, but it was more, um, materialistic. They were talking about stuff that was different, like Mercedes Benz, and I'll never forget that. My husband looked at me and I looked at him and we said, 'Oh my gosh, this is different.'

"And they didn't have solos. We loved solos at home. We would sing a lot of good solos. And then, once we finished services, we didn't have no place to go, so we just go straight home without a gathering. Because normally after church, we gathered together and discussed our Sunday. Because, you done work all week and then you go to church and give your worship. So that's your day of resting with your family and talking and conversating. But I don't see that they do that, I . . . we didn't see that they conversate after church. People would just get in their cars. Whereas when we get out of church, we stand up in the church grounds and we talk and laugh and play with the kids if you got kids. And then you would go by someone's home and eat. You know, you don't just run go get in your car."

Many Americans do not recognize their own cultural habits and needs until they leave the world where those habits are the social norm. It may be hard to communicate, hard to figure out why what seems normal isn't the way things are done. Everyday situations in grocery stores and churches can cause sudden awareness of one's own cultural difference, and that sense of being lost can stir frustration and stress. Indeed, crossing any cultural threshold can provoke culture shock, even among those who are prepared for it: Peace Corps volunteers encounter unfamiliar attitudes and ways of doing things they find vexing; anthropologists, who are especially well trained to recognize the hidden forms and silent power of culture, commonly endure some degree of culture shock in the course of their research. Their own self-awareness and awareness of cultural variations may not help them achieve understanding of uncomfortable interactions until they stay put long enough to figure out the unspoken logic behind them. It's even harder when, instead of willingly stepping out of your comfort zone, you get driven out by a storm.

The cultural patterns we take with us when we leave home are not a possession, like an outer shell of clothing that can be removed at will. Culture is a way of seeing the world that we grow up learning and internalizing, usually without explicit rules. We observe what gets rewarded, what makes people laugh, what makes people angry or hurt, what makes sense to expect from others. We learn how time is spent, what conversations are valued, and how the actions and statements of others are understood. By their teen years, most children have already become culturally competent members of their own groups. That's why children and young adults are as vulnerable to cultural loss as their parents, even if they are no more able than their parents to name precisely what is wrong. Youngsters from the bayou as well as adults felt their cultural differences when they had to accept different food, or when they had schoolmates in their temporary schools tease them about how their speech sounded.[3]

TAKING CHARGE

In the weeks following news of the storm, Connie moved heaven and earth to help her relatives adapt to the terrible circumstances, to at least live comfortably. That didn't mean she could change what grocery stores stocked. But, as in the prayer that calls on the serenity to accept what cannot change and the courage to change the things that can be changed, family members came to recognize that there was something they could do about food. It took just a few weeks after having evacuated to Dallas in late August for the elder generation of women to realize that if they were going to be displaced for months, they would fail to thrive on Dallas food. Katie and her sisters came up with an idea: the men in the family would drive back home and load up coolers with the missing foods. When it came to cooking a proper gumbo, and enjoying food the way people were used to, a one-thousand-mile roundtrip drive was a minor inconvenience. Several men volunteered to make the drive. Being on the road provided a distraction, gave them a chance to survey the damage and report it back. Such road trips also allowed them to return as heroes to the women. And, of course, they would be the beneficiaries of gifts from the kitchen.

"My husband and them went home and came back with ice chests of down-home food," said Katie, "the right crabs and shrimp. I also sent for red beans, butter beans, Blue Plate mayonnaise—they didn't have it here," she said, barely disguising her frustration. "They had Kraft and whatever. And I sent for pickled meat. And hot sausage."

The first run back was in late September, but the journeys back home weren't easy. Not only were the trips emotionally difficult, but at first, they were thwarted altogether. St. Bernard Parish remained closed to residents for the entire months of September and October. So on their early runs back to the area, the men had to get their provisions about an hour's drive southeast of Baton Rouge on Interstate 10, about thirty miles short of New Orleans. A town called Laplace hugs the far western edge of the giant estuary that sits like an oversized crown atop the head of New Orleans. Known as Lake Pontchartrain, the estuary spans an area of 630 square miles that opens to the Gulf of Mexico, which feeds its brackish and freshwater composition. Studies coordinated by various environmental agencies reported in mid-October 2005 that despite the massive surges of floodwaters into Lake Pontchartrain caused by levee breaches, it appeared that "Katrina did not have an appreciable negative impact on the ecological health of the lake."[4] That news must have been a welcome surprise to everyone missing their regular crustacean fix. For men on the family mission to stock up coolers, even if Laplace wasn't home, it was sure a good place to buy fresh seafood.

Once the parish opened back up in early November, the men were able to drive down to Verret, about thirty-five minutes southeast of downtown New Orleans, and on to Shell Beach, just a few miles farther east, on the shores of another estuary, Lake Borgne—the area where a few of the shrimpers and crabbers had recovered enough to resume fishing.[5] Going back and forth for seafood and sausage and other necessities cost time and money, and because finances were strapped after the storm, the men took turns charging what they could on their credit cards. No one complained about the cost—what mattered was their need to taste home, to reconnect to the source of what could help people feel like themselves while they were forcibly marooned a world away.

"They brought all of that back for us. So, it's a little better now, because when you make a pot of gumbo you got the right ingredients," said Katie. In Connie's kitchen, Katie cooked over the aromas she knew best. With every bead of sweat that slid down her face from her cloth head-wrap, the stress seemed to drip away. Cooking absorbed her. She closed her eyes and inhaled the steam.

All the sisters cooked, and many of their daughters and sons did, too. Traditionally, for black families in bayou communities, it was the women who spent time at the stove or preparing dishes for the oven. But by the middle generation, men too had become enticed by the complexity of ingredients and the rewards of reputation. By the time of their evacuation for Hurricane Katrina, a dozen men in the family had earned their bragging rights as cooks. Nephews, sons, and sons-in-law of the four sisters—Potchie, Doozer, Pop, Turb, Charles, and some of their sons, for example, Chuck, all enjoyed preparing specialty dishes in the kitchen. It was nearly always the men in the family who cooked outside—either grilling meats or orchestrating a seafood boil. Men of all ages grill meats, a job that is straightforward enough to offer no special status to those who undertake it.

By contrast, a good "boiler" regards his craft as an art, equal to the precision and creativity required to make a good bowl of gumbo and just as important to the group. Becoming a prize boiler requires making a great marinade that the crabs or shrimp or crawfish will boil in. Boilers use giant aluminum two-part pots that are set up outdoors. The boiler prepares his marinade and then oversees the cooking. The secret "boil" might include potatoes, onions, salt, and lemons or limes. But like making an expert roux, what matters is not just knowing the ingredients—it is knowing how much of what, in what order, and when to add the seafood and how long to cook it. In the family, there is only one woman known as a prize boiler. The rest are men.

Connie's sister Deborah and their mother, Audrey May, were talking once in Dallas with others about the food they missed. Audrey May was one of those special gumbo cooks who had, for forty years, drawn crowds of family to her home on a Sunday to eat her food. But when Deborah mentioned her own husband's boiling, her mother swooned at the memory of it.

"Oh, her husband can boil, yeah," she said with obvious understatement. "He boiled crabs that would make you bite your fingers off."

Everyone laughed. They knew just what she meant.

The labor of cooking in Dallas was no idle hobby or distraction to keep the blues at bay—the time to prepare and linger over "finger-biting," familiar food reproduced habits of home and nurtured a vital comfort zone in the middle of uncertainty and crisis. Interestingly, most of the literature investigating the relationship between food and emotion is fixated on the unhealthy effects of finding comfort in "emotional eating." But the foods that felt like "comfort" to family members were not highly processed, not high in sugar or in carbs. The family's comfort foods were whole and mostly healthy.

In fact, food traditions that feature seafood are not only steeped in cultural meaning. Logic suggests they might also promote physical health and a sense of well-being. Research documents, for example, how fish in the diet produces serotonin, the "feel good" hormone in the brain that makes it easier to adapt well to stress.[6] Moreover, fish and shellfish are the two best sources of an omega-3 fatty acid needed by the brain, called docosahexaenoic acid (DHA). Without adequate amounts of DHA, scientists have found, the prevalence of depression increases. Perhaps the reliance on seafood had always helped the family cope.

BITTER, SOUR, SALTY, AND SWEET

Some might be inclined to trivialize what it means to miss the distinctive cuisine of New Orleans and southern Louisiana. But anyone from the region relates to the comfort provided by a food repertoire that is complex and distinctive. The raw ingredients of this cuisine circulate in the Gulf Coast waters and wetlands emptying out to it, in the Mississippi, across the bayous and farmland, into the city and on up into the parishes that border the northern edge of Lake Pontchartrain. Every cultural group new to the area brought influences in the foodstuffs they knew or their styles of preparation—the French perfected sauces and the roux, the Spanish added tomatoes, Africans brought knowledge of rice and okra, Germans brought sausages. American Indians taught slaves and colonists about sassafras bark, which got ground up as filé and used to season and thicken gumbo. Cajuns brought spicy gravies and one-pot dishes, and Isleños brought *caldo*, the famous Canary Islander stew.

A century before Katrina, the seafood and wild game from the area's marshes and estuaries appeared on dinner plates in the city's most exclusive restaurants just as they appeared in the big pots and frying pans of kitchens like Katie's all over bayou communities. The unique food culture makes New Orleans one of the top international food destinations. And, like blood circulating in a body, the life force of the area's cuisine does not confine itself to the heart, the city limits. Instead, the inventiveness and craft of the cuisine flows freely in and around the entire metropolitan region.

Martha Ward, a cultural anthropologist who has made New Orleans home for the last forty years, knew just what Katie and her family were going through without their food. In her Uptown home that Katrina's flood-waters did not reach, she raised the problems of evacuees stranded in other areas of the country. These included her students and colleagues at the University of New Orleans (UNO) who were unable to return because their homes were ruined. Martha instantly grasped the hardship of the big family from St. Bernard Parish stuck in Dallas. "It's hard to imagine the culture shock that people from here are feeling living in Houston, Dallas, Denver, Atlanta, Memphis, Nashville, wherever they are. They are ripped from their homes, cast into another culture they don't understand and that, in fact, speaks another language and eats different food. . . . People are writing in by the thousands or calling to ask, 'Where's our Zatarain's mustard? Where's our red beans? We don't have this here, we don't have that here.' This huge number of foodstuffs that we're used to having here that they can't get. It's really hard. They can't fix what they consider a normal meal. There's nothing that works the way it does in New Orleans."

A local historian, and one of the few African American professionals I met who had relatives from St. Bernard Parish, Raphael Cassimere echoed Martha's sentiment in a matter-of-fact way. "You're not going to find gumbo the way we cook it anywhere else. You're not going to find the kind of meats that we have. Can't find red beans and so forth. The food is different here."

It didn't matter how many people I asked, or what color or class they considered themselves. Cassimere said it all: "Places like Houston and Dallas are not like New Orleans. And even though residents from small communities like those in St. Bernard Parish were welcome there after Katrina, and they were given a lot of support, you didn't feel at home."

Thinking more about the relationship of food to social life (and, perhaps, to mental well-being), I realized that food at family gatherings functioned both like a gift and a platform for sociality. In contrast, the most common form of social gathering I knew were potlucks with colleagues. Neither my partner nor I have any family within one thousand miles. Over the years, we gradually devolved our ambitions of hosting multicourse meals to the Colorado norm. At a typical potluck, the host provides the space, and everyone brings an individual dish to share. The dishes that converge at such gatherings share a table, but little else. Each dish is prepared by someone with no idea what others will be bringing. No one is asked to follow a theme for the event or to coordinate offerings for balance. A plate of sushi might sit alongside pizza, pork tamales, or a plate of baked brie with sun-dried tomatoes. Over there, a tray of salmon bites on crackers crowds next to hamburger lasagna, flour tortilla wraps, and Asian noodle salad. Not only do the sweet and savory flavors get oddly distributed, there is no pretense of coherence.

Potlucks save time and money because no one has to prepare more than a single dish. Hosts are spared the need to think creatively about what might fit together. Many people eliminate the labor altogether by grabbing an already prepared dish at a grocery store. As a result, the collective experience of eating together is not much about the delicate balance of tastes. People go to catch up on news and perhaps discuss ideas—a decided improvement over the ambiance of a conference room. And because everyone has contributed, there are no outstanding debts. Economic anthropologists remind us that "freedom from debt" releases those involved from any expectation that such relationships will continue to be nurtured.[7]

The bayou family members I came to know prepare food based on a different set of assumptions. For them, the food at a gathering presents complementary flavors that taste good. You know who has made something, and you understand the gift of love and time. Debt is a constant part of what holds family bonds together.

One late morning in November, nine weeks after the storm, I arrived at Connie's house to find Katie scrubbing her hands in the kitchen sink, about to launch the makings of a big pot of gumbo she would offer the crowd in a few hours. She had brought most of the ingredients with her from her temporary home in East Dallas. "What-all goes into it?" I asked her. She smiled without looking up, perhaps happy for the question since she had struggled to put together enough of the critical ingredients "to make magic." She had already assembled her seasoning vegetables into little piles—chopped bell pepper, onion, and celery, what chefs call the "holy trinity" of New Orleans cooking. Katie also used fresh garlic.

"Well, it ain't always the same, but you always got to do your roux first. You put your flour and oil in the pan—and you got to keep stirring it until you get it the right color. Stir and stir and stir, but watch out for the heat because it might burn if it's too high."

The popping of oil signaled the moment to add flour, and Katie knew just how much to put in without measuring. The popping relaxed, and a few minutes later, a gentle burbling sound rose from the frying pan. The electric stove in Connie's house made controlling the roux a little harder. Every cook in the family preferred to work with a gas oven and a gas stove, but in Dallas, nearly everyone's apartment was equipped with electric appliances, and that's what they had at Connie's, too.

"The roux is the most important part," she said, washing off a hand and glancing back at her roux with concerned eyes. "And you got to be patient with it."

I asked whether she could use a food processor to lessen the work time. "Uh-huh!" she said emphatically without explanation. Her daughter Roz clarified, "My mom doesn't use short cuts. No food processor!"

"Now," Katie said, some time later, after the roux had thickened and darkened. "You got all your ingredients—you got your crab, shrimp, oyster, hot sausage, smoked sausage, ham, chicken wings, chicken necks, gizzards, chicken hearts, chitlins." And of course, she had spent the day before getting all these meats ready—cleaning everything, picking out the crab meat, trimming the chicken parts, and cutting heads off the shrimp. "You got to fry off the meats," she said, reaching for a large frying pan.

Turb (short for Terrible News, the nickname Katie gave him when he was a rascal toddler) was just one of the younger men who loved to cook, and he had learned his repertoire from his mother. When I asked him later about making gumbo, he added a little more instruction, knowing she had provided a bare-bones recipe typical of an experienced cook who no longer thinks about each step: "You actually fry your hot sausage and then you fry the rest of your meat." The sausage went in first because the fat became the frying grease for everything else—the chicken, and then the crab and shrimp. "And you don't take a short cut because if you don't fry off the meats, you don't get the flavor; you get a pot of grease."

Katie's methodical frying seared the meats and released a new set of smells into the kitchen, sharp and spicier than the roux gravy.

"Last thing," Katie said, "is to put your meats into the roux." As Katie transferred everything from the frying pan to the big pot, the scent of gumbo steamed out into the room. She looked satisfied. All morning, she had been working inside her comfort zone, mesmerized, it seemed, by the simultaneous pleasures of smelling, listening, touching, and tasting that accompanied the art of cooking. Cooking takes attention. It is hard to worry and cook at the same time. And perhaps the immense pleasure people like Katie and Cynthia and Turb and Charles got from cooking related to this fact—that all the senses participate, and with so many kinds of perception operating at the same time, the body and the mind must feel especially alive.

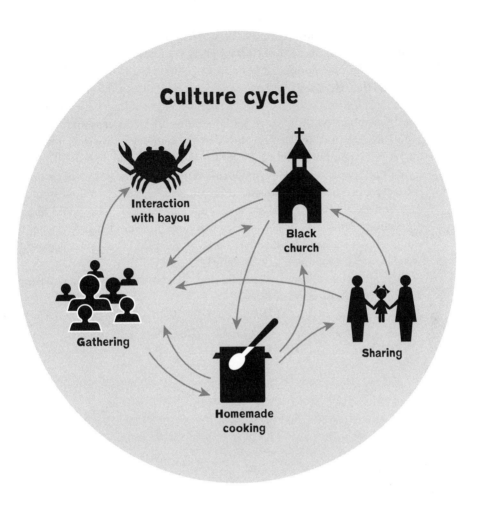

Culture cycle

Interaction with bayou

Black church

Gathering

Homemade cooking

Sharing

Circulation of cultural resources

Before Katrina, the "culture cycle" of the family depended on interaction with the bayou environment, homemade cooking, child-care sharing, front-porch conversation, black dialect, the black church, and weekly and holiday gatherings. The group's system of interdependence allowed its members a degree of autonomy from the larger world. But when Katrina hurt everyone in the family, that interdependence collapsed and activities that energized their culture cycle were compromised. At the same time, the recovery template forced family members into a new dependency on outsiders.

Fig. 21

Roz summed it up: "The way you cook is your art form, and the way people respond to the taste of your food lets you know you're a good cook."

More than two months after the storm, all variety of concerns still preoccupied their days and nights. Connie could do a lot, but she could not address the questions that no one anywhere had answers for. Every morning, family members woke up to yesterday's unresolved concerns and to new problems that constantly arose. Now that the courtesy van to the clinic no longer operated, how would they get Connie's mother to dialysis? Which tombs had been broken up by the storm? When would the power and water get restored to the lower parish so everyone could go back? Where could they find a used freezer to store more crab and shrimp? What could they do about the children who showed signs of emotional problems? And when would FEMA trailers be available? Would St. Bernard Parish ever recover? When would a good night's sleep come?

Worries weighed heavily. Good food in the company of family was the best relief for those very hard days.

II

WAVE OF TROUBLE

4

RUIN AND RELIEF

LONG BEFORE THE STORM

In 1718, in a land where a deep river flowed into the ocean and forests of bald cypress trees shielded the earth from the hot sun, French settlers came and took a look around. "Yes," they might have said, "this will do. We've got water all around us—big lakes, a mighty river, a gulf just below us, and bayous between that will supply us with plenty to hunt and fish as the local natives do. We'll harvest the cypress for lumber to build our settlement and grow what we need to eat. The river will make it easy to trade with the interior lands of the continent. We will stake our future here. Ah, but we can't do this work ourselves! We'll need slaves, *alors!*"[1]

By 1730, French sailors had shipped six thousand black slaves to Louisiana, mostly from Senegal, where the French had an important colony. And so it was that Africans arrived, without a choice. They outnumbered whites, two to one, but that hardly presented an advantage, given the severe conditions of work imposed by the French on their indigo, cypress, and rice plantations. The slaves may have said, "We have been taken from our families and everything we know in Africa. We own nothing, not our food or clothing, not even our language. But our people are clever and strong. The swamp is nearby, where no slaveholder dares go. We shall get to know the dangers so one of us can slip into the swamp and meet with runaways who have built hidden settlements. We can swap goods and build up our own independent trade. Safe with the gators and snakes, we trade secrets, too. If our children are born into this life, they will at least grow up learning how to survive."

The Spanish arrived, sixty years after the first of the French and claimed, "Louisiana is ours now. We'll use slaves to harvest cypress and also sugar cane, but we need more Spanish speakers to keep this land in our control." And so they saw to it that two thousand Canary Islanders traveled five thousand miles from their homes west of Morocco to reach southeast Louisiana around the 1780s. These arrivals, who became known as "Isleños" (the islanders), might have said, "We have nothing but the shirts on our backs. We are here because the Spanish invited us and gave us land. We brought our Catholic religion and Spanish language, our old folktales and recipes from home. We will farm for a living." And they made a new life on Bayou Terre aux Boeufs (Land of Cattle) in lower St. Bernard Parish, just fifteen miles downriver from New Orleans and next door to the plantations where the first sugar cane in Louisiana would soon be granulated.

The British also wanted a piece of the action. "Now that we have taken West Florida from the Spanish," their actions seemed to say, "we've got our eyes on Louisiana, east of the Mississippi. With a base in Louisiana, we can intercept Spanish ships and capture the gold and silver they are moving from their mainland colonies back to Spain." And so, in 1813, the British invaded the coastal area that had earlier been named St. Bernard Parish. But in 1815, forever preserved as a mythic moment in American lore, Major General Andrew Jackson beat the British back in the Battle of New Orleans. By then, the Americans technically owned Louisiana, but the Spanish and French still had their plantations, the majority of whites still spoke French, the slaves were still slaves, and many of the Spanish-speaking Isleños had sold their land to sugar planters and established trapping and fishing livelihoods in communities closer to the Gulf.

About one hundred years after Major General Jackson made his mark on history, when the cypress industry had felled most of the forests and tapped most of the profits to be gained from lumber, the oil and gas magnates stepped into the area to dig for their own bounty. One could almost hear them whisper, "We have another way to make money here. We won't need the plantations or railroads; we can pump what we find in the Gulf into our refineries. We just have to cut canals through the marshes and wetlands and lay the pipelines. No problem."

And so it was that the context of the Johnson-Fernandez family's ancestry began and evolved. Because slave records are inconclusive and many of these were lost in the storm, the earliest family ancestors who can be verified were the parents of Peachy (Alma) Johnson. Her parents were Emma Fernandez and Victor Johnson, born in St. Bernard Parish in 1878 and 1877, respectively. These ancestors constitute what I am calling generation one. Peachy and her five siblings represent generation two. They had large families of their own, and together, all these descendants belong to the Johnson-Fernandez family (see Figures 2–11).

Peachy, who lived from 1909 to 1984, had worked as a house domestic for a prominent white family in the lower parish. Before he died in 1964, her husband, McKinley, supported the family by trapping mink, coon, and muskrat. He'd skin them, dry and cure their pelts, and sell them to the markets in the city. He also caught turtles that the children sold to traders who would then resell them in New Orleans. Peachy's husband also picked moss from the bayou, dried it, and sold it by the bale as stuffing for furniture. He earned extra money by picking okra. He crabbed and shrimped and kept the home stocked with seafood.

As the generations progressed, family members sought the developing job opportunities in the parish associated with oil and gas, river trade for the Chalmette port, and small retail businesses. In the family's third generation, sisters Cynthia, Katie, Roseana, and Audrey each worked at one time or another in one of the lower-parish factories for processing shrimp, crab, or oysters. Their brothers and male cousins continued the tradition of trapping and fishing, but mostly on the side of wage work. Some grew okra, tomatoes, and turnips for household use. A few became full-time farmers. Many of the men in that generation worked as longshoremen, loading and unloading barges on the river. Men and women of generation four began to break away from the older economies attached to place and have begun to flow into the more fluid, less permanent service economy or to work as skilled labor.

Life on the bayou continued to evolve and shift, carrying along with it old habits of the heart.[2] Then came the storm.

SOON AFTER KATRINA

Stranded for months in Dallas, family members' biggest concern was finding a way back home to St. Bernard Parish. That mission became a kind of life preserver, a resolve that kept the group from drowning in sorrow. A few men had already made it back by late fall, basing themselves in Baton Rouge and then commuting to the parish during the day to return to their jobs with the utility companies or to try to get trucking work related to the cleanup. Although the parish reopened in November, there was no realistic way to go back and start on cleanup or gutting ruined homes without a place to live. The only solution FEMA offered—a trailer—became a critical resource among tens of thousands of people. In January 2006, Katie and Gray Eye and Nell and Earl were the first two households in the family to get their FEMA trailers. All the rest followed as soon as they got the call that their trailer was ready.

"There is not a livable house in this parish," pronounced Henry Rodriguez to a reporter for the *Atlantic*.[3] Known as "Junior" by parish residents, the seventy-year-old parish president had become a media presence after Katrina, distinguished by his fluff of white hair, his round shape, and his sharp tongue. He spoke candidly to reporters about the delicate topics of recovery and FEMA. No one accused him of exaggerating, except perhaps government agents with their bravado still intact.

"Trailers, trailers, trailers." Junior repeated on National Public Radio. "People want to come home, you know."

Before Katrina, the majority of the parish's sixty-seven thousand residents lived within a twenty-six-mile radius, close to the bayous that supply the New Orleans region and many parts of the country with Gulf shrimp and crab, oysters, and crawfish. According to the US Census Bureau estimates, in January 2006, only about 5 percent of the parish's former residents had returned (3,361 people), their families having managed to secure a coveted FEMA trailer.[4] Junior guessed that thousands of other former residents without a place to live commuted in during the day. There were also thousands of volunteers who set up bare-bones barracks in places like Camp Hope, a grade school in Violet repurposed as a volunteer housing and supply center.

"A lot of the people that left are going to be coming back because where they went, that is not home," Junior said as we sat in his extra-large trailer in Chalmette where he and his wife lived and where he conducted parish business. "You know, if we can get these trailers, if FEMA can just help us get these trailers in, it is an incentive for people to come back. Yesterday, I heard two people say, 'Well you know, Joe Blow is coming back on my street. I think I am coming back.'"

Junior had lived all his life in the lower parish, and for most of his adult life in the village of Verret, just a few houses down the block from Katie and Gray Eye. Everyone in the family knew him, and they felt lucky that their friend was in a position of authority.

"My wife, she wants to go back to Verret," he continued. "But she didn't want to go back because nobody was there, but now that Katie and Gray Eye are there and Cynthia and all them is coming back, well, she feels kind of safe. If you are in the community, you know your neighbor can get there in five or ten minutes. That makes a big difference." Junior pointed out what everyone in the family knew: for a community that has been broken into bits, resilience cannot manifest itself on its own. For communities like Verret, the magic formula of resilience depended on social recognition as well as membership in a social fabric and the will to maintain it.

The ordeal of getting a trailer cranked up new confusion and frustration among Katrina survivors who had enough worries to fill their quota. Connie saw to it that her family members in Dallas put their applications in at the earliest possible date back in October. From her backyard, Connie had reached Junior by phone in November. With the family members gathered around her as she relayed messages from Junior, she also learned that residents wanting a trailer on the site of their ruined home would have to first complete another round of papers authorizing FEMA to clear debris from their property. The papers had to be processed and the work completed before FEMA would assign a trailer. So people thought it was this pre-step to getting a trailer that was causing the delay. By January 2006, only a few people had been contacted.

However, there was more to the problem than the unprecedented scale of need. As early as September 9, 2005, an internal e-mail sent by White House staff hinted at the mess that would come to characterize the stunning failures of the disaster response:

> Scooter: Please see below. The trailer idea is worse than I originally thought. Per the data below, the last batch of the trailers that we are now purchasing will be coming off the production line in approximately 3.5 years.[5]

> —E-mail sent September 9, 2005, by Neil Patel, staff secretary to the vice president, to Charles P. Durkin, personal aide to the vice president, apparently destined for J. Lewis "Scooter" Libby Jr., chief of staff

The confusion surrounding FEMA trailers had become apparent in other ways. In January 2006, Connie reported that she and her sisters, Robin and Deborah, were still struggling to get their mother a trailer, with no luck. Then, out of the blue, someone from FEMA called her in Dallas to ask if they could come hook up the trailer in Violet. "What trailer?" Connie asked. She quickly called her sister. "Robin, do you see a trailer by mama's house?" Robin looked across the street and replied, "There's nothing but our destroyed house. No trailer."

Connie sighed, shaking her head. "The left hand is not knowing what the right hand is doing. So mother is still waiting for a trailer. And she is a dialysis patient, with cardiovascular problems and very sick, and she want to get back home, and live in her environment, in her so-called home, which would be the FEMA trailer."

THE PRESENCE OF ABSENCE

For our documentary film project, we had agreed to meet up with Katie and her carload of family members near Baton Rouge in mid-January 2006 so they could escort us through the parish and show us their ruined homes and communities. They had driven the eight hours from Dallas; we had flown and rented a car. Earl was driving his in-laws' Ford Explorer. Since the evacuation, the sage-colored SUV had put on thousands of miles with road trips between Dallas and New Orleans to fill coolers full of seafood and to collect the foodstuffs not available in Dallas. Katie and Nell and many of the other adults had been back once to see the damage since the parish re-opened to its residents in November. But those were reconnaissance trips—there was nothing to come back to: nowhere to stay, no electricity or water. This time, the two households were coming back to get installed in the new FEMA trailers they had been assigned. Ginny had hopped in their car to film them as we entered the land of ruin. As Earl drove, Katie narrated from the front seat, Gray Eye and Nell offered occasional remarks from the back. I drove alone, close behind.

The traffic was heavy and moving at a creep. We passed the town of Kenner just east of the New Orleans International Airport and slowly continued on through Metairie toward the city. On both sides of the highway, I could spot the damage from the ragged edges of the storm: garages blown down, windows knocked out of apartments, roofs pushed off shopping malls and public buildings. But these areas only foreshadowed the more dramatic hurt that lay farther ahead in the beloved city of mayhem and, beyond that—toward the Gulf—in St. Bernard Parish. It was hard to keep focused on the road. Off to my right, a sea of blue tarps flapped at their corners in the gusty wind. They covered ruined roofs—signs of effort already in motion. The visible impact of the storm roused my affection for New Orleans in a way that I imagined everyone else on the road was also feeling that very moment. Together, we were all voyeurs, and we were all people who felt allegiance to a community that celebrated life. I didn't want to drive off the road, but I needed to look at all the ruin those broken levees had caused.

We merged onto I-610 toward Slidell, and within a few minutes, exited toward North Claiborne, taking the one-way street that directed us through the Upper Ninth Ward and Bywater neighborhoods with their sodden shot-gun homes and wide front porches, once charming, once elevated several steps above ground. Block after block after block of established, historic neighborhoods marked with the special language of disaster-relief workers—a big spray-painted X on every home provided a quick shorthand for key messages. Often the X was orange, corresponding to the color of international search and rescue. The "X" itself is FEMA's own symbol for urban search-and-rescue efforts. Each quadrant of the X reserves space for abbreviations and symbols that communicate critical information: top center indicates the time and date the rescue team left the structure; right shows hazards in the structure; bottom center records number of live bodies (LB) and dead bodies (DB) found in the structure; left is the rescue-team identifier.

Our two vehicles crossed over the Industrial Canal bridge that leads from the Upper Ninth Ward to the Lower Ninth Ward, and on to the parish. The Industrial Canal, which empties into the Mississippi, was built in the 1920s to connect the river to Lake Pontchartrain. During Katrina, its levees were breached in three places, just as other levees had failed all along the notorious seventy-five-mile shipping canal: the Mississippi River Gulf Outlet. The MRGO runs all the way up the eastern side of St. Bernard Parish from the Gulf until it meets the Industrial Canal. The failures of these and other levees allowed the water in Lake Pontchartrain and Lake Borgne to fill the bowl of the city and its surrounding low-lying parishes with a toxic soup.[6] The horrific zone of devastation stretched out mile after mile, surreal in the jagged contours of former communities, still occupying space, but with a scrambled footprint and gutted soul.

I kept driving, my hands now damp. I wanted to lighten my grip, but the wheel was my anchor and its resistance helped to keep me focused, oriented in a disorienting landscape. Street signs and traffic lights lay crumpled on the ground, ripped from their sockets. The only indication I was leaving the Lower Ninth Ward and Orleans Parish was a big welcome sign, bent over and barely readable: "Welcome to St. Bernard Parish." Katie's voice murmured in my head. "We not from New Orleans. We from St. Bernard Parish!" This was the place, a place treasured by people I had come to know in Dallas. It was just a sign, but in its simple broken way, it distilled the trace of human pride, and the assumption of everyday life that broken levees had betrayed.

As we drove south through what remained of Chalmette, the mighty Mississippi was a few blocks to the west, and the killer canal, the MRGO, a couple of miles to the east. With all the media attention on the levee breaches, no one seemed to be reporting about the coastal land loss in Louisiana, according to some scientists the fastest-disappearing land on the planet. After all, this loss of land had contributed significantly to the damage caused by Katrina.[7] The wetlands had always slowed down hurricanes and helped buffer the impact on human settlements in the past. But since the 1950s, these buffers had been eroded at alarming rates, dissolving into water, in part because of the thousands of canals etched through their vegetative skin, permitting saltwater from the Gulf to enter and destroy their balance. The MRGO's long gash in the wetlands was the single biggest of these canals, a broken promise of a boon for business. No boon at all, the canal performed double duty to destroy the parish: building it had not only removed thousands of acres of wetland buffer, but its long profile also served as a perfect funnel to whip up gigantic twenty-five-foot storm surges and breach the levees. All that for a misbegotten shipping shortcut.[8]

At four and a half months after Katrina, the four-lane St. Bernard Highway was still crazed with gaping cracks and pocked with deep potholes. Many of the smaller roadways were not even passable, blocked by felled trees, upended vehicles, and a great variety of debris. The furiously churning water had deposited stray household items in front yards, on sidewalks, in the roadway's brown median grass, and in vacant parking lots. Mangled pieces of roofing, fencing, shopping-center shelving, backyard playground equipment, trees, and signage, all had swept their way into a no-man's-land, like the haphazard array of pieces to a jigsaw puzzle still awaiting placement. News reports indicated that already tons of debris had been cleared from the parish, but thousands of tons remained. On some blocks, big clawtoothed machines had scooped up random remnants and dumped them into heaps of waste, shoved to the side of the road for pickup later. Mile after mile after mile, a "terrible wilderness of ruin."[9]

Every inch of visible earth lay blanketed with muck and sludge. More varieties of damage appeared the farther south we drove, owing to the more numerous canals and boats in the lower parish. Pitched up into limbs of dead trees still standing and onto roofs or telephone poles were car seats, fencing, shards of buildings, furniture, boat netting, and clothing, hung like ornaments for a bizarre-themed parade. Mighty steel poles that banked electrical lines had bent and broken in submission to two-hundred m.p.h. winds and twenty-five-foot storm surges. The poles were one thing, the circuitry another, and by this time, the wire cables had been eaten up by the infusion of saltwater. Lakes of standing water stood their ground and the water inside structures stubbornly resisted evaporation. Just one inch of standing floodwater inside a structure could unleash toxic mold that would overtake the entire building. I could not escape the stench. Or the stillness. The presence of so much absence. A morgue landscape.

When Earl turned onto one of the desolate blocks in Violet, I stayed behind for a moment to collect myself.

I stepped out of the car and looked around me. It felt as if the world had stopped breathing. There was no sound. There were no gulls, no doves, no pelicans, no sparrows, no squirrels, no cats, no children playing in yards. No breezes. Only ruin. Stink. Putrid water. Organic rot. Savage wounds, as nasty to the nose as they were to the eye. What could survive in such an incongruous jumble of remnants and death?

I got back in the car and caught up to the family ahead of me. I watched as they surveyed the ruined Violet and scouted for familiar faces. As Ginny filmed more of the damage, family members would hoot and holler to people they knew, even when they spotted someone at a distance. Their joy filled every shout. I saw no tears, only smiles and laughter. How could their spirits be lighter than mine? This ruin beyond imagining was their home. That's when it clicked: what I was seeing was not what they saw. Their love of home, all the interactions and life experience that had been part of this place had equipped them with another set of eyes, a soft-focus lens made of memory. Theirs was like a double vision: they could see the mess, but through the lens of their hearts, they could also see home. I was an outsider, and seeing the place for the first time, I could only experience the rawness of the devastation with an outsider's eyes, nose, and ears. I thought about something Junior had said, about the way people made up their mind to come back based on what their friends and neighbors were deciding. It made sense. For people from the parish, every person who had come back was a vote for hope, and that hope formed a special unity among those willing to face the task of reclaiming this godforsaken land.

Leaving Violet to head farther south toward the Gulf and the oldest part of the parish, we turned onto the other primary road that led from the upper to the lower parish—the four-lane divided State Highway 39, also known as Judge Perez. We followed it until we reached the junction of LA 46 and LA 39, where we turned left, away from the river and east toward the MRGO and Lake Borgne beyond it. Close to the turn stood a big outdoor stadium, what had been a high school football field. Before the storm, high school students and much of the rest of the community attended Friday-night games. The rivalry between their Eagles and the Chalmette High Owls brought big crowds and channeled the tensions between up-the-road and down-the-road populations into a healthy competition. After Katrina, St. Bernard High School had been closed by the parish school district, and students from down here had to be bused up to Chalmette, where, since October, the high school temporarily housed all grades, K-12, under the name of St. Bernard Unified. Beyond the high school, we passed a small cemetery and then, at a beat-up structure that had housed the Verret Fire Station, we turned right, and then right again, heading west on Bayou Road.

So this is Verret, I thought. It is situated at a midpoint in the dog-legged Bayou Terre aux Boeufs, the bayou made famous by its colonial plantations and small Isleño settlements that ran on either side of its borders (see Figures 14 and 27). The bayou lay at the center of a tongue of land about a mile wide and twenty miles long, beginning at the Mississippi River to the west and continuing east past Verret and then south toward Delacroix Island, the "end of the road," where it emptied into the Gulf.

It was on this fertile bayou land that the Isleños, Junior's ancestors, had originally pursued subsistence farming on their allotted parcels. But gradually, with the help of the black slaves, the Isleños learned to adapt to the swamps and marshlands. They became expert trappers, fishermen, and boat builders.[10] Long before Katrina, the Isleño fishing communities and presence had come to dominate the white ethnic character of the lower parish.[11]

Verret was located just inside the parish levee system, a ring of earthen mounds that encircled all but the smallest communities located beyond Verret toward the Gulf (see Figure 14). The three sisters—Cynthia, Katie, and Roseana—who lived in Verret lost their homes completely. "The village," as family members refer to it, was still regarded as the family's epicenter, the rural version of an important hub city where people came on weekends, and especially on Sundays.

BAYOU ROAD

Bayou Road runs alongside the Bayou Terre aux Boeufs between Poydras near the Mississippi River, to Verret, and then on another nine miles south to Delacroix, its terminus. Unlike the flowing stream and transportation waterway it once was, the Bayou Terre aux Boeufs had long been choked from too much algae and had become an abandoned channel off the river. Nonetheless, the bayou that ran through Verret remained a place where family could easily walk to net a crab or crawfish dinner.

There are no curbs or gutters on Bayou Road, and the short, single-lane stubs of asphalt off this road in Verret housed just handfuls of people. It was clear that whatever the village had been in its most populous and energetic days had shifted to a home base with a few anchoring members of the

Loss and ruin

Only devastation met family members on their return. Still, it was home.

Nature's recovery effort worked faster than FEMA's

Katrina's power upended and emptied above-ground concrete tombs

Hymn 489: "Wade in the Water"

Cynthia, relieved to recover her mother's photo from her ruined home

Fig. 22

The storm-tossed sanctuary of First Baptist Church in Verret

family. Their children had grown up and moved out, mostly to Violet, but the three sisters still lived here, just a block or two from their First Baptist Church. Their frame homes had been modest but, by all reports, well kept. A few Verret homes were brick, as was the church, but none escaped terrible damage. Some homes had spun off their foundations, some roofs had caved in or been swept off to another lot or another block.

There in Verret, Katie began the explanation of where we were and what we were seeing. On the right, she pointed to what had been Junior Rodriguez's home. He was no celebrity to them—just someone they all knew and liked, someone who used to fish and hunt with Katie's brother, Raymond, and who later taught Raymond's son, Buffy, to fish. Like other Isleños, Junior's family was Catholic, so the issue of white and black churches got sidestepped. Everyone just accepted the idea that blacks down here were Baptists and whites were Catholics. The relationship between Junior's family and Katie's generation of the Peachy Gang illustrates exactly why race relations in the lower parish can't be mapped onto US politics. That's why when city folk look at the parish as racist, they are missing the lower-parish piece of the story. Families interacted; they had children in the same schools and met as parents. Race relations here are more complex because black and white families have lived alongside each other for generations.

But proximity serves only as the visible part of a fuller context for this complexity. Having a Creole heritage meant that families with deep roots were likely to be intertwined, a reality that helped buffer the racism of the larger parish. On Peachy's side, some believed that Peachy's mother, Emma Fernandez, had had at least some Spanish blood. In addition, the man Peachy married, McKinley James, was part Indian. Katie was quick to add that he had "good hair" and wore it short, in a pompadour. She told me once that she had asked her father, "How come you so dark?" He told her his mama was dark. *Creole* is a knotty term because it is used differently by different groups. But the most basic understanding refers to having been born in the local environment, whether that refers to people, language, or food.[12] No one in the family called themselves Creole; it simply had no meaning to them.

The tour continued.

Junior's home fit the typical village residence—a large, one-story frame house that appeared to have been comfortable but not showy. It had been medium gray with red trim around the windows, perhaps not what many an outsider might expect for the residence of the parish president. But Junior was not your everyday politician.

"There's our church," said Katie with a flat voice, looking ahead and to the right, the Lake Borgne side of the road. The broken "First Baptist Church" sign had collapsed in the weedy parking lot fronting the church. The structural damage appeared minimal from the road, but we would learn again and again that seeing the breathtaking devastation from a flood requires opening the front door.

Between the church and Katie's home sat a small, ranch-style brick house where children with disabilities had lived, a place Cynthia knew well from her years of work with the residents she cared for. We inched forward to see what was left of the home Katie and Gray Eye had built and lived in for twenty-three years. The baby-blue paint with white trim matched the exterior colors of Connie's Victorian home. Family members had seen the damage on a previous trip, but their silence seemed to express something deeply private, and it distanced us from them. We walked around the house to try to see how it had been knocked from its foundation and how the roof had blown off. In front, there were concrete steps that had once led up to a porch that now led nowhere. In this parish, and throughout the region, the porch with its chairs and orientation to the street was a place for conversation, the interface between one family and another family. As a material manifestation of a cultural bent toward hospitality, porches softened barriers and helped neighbors stay connected and genial. Everyone says hello from their porch. In FEMA's post-Katrina society of cultural irrelevance, however, the wobbly aluminum steps of the trailers led directly inside.

At the side of the house, Gray Eye helped hoist Katie up two feet into the easiest entry to the inside. Without turning around, she beckoned us inside. I swallowed and braced before entering the grave site of so much loss. Gray Eye stood by with a hand to help us step up into the living room. It was hard to imagine that Katie had hosted dozens of family members here just days before the evacuation. The musty, moldy smell made breathing hard. What had been the primary public space resembled an abandoned junkyard, crowded with incoherent, topsy-turvy furniture, all of it framed by black mold that had found a hospitable environment. Spawned by the slow, insidious rot of standing water, the creep of opportunistic, splotchy mold had invited termites to take up residence in the idyllic damp environment. Within weeks, the black mold penetrated the walls, rendering them forever toxic.

Katie put her hand on what had been an island counter as if to balance herself. She said nothing, but she turned to look at something on the wall. Her eyes were fixed on a school pennant hanging with red and silver rib-

Black mold

Standing water served as a breeding ground for mold to grow and creep up the walls of homes and other structures throughout the parish. Black mold releases mycotoxins that can damage lungs and, in some cases, cause death.

Fig. 23

bons attached to it, probably a child's achievement she had showcased for all to see.

We made our own path through the tumbled chunks of mud-caked furniture to look into the next room. Katie said softly to herself, "This is where I made my magic." The big kitchen looked scorched with blackness, consumed with black mold. The stovetop had all but disappeared under the muck. We paused in reverence for what seemed the most important loss, then looked into the front bedroom, where Gray Eye was standing, looking down at the floor of rubble. Katie gently tugged a dresser drawer open to find stacks of mildew-infested records. She loved music. She pulled out two random 45s. "Etta James," she said, then glanced at the other one. "Turn Back the Hands of Time," she said, shaking her head, voice barely audible. Then she spotted a framed photo of her mother, the woman her children and nieces and nephews knew as Big Mama and everyone else knew as Peachy. Peachy's photo looked more like a ghostly watercolor than a photograph, but it seemed to be recognizable enough to mean the world to Katie. Nothing else was salvageable.

The scene inside Katie's home took my breath away. This was the first interior I had visited in person. We had looked through hundreds of pictures in Dallas, but this was the full sensory experience. The turmoil of a violent storm hurling people's material lives like bits in a blender had left a scale of mess that I had never witnessed before.

We walked back outside. Katie broke the spell. "I sent my husband when he first went home," she said. She had collected herself and wanted to talk; she was not going to cry. "I told him, 'Get me some pictures.' He got the pictures. They put them all in the plastic bag, but some of them was wet. I lost a lot of them—all my kids' graduation pictures. And my granddaughter was the queen of homecoming. They ran so much that you could just see a little part of her face like this," she said, holding up the photo of her mother that she had kept in one hand. "I mainly wanted my son's pictures. He was killed in a car accident on his way to work on a Sunday morning, and he was twenty-one years old, and I wanted his picture. And they got that one. But everything else gone. Everything."

Heirlooms and photos that had documented shared memories had been swept away right along with old newspapers and clothes. Katrina had no regard for what was sacred. "My sofa was climbing the walls, my freezer was laying up in the middle of the floor. I didn't see the kitchen table. I lost everything. He couldn't find nothing. Under water all that time, I guess, you know."

Katie and Gray Eye sat on the steps that led nowhere, looking around at what had befallen their community, their own home. But just to be back lifted their spirits and calmed their anxieties. Their trailer was due to arrive. Hope was in the air.

Gray Eye shook his head side to side as he often did, "I never did give up on coming back where I lived. And, believe me, I love where we were [in Dallas] because it was wonderful, because everybody treated us well. But it was never like home. Morning, noon, or night you wake up, think about home. Anybody got any kind of understanding, you know what I'm saying, they would understand that."

Katie had her own way of putting it. "Oh, well, I knew that the house was gone," she said. "But just to be home, that is the important thing. To see people you know. Now we didn't have any problem with the people in Texas. The people were beautiful to us. But it's not like being home."

THE POWER OF COMMUNITY

Driving alone down through the parish had sent prickles through my skin, as if my cells were conducting a reality check of the morbid landscape surrounding me. But the brown wash over everything in my sights shifted to the background as I saw people reaching out to each other, waving furiously to passersby like us, even when they were strangers. The moment made me realize that what really mattered was not the absence of everything that had been here, but the presence of what was here—the humanity of a badly hurt community whose members were coming back, claiming the devastation: their loyalty was bigger than the defeat of all that property. I saw ruin. They saw familiar ground, comfort, and recognition. Their joy shook me loose of my outsider's single vision. The power of community was wrapped up in all these invisible, dense connections. That connectedness could hold up hope and allow people to stand, even in the need of so much.

A honeymoon phase is predictable following tragedy.[13] The affected people seek each other's company for comfort, and spontaneous "therapeutic communities" arise to cope with the collective blow. This common experience, disaster researchers tell us, involves an intimate but short-term bond, one that dissipates as the circumstances that gave rise to it change.[14] But if unifying responses to a disaster are typical in the immediate aftermath, the form and duration of such reactions vary. In the case of the Peachy Gang and the larger Johnson-Fernandez family, the sense of community was heightened by the disaster, but it was not fundamentally tied to it and did not, therefore, dissipate over time. The family rhizome, with no beginning and no end, had always been rooted to this soil, and its rootstock reached across family branches and across generations. When all the people in the group lost the material contents of their former lives, their collective system of organization simply made room for another layer of connection, on top of already-existing bonds formed and reformed by their shared dependence on the bayou, and their relations through church, neighborhood, family, race, and class. The density of these myriad pathways to each other provided confidence in a future together, a true union of "people, place, and premise."[15]

THE MIRAGE OF RELIEF

Every week after January 2006, when Katie and Gray Eye and Nell and Earl had come back, newly returning family members who had secured their FEMA trailers also began to settle in. I asked Buffy what made the choice to come back the default assumption. He smiled as though he realized the answer might not be self-evident to outsiders. "Well, I think that why people are coming back, number one is home," he said. "Okay, number two is we have roots down here to where we are family oriented, and once you see your family, it says a lot. If I am by myself, I can go by my Aunt Katie and go eat. Or I can go by my Aunt Cynthia and eat or go by my Aunt Roseana's or even by my Aunt Audrey, you know. There are so many places that I can go eat and not worry about where my next meal is at. But if I am in an area where I am by myself, it is no such thing."

At the same time different households in the family were making their way to their new FEMA trailers, Connie remained in Dallas, puzzled by the near-complete reverse evacuation. Everyone had headed back just as soon as they could make arrangements for their trailers to be delivered and hooked up. Connie felt anxious about what was happening and disappointed that her family members didn't realize the opportunities they were turning their backs on to return to the parish. Of the several hundred family members from the parish (including those who had stayed in Houston or Atlanta or elsewhere), only two of Audrey's daughters decided not to return.

"Even though everyone got to see another part of the world," Connie said in dismay, "they still wanted to get right back, to St. Bernard Parish." She paused, wanting to be respectful. "And I wonder, why are they going back? Why are they going back? I don't see jobs, I don't see nothing there but their environment. To me there's nothing there." It was like she was talking to people in a foreign language. Her family was polite, but they didn't absorb her words. "Dallas is a city with better jobs for blacks, and there are better schools for the kids."

Connie's single vision of the parish was more like mine than the double vision of her relatives. It had been too long, and her own memories existed in a different time. Connie felt bewildered and pained by the sweep of the collective to move back to ruin. But she was not ready to give up being involved in their struggle.

"They going to need some form of support," Connie said, turning a corner on her disappointment and readying herself instead for action. "They going to have to have someone there to intervene, a planner. You need somebody to be able to help them to structure, give them a protocol, how to go back and reorganize your life again. We have senior citizens that need some form of guidance." Connie had demonstrated the art of culture brokering in Dallas. She could do it in St. Bernard Parish, too, she thought. If they insisted on returning, maybe she could help make some changes so their lives could be better, freer from the racial bias that was so obvious to her.

Her strategy was to visit the parish and explain the problems to Junior from her perspective and then offer herself for a time to help get change in motion. The passion of her position inspired us to ask her and Junior if we could film their conversation. Everyone agreed. Maybe this was our moment to get race issues on the table. But Junior politely deflected Connie's plea for blacks without missing a conversational beat. Even if he was sympathetic, he explained, he had emergencies on his plate and changing the racial climate in the parish was not one of them. Connie had expected her family's support. To our surprise, however, none showed up for the interview in Junior's presidential FEMA trailer. No one was interested in confronting authorities, much less a family friend like Junior, about racial bias. But that did not mean that their awareness of racism in the parish wasn't broad and deep.

HONEYMOON DREAMS

Eight of Robin's cousins squeezed into her new FEMA trailer that same day Connie visited Junior, unconcerned about the crowding. After being spread out in Dallas and Houston and Atlanta, they couldn't be too close. Those coming back had calculated what they were leaving behind, such as better schools, better job opportunities, less racism.

Robin stood in the kitchen giving another stir to her fresh pot of red beans as she tried to explain to Connie why everyone wanted to be back home. "You feel comfortable when you at your own," she said.

"But coming back here, to me," Connie countered, "it's like a Third World country."

Robin kept stirring. "I could have riches and don't be happy. I don't need the house, I don't need the car."

Cousin Dale (daughter of Connie's mother's sister) interrupted, "You know, maybe this is an opportunity for better." To which Connie immediately continued her thought, "Yes, restructuring might be better. More modern, more with the times."

Dale delivered the bottom line, "You know, people say, 'I wouldn't go in that parish.' Yes, it is a little racist. But I still love St. Bernard Parish and this is truly where I want to be."

It wasn't as if the family did not notice that life on the bayou was hard. Parents were aware that local schools were poor, particularly after having children in school in Dallas or Houston. In a different trailer that same spring, Roz, Katie's daughter, explained to several of her cousins, "Treyvon really learned things out there. His teachers actually paid attention to him, and I saw a difference in him." The experience with better schools during the evacuation phase had made it impossible to deny the problems of local schools. But her sense of place and familiarity trumped all.

"Other people in different places don't understand it, but this is where I want to live. This is where our heart is. And we not going nowhere else."

One day, after the trailer gatherings, I met with Robin and her younger daughter, Precious. We walked across St. Bernard Highway to the Violet Canal, where she explained what made life in the midst of ruin so acceptable. The double vision that I had begun to understand from conversations with Katie and Buffy was the lens of saturated experience, a lifetime of meaningful exchanges, a place that held one's reputation and connections, and where people cared about you and kept up with your life. "It's just so good to be back," Robin reiterated, "where people know who you are."

I asked her what she might want to say to her neighbors who had not yet returned, leaving the community with a conspicuous absence of people. "I'd tell the truth, I'd tell them, come home, you won't get treated different, like they treat us in Dallas or Houston. You know it wasn't so much racism there, it was, 'You're from New Orleans.' And all the looting and everything was going on—they watching you, even though you wasn't there at that time, it doesn't matter. And that's why I tell everyone, 'Come home, we won't watch you. If anything I come sit down and talk to you.' But they scared of the hurricane season. Can't take the fear from them."

Just as we were nearing Robin's trailer, Robin's cousin Deirdre, who had been rescued from her roof, drove up. Robin laughed as Deirdre called out from her window, "Good morning, how ya'll doing?!"

"I just was telling them about you on the roof!" Robin called back.

Deirdre smiled and replied, "Yes, I was on the roof, it wasn't pleasant, but next year I will leave quickly!"

Robin asked Deirdre if there was something she needed.

"No," she said, "Just passing, saying good morning." She reached to touch Robin's hand and drove off.

In triumph, Robin turned and said, "See? That's home. That's family. She didn't need anything. She just came to make sure I was okay. Good morning. You can't get that nowhere else. I mean, I stood there in Texas for ten months. I got one gentleman to tell me he wanted to say good night. He was a Mexican. He told me happy night. Here, no matter how many times they passing on the street they going to wave, 'Hey, Robin!' I mean, how many cars have passed, and my hand always up. That's family."

5

TRIAL BY TRAILER

For members of a large family accustomed to interacting and circulating and gathering together often, living in FEMA trailers piled on stress. It had been a challenge for them to adapt bayou life to the foreign environment of Dallas, but once they got back home, the constraints imposed by trailers cut off even more forms of sharing. Living in the individuated spaces of FEMA trailers compartmentalized people in unfamiliar ways and, over time, undermined family life as they knew it. In fact, as the promotional language used by trailer manufacturers, dealers, and users suggests, these trailers were never intended to be installed as long-term living quarters in residential communities.

"The tubs," Katie winced as she shook her head. "I know this is a little trailer with little tubs. But I have a hard time getting in. You fall getting in; you fall getting out."

Katie was an upbeat person who didn't like to dwell on her troubles, but she didn't pretend things were easy. Having lost half a leg to diabetes made it harder. "Oh, it is a good thing the wall on the shower is kind of sturdy." She smiled as if to say she was not really complaining. "Because you've got to hold on. And with this knee not too sturdy I've got to get on this one and then hold on to the tub to try and get out."

"She used a shower chair before," Nell piped up, unamused. "Shower chair can't even fit in there!"

"I am a shower person," Katie offered gently. "I can't take no shower now."

"You still storing your cooking pots in the bathroom?" I asked her.

"There ain't no room in the bathroom," she scoffed, giving way to her frustration. "They under the bunk beds. And it is hard on crutches because you know you got to get down there and get them."

During my first visit to the parish in early 2006, I'd gotten a look inside these miniature living compartments supplied by FEMA and concluded if

The 2006 GULF STREAM CAVALIER
Travel Trailer

User testimonial:
A lot of camper for the money!!!

Manufacturer statement:
When it comes to construction
no one does it like we do.

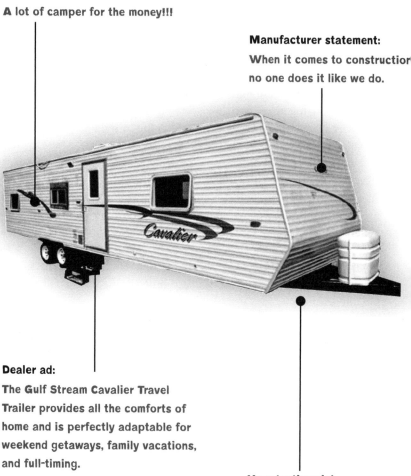

Dealer ad:
The Gulf Stream Cavalier Travel
Trailer provides all the comforts of
home and is perfectly adaptable for
weekend getaways, family vacations,
and full-timing.

User testimonial:
Beautiful R.V.! Loads of
storage, great bunk room for
the kids, love the tub and
shower combo. Pulls nice.

Fig. 24

there was one good thing about the delay in getting a trailer, it was that waiting had forestalled the nightmare of living in one. Trailers like these were
made for weekend camping trips, for happy camping families that mostly
stayed outside, fishing, hiking, hunting, swimming. That's why the formaldehyde lurking in the walls of these cheaply made homes was never an issue
before the storm—until that point, people didn't use travel trailers for real
homes, for their day-to-day, year-in, year-out lives. Because of the mobile
nature of their purpose, these kinds of trailers, the kind FEMA delivered to
Gulf Coast survivors of Hurricane Katrina, were not subject to Department
of Housing and Urban Development (HUD) inspection.

With more than 320,000 homes damaged in the metropolitan area of
New Orleans alone and 515,000 statewide, FEMA contracted sixteen companies to manufacture emergency dwellings.[1] These companies together
supplied FEMA with 145,000 trailers at a price tag of $2.7 billion. Another
story.[2] By May 2006, nine months after the storm, ninety-eight thousand
trailers had been delivered to the wrecked areas of Louisiana and Mississippi. The trailers were built according to one of three plans, but most were
thirty-two feet long and eight feet wide, a total of 240 square feet of interior
space, enclosed by aluminum, fiberglass, and particleboard.[3] This compact
trailer is known as the "park" model.

One of the FEMA contractors, Gulf Stream, produced fifty-five thousand
park trailers called the "Cavalier," a basic travel trailer without the usual bat-
tery system or holding tanks, per FEMA specifications. FEMA had directed
the manufacturers to disable the unit's travel capacity, and by requiring on-
site hookups to water and electricity, there would be no way for a Cavalier
to function as a self-contained unit on the road. Never mind that they came
with wheels. To make the requirement for un-roadworthiness clear, FEMA
threatened legal action against anyone attempting to relocate a trailer from
the site where it had been delivered and installed.

The inside of a FEMA trailer came "ready" to sleep six with a queen bed,
two single bunks in the rear, a foldout couch and a dinette table that converted to a single bed. The kitchen had a double sink, an oven and stove
top, a microwave, and a full-size refrigerator. There was one bathroom with
a tub-shower, a sink, and a toilet. Despite the immobility of FEMA trailers,
they still arrived with travel-ready interior standards, including furniture
that was fixed in place. The uniform design and dimensions of these trailers
ensured their predictability, like a Big Mac from McDonald's: same dimensions, same contents, same health consequences.

It was June 2006, ten months after the storm, and on this filming trip
back to visit the family, we found that almost everyone except families

with kids in school had returned to the parish and installed themselves in their respective FEMA trailers. While we waited to talk to Robin, who was busy explaining to a neighbor where to find eyeglasses, I stood outside her trailer, looking out on storm-torn Violet, a town that had over the years drawn the largest share of the African American population residing in St. Bernard Parish. I looked up and down the street to see who else was out in this steamy hot weather. Toward St. Bernard Highway from Robin's place, I spotted an elderly white woman sitting in a white plastic chair on the landing to her trailer door, looking out across the street at two black youngsters chasing each other in an everyday game of tag. The residential mix of white and black in lower-parish communities and the long-running relations between them complicated easy assertions about race. However many times scholars tried to shame a nation about how "Katrina exposed brutal inequalities of race," the family had taught me that the ocean of truth about race could not fit in this thimble.

I stepped out into the narrow, once-paved road, now heavily potholed and unevenly patched from different eras. There were no gutters and no sidewalks. From an outsider's glance, this older section of Violet had noticeably less going for it than other blocks of the town, equally mixed, with curbs and gutters and modest, attractive brick homes. But as Robin made clear later that day as she gave us a tour up and down the street, her neighbors were people who cared for each other and who lived with dignity. She pointed out her mother's home across the street, where she and Connie and Deborah had grown up, now completely collapsed in on its right half and not yet fully gutted. She recounted the way people worried about their kids and about how older folks told such good stories about growing up in Violet long ago. There was love here and no less attachment to home than in any other community with deep roots.

I let my eyes relax, continuing to scan slowly without searching, looking across the street and to the right, as far to the right as I could see. Then to the left, and farther beyond, to the river, made invisible by a fifteen-foot dirt levee, just past St. Bernard Highway. I could make out the faint outline of a dull-green freighter, an army issue, docked at a makeshift port to deliver goods. When you see so much laid bare, it's hard to grasp the hope and pride that had animated the contents of homes. The material remains of "what was" now lay belched out onto the street and renamed "debris." Separate household heaps of furniture, dishware, clothing, toys, appliances—items ripped, shredded, twisted, and broken, bearing no sense of the knots of meaning binding them into specific lives. The stuff of the living lay dead to the present, of interest only to insects and vermin and reptiles.

I had already heard that snakes were paying house calls to peoples' trailers. One day, as we sat inside Katie's trailer in Verret, Katie said to Nell, "Had a snake on Sunday."

"I had a snake Tuesday!" Nell cried back. Nell, like Robin, lived in Violet.

"Right there," said Katie, pointing to a place under the dinette table. "Little bitty one, though. Dude [Trashell's boyfriend] say he wanted to stomp him, but I said no. He was a little king snake. Wasn't much."

Cynthia was someone who would cook anything—coon, muskrat, turtle—yet she was the one most afraid of snakes. The thought amused me.

"Then, Earl took Cynthia home, and the same day that I found my snake," Katie said, raising her voice in disbelief, "she opened the door and down fell a snake before she'd got inside. She didn't know where he fell from! How he got up in the trailer? And she is terrified of snakes. She is not a snake person. She can't even look at them on TV!

"She was hollering for Earl, but he couldn't hear her cause he had his music on and his windows up. So look, she taped it all up. She taped up everything. All the vents. Because she isn't going to be able to stay in there if she thinks snakes can get in."

One day later that summer, as I stood in the motionless street where we were filming the scene of a grappling truck's mechanical jaws reaching to snatch up a portion of a debris heap, a workman yelled at us to move away. I walked over to ask if there was a problem with our filming the cleanup work.

He said, "Well, if you don't want a snake to fall on you, I'd say you better stand back a good way."

"You finding a lot of snakes in these piles?" I asked.

"You wouldn't believe!" he said. "They wriggling somewhere in every pile you see."

No surprise. After all, months had gone by with all this destruction and all these unoccupied, waterlogged homes. No human deterrents. Plenty of time for bayou inhabitants to inspect new opportunities for food. Alligators, armadillos, raccoons, foxes, and nutria—along with the snakes—all made appearances in record numbers that first year.

This storm had thrust together the momentous and the minute and mixed them up, in inseparable scales of destruction. Yet against this sludgy backdrop of gray and brown, the white and sterile FEMA capsules appeared, demarcating past from future. The irony seemed too much: in all this ruin of realness, only the tin capsules held life and only the capsules promised another day. Their ubiquitous presence by summer 2006 seemed to announce the control of an otherworldly presence. Family members recognized that making do in these shrunken boxes was a necessary evil, which they believed would last only a short time. But short became long; long became longer.

Research about space and human needs could have predicted the stressfulness of life in a FEMA trailer. FEMA emphasized that their trailers were "temporary living quarters" but also acknowledged that people might occupy them for up to eighteen months. In fact, many of the family members I followed were forced to make these trailers home for three years or more while they waited for insurance settlements and Road Home checks in order to rebuild.[4]

Robin sighed when I asked her how things were going. "It's hard. When my mom comes over, it's, like, we got to get out of the bed so that she can sleep in the bed and be comfortable . . . And the top bunk has stuff we store up there, so one of us has to sleep on the bottom bunk and one on the couch."

That left Trietha, Robin's eighteen-year-old daughter, to sleep on the floor. "I don't mind," Tri said, "as long as I know that when somebody have to go to the bathroom they're not going to step on me, because I'm on the floor, somebody's on the sofa, another person's in the bunk bed, the clothes on the top bunk, two people sharing the master bedroom . . . I don't really want to get stepped on!"

Tri had graduated from high school just before Katrina. She is smart and big, a lot like her mother, Robin. Tri made no effort to gloss the problems. "I hate the FEMA trailers, they aren't big enough—it's like, if you a big person trying to go to the bathroom, your knees literally hit the bathtub. Or you have to put your feet in the bathtub and go. And . . . I hit my head so many times trying to take a shower, because they give you a little vent, and you can open it, but you can only stick your head out so far (laughing) and try and clean yourself, and then, you only get a little bit of propane, and you know, the water got cold as soon as you get in there."

Day in, day out, what was cramped became more and more crowded, and personal space got overrun. Inside the family's trailers, the tiny closets were quickly filled up by essentials—sheets, towels, laundry baskets, cleaning supplies, toys for children, uniforms for church ushers or wage workers at Home Depot or a dollar store, and Sunday clothes for attending the funerals announced each week. Every single item anyone brings into the trailer crowds the space for sitting, bathing, sleeping, or just plain moving around.

Cynthia, the oldest of the four sisters, lived alone and by all accounts had kept a tidy, lovely home, a home where Saturday breakfasts took place and where family loved to gather on special occasions. Every time I entered her trailer, she apologized for the mess she could not come to terms with—the

A typical **FEMA** trailer home

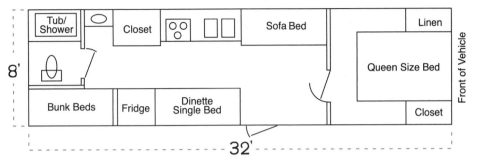

Tub/Shower · Closet · Sofa Bed · Linen · Queen Size Bed · Closet · Bunk Beds · Fridge · Dinette Single Bed · Front of Vehicle · 8' · 32'

Wilt Chamberlain's wingspan
is about the same width as a typical **FEMA** trailer

2 Chevy Suburbans
are longer than the length of a typical **FEMA** trailer

Standard box car
is 36% longer and wider than a typical **FEMA** trailer

Fig. 25

loads of laundry and stacks of cookware shoved into corners, plants she tried to keep alive that lined her walls, the clean clothes piled up to iron on the bench seat bolted to the table and floor.

"Child, I got no place for all these things. Look like I'd be better off without them!" She laughed uncomfortably, determined to keep her lightness no matter how hard things got.

FLOW AND CIRCULATION

The physical reality of a FEMA trailer strained the family's everyday rituals and limited their usual strategies for coping with life—cooking and sharing good food, taking care of each others' kids. Katie and her sisters knew that cooking was the surest way to supply comfort for others and bring people together. Once she was moved into her trailer, I asked Katie about the long-handled spoons and big pots she had told me were key for cooking right.

"Have you got the spoons and pots you need?" I asked her.

"Uh-uh," she replied. "I got one good-handled spoon, but the pots I got are like what you use plastic with you know with—like, Teflon on the inside. I need the one where you can stir your pot in and, you know, we are just not used to living like this. If you go in there," she said, pointing the direction of her former home that would soon be demolished, "and go look in my spoon drawer, I got so many spoons in there you can't hardly open the drawer. You know, cooking spoons. Like if we have a function at church, we cook for the church. So you know you got to have the big pots and long spoons. But you don't have anywhere to put all of that in there," she said, thrusting her chin in the direction of the cabinets by the sink. "No way."

Cooking familiar food for a lot of people requires more than big pots and long-handled spoons; it also requires casserole dishes, lots of spices and seasonings, big burners, a full-sized oven, and a freezer with room for several dozen pounds of shrimp and crab. Then, assuming you can somehow get the food prepared, where do you put the people? FEMA trailers feel crowded with three people. There were no options for giving more people a comfortable place to sit, and no way to keep all the food hot once you had prepared all the dishes in small-burner sequence.

Desperate for a family gathering spot, Katie realized her old carport could be useful. It was still standing after the storm, beaten up and unattractive, but functional. The day the crew arrived to demolish her home, she hailed them not to dismantle and junk the carport. "Keep it there, just like it is," she yelled. The crew leader flashed her a quizzical look, but with a stern nod, she reassured him she meant what she said. When it came to knowing what family needed, Katie was special. By preserving this cover over outdoor space, she could extend a familiar welcome to anyone passing and to groups that wanted to collect. At fifteen feet square, the space under the carport provided an opportunity for comfort, a gathering place out of the rain. It became the spot where crab or crawfish boils could take place, where three picnic tables could be lined up to seat people, where people could enjoy the shade and each other's company without having to stuff into someone's trailer. The carport presented an imperfect solution to an imponderable problem. Katie used this battered relic of the material past to assert a place for family continuity, a bridge to a new future.

Over the spring and summer of 2006, I entered more than a dozen trailers assigned to various family members. Every time I witnessed the same signs of compression, with "stuff" spilling out into the living spaces. Beyond problems of movement and storage, the chronic lack of space also meant parents of young children were denied their expectation of help. As far back as anyone remembers, children in the big family moved around, living with aunts and uncles or grandparents for days or weeks or even years. This flexibility allows many black families to adapt to shifting resources and the time constraints of jobs. It's also how they eliminate paying for formal child care. But fluid household systems like this one depend on easy flows between people who have space to share. It also takes space for grandchildren to enjoy their sleepovers with grandparents, and for young boys or young girls to host slumber parties at each other's homes. These child-sharing practices and sleepover events were not incidental to cultural life. They came packed with opportunities to socialize children, and to remind them about the principles of family life: that cousins are your friends, that elders know things and are important people to your parents. The lessons for a young generation come from just these kinds of interhousehold movements, invisible to outsiders. The needs of parents for help with children could have been addressed by agents of recovery tuned in to the cultural practice of child sharing.

When asked what she needed most, Katie did not hesitate: "Space. I need space. Miss having my grandchildren stay over. Miss a lot of things."

In cultural settings where built space is made to accommodate the flows and circulation of lots of people in and out, the need for space is no luxury. It is basic. Researchers have shown that the perception of ample space and flexible space plays a big role in a person's sense of well-being. FEMA trailers are not ample, and they are not flexible. The dinette table, the bench seats on either side of it, the couch, the queen bed—everything that could move doesn't. It is true that movable furniture makes no sense in travel trailers headed for the mountains or the woods or the lake. Happy campers need to know that the furniture in their mobile dwelling is not going anywhere. But FEMA trailers do not travel.

"I need space," was more than a simple lament. Scholars from different fields—geographers, urban planners, interior architects, and health psychologists—study how we interact with space. Their studies back up the commonsense appeal of movable furniture in public spaces. A public park and the interior of a FEMA trailer are hardly similar, but the principle of control over space is the same—when people are able to alter the arrangement of items in an environment they occupy, they invest more in being there, feel a greater sense of well-being and health, and report lower levels of anxiety over minor annoyances.[5]

FEMA trailers violated all the basic understandings of what makes space comfortable:

- The furniture was bolted to the floor and impossible to move.
- It was illegal to rearrange the interior space, even if it were possible.
- It was illegal to paint anything—interior or exterior.[6]
- The bedroom was so tightly spaced, it was hard to enter the bed normally.

If controlling one's space promotes well-being, then lacking that control can undermine it. Studies show that the costs of too much self-restraint and too much loss of control result in fatigue. It's exhausting to wake up every day in an environment that forces you to stuff your frustration, an environment that compels you to deal with outsiders who control things you are used to controlling.[7] Fatigue interferes with good decision making and interferes with the desire to actively problem-solve, to try different approaches.[8]

In spring 2006, I asked Lolis Elie, reporter for the New Orleans daily newspaper, the *Times-Picayune*, to identify what he thought were problems that the general public did not understand about what people impacted by Katrina were going through. His answer was swift and spoke to a loss of control.

"It's really impossible to convey to people the extent to which this is a 24/7 problem for us. Under most circumstances, no matter what you may be going through personally, you have friends and relatives that are not suffering that exact same thing. So it's possible to get some kind of assistance from them. Well, we're in a situation now where almost everybody is in the same kind of circumstance.

"Between dealing with contractors, dealing with insurance companies, dealing with FEMA, dealing with the Small Business Administration, which is handling various types of loans, trying to keep up with the kinds of things the government is and is not doing. . . . Trying to address your own grief over the loss of your community, over the loss of your loved ones. Trying to deal with the power company, the phone company, the cable-television company, to get these services turned back on. This consumes us constantly, all day every day. And it's difficult to explain that to people. I mean, who wants to hear that you sit on the phone for a half hour waiting for the power company to come on the line? It seems like a minor problem. But in the context of everything happening, it's a consistent burden, it's a consistent barrage coming at you from various fronts."

Everything about FEMA trailers was contraindicated for the recovery of the family collective: the tiny space, the lack of ventilation, the immovable furniture, the small stoves, the lack of storage, and the lack of seating. No one in the family knew whether their own trailer also carried toxic levels of formaldehyde, found later in 40 percent of the trailers.[9] Like wrong medication prescribed by a doctor unfamiliar with the malady, the individualizing space forced family members to set aside cultural values when the comforts of gathering and talking, cooking and sharing children were needed most.

Indeed, had keepers of the recovery operated from a best-practices mandate that called for attention to meeting cultural needs for comfort, one solution would have been to install inexpensive temporary shelters that could have been used for community gatherings.[10] International experts devoted to creative post-disaster solutions have pointed out, "Evidence suggests that affected communities . . . have the most extensive knowledge of their own needs. However, reconstruction is often delivered in such a way that at best responds to the requirements of its implementers rather than to those of the affected population."[11] The capacity to cook and gather would have provided a critical source of comfort in the no-relief disaster zone.

ADDING INJURY TO INSULT

The confining and inflexible space in a FEMA trailer represented just the beginning of indignities imposed by the outsider recovery culture. The impact of these problems alone created undue wear and tear on all family members; but for Katie, the indifference to human need would prove ruinous. She had one leg, so back in October 2005 in Dallas, Connie had helped her order a trailer built to Americans with Disabilities Act (ADA) specifications to put on the lot where her destroyed home sat. Finally, after almost four months, FEMA called Katie to say the agency had assigned her a trailer. But it was not the "accessible" trailer that she and Connie had ordered and that she qualified for under ADA law. Never mind, she told them, she'd take what they had for her. She figured the mistake could take weeks or longer to correct, and she could not bear to wait another day to get home.

Katie hadn't been on crutches when I first met her. In fact, it was weeks before I realized that she wore a prosthetic leg. That leg was the first thing the FEMA trailer claimed. Not getting her accessible trailer didn't undo Katie until it took away her mobility. She knew the aluminum steps up to the trailer door were not sturdy, and as soon as her daughters Roz and Nell saw what they had installed, they asked FEMA to come back to fix them or better yet, exchange the stairs for a ramp to the front door as they saw on so many other regular trailers. No one knew why officials wouldn't respond, so Katie did something about the problem herself. "I went and found some slip-guard tape, and I put it down on the steps myself." But Nell said, "Everyone still trips going into the trailer and coming back out because there's a gap between the end of the steps and the door. But they won't come fix it."

Then, it happened.

"It was a Sunday," Katie said. "I went to church. My leg was bothering me. Monday morning it still was bothering me so I took the leg off. I sent one of the kids to go in there and get one of my crutches. So I was on the crutches. I was going up the steps, and I fell trying to hop from the porch to the inside of the trailer. I fell on the iron bar, and Lord, I tell you about excruciating pains.

"I haven't had pain like this! Every night I have to take something to go to sleep. I went to the free clinic after I saw it was doing no good. I went to the free clinic up by FEMA, and the doctor told me they didn't have an X-ray machine, and so he felt to see if the bone was broken. It wasn't broken. And they gave me a pair of crutches. About a week later, it wasn't getting no better, so I went back to the free clinic, but it wasn't free anymore. They turned it into a little hospital. You had to pay.

"The doctor said to keep it bandaged, and he recommended me to go to the surgeon who did the leg. So I got an appointment and went to him and, let me show you, it had got like, it was deep, deep down in there it was, like, a hole. It was hurting so bad, I was holding on to the bed and every time he would say, 'Oh, I am so sorry.' He said, 'I got to go all the way down to the bone to see if the bone is chipped or if there is blood in the bone.' And baby he dug and dug in that thing, and he gave me some prescription for some Vicodin, and it didn't do a thing for me. I was crying every night. I never had so much pain in my whole life. I never knew something could hurt you that bad.

"But after that it still wasn't doing no better, and I went back and he told me to go see the surgeon. And I went, he did the surgery and then I had a home-help nurse come until my insurance company stopped them.

"Then, I went to the FEMA office in the parish and I ask them to help me pay for the medicine and the doctor visit and they said, 'Don't you have insurance?' and I said 'Yeah, I have insurance, but I fell on your steps. You could just do something.' And they said they just didn't know, and that is when I thought about a lawyer. Because you already know your insurance will go up. My insurance is 80-20. My medicine bills already is, like, $500 a month. I pay for regular medicine between me and my husband, and I mean with extra, that is why I am trying to get some help.

"They asked me why I didn't have a ramp. I said, 'They didn't ever put one in even though we tried to get one.' I was standing there on one leg with bandages on my stump, but they wanted a note from the doctor saying how I fell, and I said, 'The doctor wasn't there. He wouldn't know how to tell you.' You know, every little place in that FEMA, they trying to turn me down. The lady say, 'I am so sorry,' and I say, 'Don't be sorry because everywhere I go in this place they turn me down.' I went to the food stamps. I went to the Small Business Administration.

"I went back to the doctor. I told him what they needed, and he said, 'They want a note? For me to tell them how you fell?' And I said, 'Yeah.' And he said, 'I don't know.' So I told him to put it down on the prescriptions to say, 'Whatever else you want to know, call me.'"

Katie continued to call FEMA; her daughter Nell called FEMA. They begged for the accessible trailer she should have had in the beginning. Nell said, "You got to act like you a crazy person just to get anybody to listen!"

Weeks later, a carload of six FEMA employees showed up to take pictures of the step and prepare the paperwork for Katie's new trailer. Nell looked at the men in disbelief and cried out, "Why you want a picture of the step? You see she ain't got but one leg. What more you want?" The men left. Months passed. No word, no accessible trailer.

By the time of our next visit in early June, no trailer swap had taken place. I asked Katie what the holdup was. She just shook her head, signaling she had no idea. Nell didn't hold back: "My mama still here in the same trailer, using the same steps, still no ramp. We still in the same boat three months later."

One day we had moved inside her trailer to film her cooking and to see how she managed to cook on crutches. She hopped to the stove from the table where she was chopping onions to demonstrate, and we captured this on film. "Well, you see, you can stand up by the stove," she said. "You don't have to use the crutches," she continued, picking up the ladle from the counter and stirring the pot of gumbo she had started that morning. "You can stand by the stove. Lean a little bit. It is not hard." She looked around for her rice cooker, which was not in sight. "The thing is moving the pots. Moving the pots from one place to the other—that is hard."

A few weeks later, after Katie had become more aware of just how wearing her confined space would be, she said, "I met a girl at one of the help camps where they give out supplies and things. She got a three-bedroom trailer," and drawing the long distance with her pointer finger, continued, "maybe big as from my house to here." She paused to reflect. "And she got a ramp all the way to that side and all the way to the highway on the other side, and I asked her how did you get that big trailer? She said, 'I told them I got a bad knee.'" Katie bent over, smiling in disbelief. "I said to her, 'You had a bad knee and you got a big trailer like that?' And she is just one. She is by herself."

Katie shrugged off her bewilderment, but her high-pitched voice showed that it stung. She continued, "I told the girl, well, I got one leg and they give me a little Cavalier." And she laughed. "That's what they call it, a Cavalier, that's the name of it."

In July 2006, five months after her fall, FEMA delivered Katie's handicapped trailer. By that time, the stump of her leg was so badly compromised that she was never again able to wear her prosthesis. Katie would not be defeated. She got herself around using crutches and a wheelchair.

BAYOU SPEECH AND BAYOU STYLE

It took a lot of goodwill to adjust to living in an aluminum box too small to accommodate the essential circulations of a big family. But the material mismatch to local needs was nonnegotiable, so people did their best, hoping that the punishing sentence would be short, believing that their own government would not allow hundreds of thousands of homeowners to live like this for long. Meanwhile, the chasm that separated the worlds of recovery authorities and local residents became particularly apparent in chronic failures of communication.

In helping people recover from disaster, what could be more basic than ensuring that communication is clear and that people are not left to guess what is happening?[1] Central to the definition of a language is that its speakers are mutually intelligible to each other. But what happens when what a speaker says is not what the receiver of the message actually hears? What are the stakes of these communication disconnects? No one in the family expected that in their own home environment, their ways of expressing themselves would become an impediment to their recovery.

WE SPEAK BAYOU

Bayou dialect and bureaucratese have nothing in common, even if they both belong to the English language. Bureaucratic language, both spoken and written, suffers from what linguists call "gobbledygook," inflated words and impenetrable phrases that might as well have been gobbled out by a pompous tom turkey.[2] The printed forms of FEMA documents can bring the best educated among us to a dead stop in a paralysis of incomprehension. In Dallas, Connie helped family members interpret questions on the paperwork FEMA required for them to get registered. But once people returned to their bayou environment, there were no translators to help them decipher the turgid wording on forms required by FEMA or Road Home, the state of Louisiana's office designated by HUD to manage compensation for homeowners. On countless occasions, I witnessed family members' frustration with not being able to follow bureaucratic language and feeling that they could not get through to the people who had charge of their lives. Individuals explained these frustrations differently, but they all reported that meetings or phone calls left them feeling humiliated, confused, and dismissed.

Robin had initially expressed relief about being back in the parish, where she didn't have to explain herself all the time. "Where I don't have to say things twenty-three ways for somebody to understand what I want or even what I mean." Ironically, though, the language problem she and many other family members felt in Dallas was nothing compared to the difficulties they faced back home with FEMA and Road Home.

Robin and her family use speech that linguists call "marked," a noticeable deviation from the "unmarked" Standard American English.[3] Unmarked American English sounds like the Midwestern, newscaster type of speech, assumed to be "proper" by the white middle class. Members of the bayou family speak a black bayou dialect, a version of English. Their language has a distinctive history, one most Americans aren't aware of. Black dialect did not evolve from English alone. Most recently, it came from a plantation Creole spoken by slaves. In this case, it was a French Creole, a distinct and fully complex language born naturally from the tongues of West African slaves and European sailors and planters. As with all Creole inventions, the syntax of the Creole relies on the invisible grammar of the subordinate group, while the Creole's vocabulary draws on the lexicon of the European power—in this case, French. Over the generations, as contact with English speakers on plantations and in the bayou environment increased, the Creole of slaves evolved into a dialect of English. Still today, though, black English, also known as African American Vernacular English (AAVE), retains some features of Creole, which had itself retained elements of West African syntax.

The communicative power of the family's dialect was unmistakable. In the company of a group of family members, rapid banter, overlapping voices, and verbal shorthand animated exchanges. The dynamics of in-group expression set off my own speech as conspicuously different, not just in the words I used, but in my slower rhythms and training to avoid interrupting, not at all how their culturally conditioned interactions work. My own Midwestern speech patterns and style of interaction made it hard to fit into the flow of conversation and required me to "bend my ears" to unfamiliar cadences, word choices, and pronunciations. In West African languages, for example, there is no "th" sound, and in fact, "th" is a sound rarely used in any of the world's languages. So, just as the English "th" sound in "this" becomes a "zis" in French, it became for African Americans, "dis." The "th" sound varies depending on its placement in a word: "brova" for brother; "wit" for with. In addition, family members used a set of words and patterns that distinguish their dialect. To go "by" someone's house meant "to visit" (We go by Audrey's for Mother's Day); to go "for" 7 o'clock or to go "for" a place meant to go at 7:00 p.m. or to go to a place; to "stand" somewhere meant to stay there (We stood by Connie's for months).

The black bayou speech of family members sits on a continuum alongside dozens of dialects of English, including the many rich varieties in the New Orleans region—Cajun English, Brooklyn "Yat," Garden District English—as well as dozens of other varieties in the United States, the United Kingdom, and around the world, for example, Australian English and South Asian English. A dialect is simply a variation on the unmarked standard in terms of accent, vocabulary, and/or syntax. Those unfamiliar with the black bayou dialect and inexperienced at the deliberate effort required to listen to a distinctive accent might unwittingly resort to completing portions of sentences with what they imagine is being said. When speakers of Standard American English travel to other English-speaking countries, such as Scotland or India, unless they bend their ears, they risk misunderstandings based on the different accents or vocabulary.[4]

Linguists point out that judgments of speech and speech style are really judgments about speakers. British English, for example, is a marked variation from the American standard, but it is prestigious because we have high regard for British people. The marked speech of black bayou speakers, by contrast, is stigmatized because many in the United States still hold a prejudice toward black people.[5] When institutional authorities work in a cultural environment that they don't understand, when they encounter speech and styles of communicating that are not familiar and are commonly stigmatized, it is all but inevitable that their judgments and biases will inadvertently (if not consciously) impact how they view, and perhaps treat, those in need.

In a disaster situation, the burden of understanding is never symmetrical. Representatives of recovery institutions must recognize their obligation to do whatever it takes to understand what people say and what they need. Every member of the Johnson-Fernandez family understands Standard American English because it is the dialect of major media. But most do not aspire to sound like TV anchors because their own bayou accent and dialect is the currency of their everyday world.

THE BUREAUCRATIC TIN EAR

Even in the best of circumstances, it is nerve-racking to try to work with bureaucracies, or even large companies with multiple layers of customer service: "Press 1 for this, press 2 for that. Sorry. You'll have to call back later. We are experiencing a high volume of calls." Trying to wrestle attention from a utility company to handle a billing problem or an insurance provider to explain a rejected claim sucks up time, energy, and patience. Consumers routinely feel as if they have to fight for what is clearly owed them, as public advocates attest.[6] The stakes may be small, but keeping a cool head in the face of what seems like willful incompetence requires abundant self-control. If these experiences are charged with irritation and difficulty for those with well-developed linguistic tools and an "unmarked" white accent, it is hard to imagine how someone without these resources could cope with the powerlessness such conversations produce.

During the recovery, the bureaucratic norms of communication practiced by recovery authorities did not bend to black bayou dialect or ways of talking, and the resulting failures of communication presented a confusion people didn't even know how to identify. Robin never struggled for words, but her speech is heavily inflected with bayou rhythms and black dialect, just like everyone else's in the family. In her view, she was making herself perfectly clear, but she had had trouble communicating with Texans in Dallas and unexpected trouble communicating with caseworkers on her home turf.

Most family members had had only a few occasions in which they interacted with a government agent: getting a driver's license or a marriage certificate, or registering to vote. When people suddenly had to talk to strangers from FEMA and Road Home in ways that involved big stakes, their normal style of communicating did not translate well. Connie had been able to serve as the family's culture broker precisely because she had gained experience in Dallas speaking to outsiders and conducting work in institutional settings such as in the higher education system and hospitals. By the time her family landed on her doorstep in 2005, Connie had spent twenty years speaking to people who had no bayou roots. She knew how to change her register and cadence with middle-class whites, and she knew what questions to ask. She could sound familiar to the agents on the phone, and that got results.

Judging by the existing literature of disaster studies, it appears that few scholars have explored how a group's local dialect or style of communication can help or hurt their recovery.[7] However, a growing number of language studies demonstrates the devastating consequences of communication failures in settings where an institutional gatekeeper is involved. The classic study is by John Gumperz, a linguist who recorded a set of exchanges between English speakers who could not understand each other—a British banker speaking to a South Asian customer. Although both parties were speaking their native English language, the variety of miscues and different styles of speaking led to complete misunderstanding and a feeling of animosity.[8] "People speaking the same language but having different communicative backgrounds," said Gumperz, "may run into intercultural problems derived from the different cultural assumptions, different ways of structuring information, and different ways of speaking they bring to the interaction."

It's not just what people say or don't say, it's how they sound and how they engage. The consequences of such intercultural problems are especially insidious because both parties assume they are intelligible. (Or, as George Bernard Shaw put it, "The single biggest problem in communication is the illusion that it has taken place.")[9] The damage in the recovery process caused by conscious or unconscious judgments and decisions that flowed from the disconnects between recovery authorities and the survivors of the storm and its aftermath is impossible to calculate.

FEMA's standards for communication failed. "Sherry," a FEMA employee who requested anonymity, said, "I tell you, FEMA does the worst job educating the public." She then explained how FEMA hired locals from temporary services agencies and paid them an hourly wage, like her.[10]

"We were basically cheap labor," she said, "because they weren't having to pay the expert to be down there, or paying the travel of that expert." She explained that although local hires were theoretically valuable, the way FEMA used them made them a wasted resource. "They send these local hires out there who aren't armed with information or resources they can refer these people [the residents] to. FEMA didn't put emphasis on getting the story out or getting the local hires to perform. I mean, if you sit down and try to read their letters, it's all 'therefore,' 'whereas,' you know. Then, they also don't do a good job of following up to verify that something actually happened."

Lack of continuity was another problem that a different FEMA employee identified as interfering with communication. "Jonathan" said, "Every time you call, you get someone different, and it all depends on how they interpret things to be. If FEMA had one caseworker assigned to that person, and your duty and responsibility was to find them the help that they need, I think that you would have people way more far along in their recovery than they are now."[11] The bottom line, Sherry said, is that, "FEMA wasn't advocating."

Another telling point Sherry made concerned the local need for face-to-face exchange. "That person assigned to you needs to be on the ground, they need to do face-to-face," she emphasized. Any research methods' text explains that the main drawback of surveys administered by phone or mail is that you lose all the information in a person's face, all the ways people communicate without words. And for the family, conversation occurs in the flow of activity—minding children, eating together, sitting on the porch. A phone call draws attention to an exchange in a way that amplifies verbal speech and eliminates all the other cues for reading the communication. You have no way of knowing if someone is smiling, tearing up, staring blankly, listening intently, or sending a text to someone else. Linguists tell us that between 60 and 80 percent of all communication is nonverbal. FEMA's missing that much of a message plainly hurt people already at a disadvantage because of their stigmatized speech.

The challenges people faced in communicating with recovery authorities were at the heart of what made recovery so wrenching. Even in 2009, after most family members had settled into new or rebuilt homes, when I asked some of the cousins to reflect on what had been the hardest part of the whole experience of Katrina, they didn't mention the loss of a house and their possessions: it was the sting of not being understood and fighting for respect in communication with recovery authorities that burned the most. Around a table at Melanie's rebuilt home, cousins Mel, Roz, and Janice discussed the unfair treatment. Audrey, Melanie's mother, came in after the conversation had begun and took up her position on the couch a few feet away.

"They talk to you, degradingly, like, you know, as if you were nothing, had nothing and weren't nobody. That's how they spoke to you," Melanie said.

Roz nodded and added, "They talk to you just, like . . . They don't realize we was workers. They act like everybody is a welfare recipient."

"That's right," said Janice. "We all had jobs, we weren't on welfare with fifty children. Like how they made Donnatte feel when she called."

"Girl," said Melanie, "they made Donnatte cry, made her cry. Made her feel like all of us were the same. They made us feel like we weren't people who work, we just wanted handouts from the government. And knowing that we worked, that we were people who worked, they made you feel like, like you was just beggars. You know. Like we, we didn't need it, we just wanted to get it because it was there and it was free."[12]

Roz spoke so quietly, it was hard to hear the hurt in her voice. "It may not be for any others to see, but I think mentally this has really been hard," she said. "We was brought up in the church, we faith believers and Christians, we can better deal with it, but, but . . . I think that mentally, it hurt everybody." Her aunt Audrey nodded, staring into space from her seat on the couch.

Janice laughed. "Oh my, oh baby. When I talk to FEMA, those people ask me so much, so many questions, how much I spent on toilet paper how much I . . . I was, like, mister, don't worry about it."

Roz turned to me to say, "Now she got to practically give up every secret she has for some organization to just help her with appliances in her house. People never been on welfare, never had food stamps, you got to go in there and practically tell them to pull off your drawers to get a meal on our table."

One problem with the easy pigeonholing of black bayou speakers might have been mitigated if, as Jonathan the FEMA employee suggested, the caseworkers assigned them had been the same individuals over time. However, as Sherry indicated, the local hires weren't trained to understand anything about the big picture, and they were not allowed to deal with a "whole case"—only with a specific issue. A constantly rotating assistance voice on the other end of the line left people in need without consistent, reliable help.

When a disaster context requires two culturally divided worlds of actors to interact, communication failures will occur unless there is an explicit, intentional effort to bridge those divides. The chronic communication failures may result from speech differences, perceptions based on those differences, or from dissimilar styles of interacting.[13] And language divides are not just about speech—they are also apparent in actions that consciously or unconsciously send messages that mislead, disempower, or exclude those impacted from control over their own recovery. The details of flawed interactions varied, as the following demonstrates. Family members—hard as they tried to be understood—never got an even break.

THE "WE DON'T HEAR YOU" RESPONSE

Buffy had stayed in the parish during the storm to help rescue those he knew would be stranded and could not help themselves. So for him, the frustrations of depending on outsiders who seemed uninterested in communicating with him began immediately after the storm. No rescue teams showed up in a timely way to help him or his fellow parish employees left stranded on a roof, desperate for food, water, and sanitary provisions. Yet FEMA and emergency responders from the US government had ample warning of the likelihood of Hurricane Katrina's colossal impact on the region.[14] What was lacking was readiness, a communication plan, and quick action. The incompetence of the response infuriated Buffy, but he let go of his anger. More important than what had just happened, he told me, was what needed to happen next. He turned his attention to how he could help his parish. As a man of action, he had no intention of letting his nation's failed response to dire need incapacitate him.

Once the floodwaters had receded and it was time to begin cleanup, Buffy's role as road-crew supervisor seemed straightforward. He pulled together the few crew members he could, and together they undertook a big cleanup of the "yard" where their equipment was stored. It wasn't easy to sort the odd fragments of plastic, concrete, iron, and metal from machine parts, or the broken and uprooted trees from the debris the storm blew in. But they did it, loaded up their trucks, and proceeded to drive the waste to a familiar landfill an hour away, across the river. There, FEMA undid all their progress.

"We went to the landfill to dump it, where all the trash at," Buffy said in March 2006. "FEMA made us bring it back, put it back on the ground, so another crew could come over and inspect it to pick it up."

Instead of completing what seemed like a good idea, Buffy was told by FEMA authorities in charge that they had their own procedures for getting things done and their own lists of approved contractors. They had no idea who Buffy was or how he was capable of helping.

Yet by FEMA's own account, in St. Bernard Parish, some 3.3 million cubic yards of debris needed collecting, and more than twelve thousand homes and other structures needed demolishing. Their turning down local help made no sense to Buffy. If FEMA personnel had reasons beyond "We don't hear you," or "This is the way we do it," they made no effort to articulate them.

"We can't do street repairs, clean up trash, can't do much of anything. We could clean up this whole area," he said, sweeping his arm across from left to right, "all the trash." He went on to say that if FEMA wanted to get things done, "I firmly believe—someone that's from down here that know what to do, at least listen to them."

FEMA and its contractors summarily occupied the disaster zone where

Buffy's family had lived for six generations, longer than FEMA had existed. The agency moved in without asking any questions, without knowing anything about local people or the communities, without tapping local networks of people who needed work and offered skills. That's how it seemed to Buffy, who expressed a whole new bewilderment at his government, this time for the arrogance of ignoring local residents who wanted a chance to participate. Taking direct action, not waiting for somebody else to do a job—that's the local style of expression.

FEMA is authorized by the Stafford Act of 1988 (an amended version of the Disaster Relief Act of 1974) to assume responsibility for a federally declared disaster by coordinating relief and recovery. The act specifies the ways FEMA is authorized to provide orderly and systemic help to state and local governments and aid citizens and their communities following a disaster. It is through FEMA that cleanup and debris removal happens, and that temporary housing is made available. Through FEMA, funding flows to states for the restoration of public facilities and infrastructure, the rebuilding of damaged or destroyed homes not covered by insurance, and the assisting of individuals in need of short-term help.[15] The Stafford Act also mandates that post-disaster contracts issued for recovery work must be preferentially awarded to local, small, and minority-owned businesses. Such preferential treatment rarely happened, however, as a Senate Bipartisan Committee reported in 2006.[16] Even if contracts had been awarded as legally required, it would have made no difference to any of the residents I knew in the parish. That's because, according to the Department of Homeland Security, a "small" business is one that doesn't earn more than $35.5 million annually or employ more than five hundred people. Clearly, the "small" business operations run by men in Buffy's family qualified in a technical sense. Just as clearly, these microbusinesses were far too small to compete. So, however local, small, or black they might have been, they did not fit the profile.

In fact, most of the FEMA contracts went to multinational companies, among them the Louisiana-based Shaw Group.[17] "The way it is," said Buffy, leaning up against an outside wall of Katie's ruined house, "there's a pyramid." He used his hands to separate the space at the top from the bottom. "And Shaw contractor, they at the top of the pyramid," he accentuated with his one palm slicing the air at the top of his imaginary triangle. "Now they might have two people under them." He started segmenting the vertical space with a couple of layers. "And those two people might hire two more people, so there's a trickle down to four people. Then before you know it, it done jumped down to sixteen people," he said, slicing lots more layers of air with his palm, moving toward the ground. "And by the time you get down to the people working, then there might be, like, twenty boss or sixty boss on top and they at the bottom of the totem pole. That's how little money they make. It's like contractors subbing out to another contractor, and another contractor subbing out to this one. And, that's how it working now."

Sherry, the FEMA employee, responded openly to my question about the pyramid system. "It's all political when you're talking about contracts and debris removal and bringing in FEMA trailers and all of that," she said. "Your groups like Shaw, All South, DRC—all these groups have political ties."

So in effect, it becomes almost impossible to get work if you aren't already on somebody's "list." "Besides," she said, "The federal government makes it very difficult for small organizations, as much as they try to promote it. They make it very difficult when it comes to providing the right documentation."

Potchie Smith, grandnephew to Peachy, owned a heavy-duty rig and had been a professional trucker for twenty years. He said, "There not a black-owned company I know of that got any contract down here to do constructing. None. No blacks at all. We got some work, but we worked under someone else that got the contract. They had to sub it out because they had no equipment for the job." I asked him if he made money being at the bottom of the pyramid. He smiled, but looked at me like I was crazy. "Yeah, well, by the time it got to us, I mean, sometime we lost money."

Eventually, Buffy got a little side work at the bottom of a pyramid, but only a fraction of what those earning money above him made for—in his view—doing nothing. And worse, he said, the real work went to people who weren't locals at all. "There's contractors in here from I don't know where, every state is down here getting the work," he said, exasperated. "Now, the local people is trying to make money as well, but they not getting the work that they should be getting because they [the contractors] making sure all the out-of-towners is getting the good areas. It's, like, the one with the most trash in it, that's the ones the out-of-towners is getting and local is getting an area with hardly nothing in it."

Buffy explained that the best work was in areas where there was the most to do. That's because workers are paid by the tonnage of the load of debris they bring in. So if there is an area full of trash, it is not only quicker to collect it and deliver it as a full load, it is also an area that can sustain a crew for much longer than areas with little debris. "Someone from North Carolina, or Tennessee, or Texas, they out here working from seven to seven, and getting twenty loads a day and we can only get four."

"Why they excluding the local people or giving the local people a run, a hassle?" he asked, unclear himself about the answer. "It's not only with the trash, it's also with the levees, the FEMA trailers—the local people is not getting the work they should. I purchased two trucks to haul FEMA trailers. I pay $1,100 a month for insurance."

The direct-action style of local expression got shoved aside by the system FEMA put in place and failed to oversee. The system promoted inaction and layers of players who simply sat, "managed," and collected fees. The Department of Homeland Security issued a report in 2008 defending FEMA's multi-tier subcontracting program, noting that there was no legal limit to the number of tiers of subcontractors permitted by FEMA contractors. But because there was no effective oversight of these layered contracts, rampant fraud, waste, and abuse occurred within these pyramids, and skilled and unskilled residents could not hope to get hired.[18] The message received, whether intentionally sent or not, was, "We don't know you, we don't need you, we don't hear you," leaving capable residents with the shortest stick in their own neighborhood.

FEMA's lack of oversight also allowed inflated prices to drive the recovery effort, picking taxpayer pockets. For people impacted by the disaster, the economic hurt multiplied. And beyond economics, pride and self-respect took a hit. Men in the family were used to earning status from having a steady job, doing good work, and offering to help others.

"FEMA has took over this parish," said Buffy. "We know what we need to do and how to do it, but you know, what can we do when somebody else is calling the shots?"

The clash of operating systems resulted in the failure of many messages sent that were not received or not acted upon. The cousins' style of direct action and the expectations of positive feedback got slammed again and again. One evening when Buffy and two of his cousins and I stood outside the parish civic center in Chalmette, they recounted another story. We had all just attended a meeting about FEMA funds and how they were getting disbursed in the parish. Alton, Buffy's cousin who ran a car-repair shop in Violet, shook his head over the way FEMA had led him and other cousins to believe they could get hauling contracts. Men in the family were experienced truckers. That's how many made their living. Some of them had pooled their resources a couple of months after the storm to outfit and insure their rigs in order to haul FEMA trailers into the parish. That was one thing they thought they could do to earn a little money at the same time they were helping supply desperately needed trailers. The logjam for delivery of trailers from other states was a big problem. So it made sense that a few more qualified drivers could help. Alton, Buffy, Charles, and several other truck-driving cousins got ready for work.

"We bought big dualies [pickups with dual rear wheels] to haul FEMA trailers," Alton said. "They told us okay, you'll get the contract." He paused and turned to me. "Ask me how many FEMA trailers we pulled."

"None?" I guessed, correctly.

"I had to put $30,000 worth of coverage on that truck," Alton said with disbelief in his voice and his eyes. "I had to go across the river and . . . ," gesturing with his chin toward Buffy. "He could tell you," he said. "He went for trailers, too."

"Right," Buffy added. "I didn't pull not one trailer. But here somebody else that got a ole' raggedy truck, barely making it, pulling ten trailers . . ."

"What?" I asked. "So how do you guys explain that?"

Buffy shook his head. The hurt smarted. "We're not used to that, you know, because they say we taking money from the contractors."

Despite their need for work, their professional experience with trucking and hauling, and the rigs they invested in to make themselves more marketable to outsiders they didn't know, the men of the family had difficulty realizing that FEMA was not the slightest bit interested in them. Their desire to work and help relieve a logjam that was delaying the return of family members met with another scripted response: "We don't do things that way." The men had no idea what to say to get through to the logic of the recovery culture, no idea how to position themselves to get the work they and other local residents should have been first in line to get.

THE RHETORIC-ACTION DISCONNECT: FEMA WORDS AND FEMA ACTIONS

To read FEMA literature, one might have felt heartened by the twenty-first-century shift recognizing the value of engaging "local" communities in the process of recovery. The movement to involve disaster-struck communities themselves has gained momentum across fields of disaster planning and is now reflected in the common slogan used in emergency management training: "All disasters are local."[19] In 2004, FEMA named a new series of Emergency Support Functions (ESF), sixteen in all. One of these, ESF-14, specified FEMA's new "local" approach to disaster, by establishing a Long Term Community Recovery (LTCR) plan that would reach out to local communities and residents and work with them to achieve recovery goals. The plan was organized, expressed in impeccable bureaucratese, to "promote the successful recovery of communities by helping create a shared understanding of the problems facing communities, facilitating an inclusive community-wide dialogue that launches a strategic recovery road map, and assisting with the coordination of State and Federal agencies, private sector organizations, and non-profits to achieve optimal recovery."[20] At FEMA's instigation, a Long Term Recovery Group was on the record as having been established in St. Bernard Parish in 2005. Over the years that followed, FEMA, its contractors, and the Long Term Recovery Group promised to ensure the recovery of parish communities by working with those communities.

But family members and other residents I interviewed never heard about a Long Term Recovery Group in their parish. Jonathan, the salaried FEMA employee working on the ground in St. Bernard Parish, explained that "the Long Term Recovery Groups that FEMA helps set up aren't really local people in the sense you mean. They're nonprofits and faith-based groups with an office in the vicinity, but their people aren't necessarily from the community." In St. Bernard Parish, reports indicate that the LTRG was composed of thirty-eight individuals who were drawn from "stakeholder organizations" in the parish, including authorities in various branches of parish government, the school board, the port, banks, commercial fisheries, oil companies, and service organizations like the Chamber of Commerce and Kiwanis.[21] No ordinary residents had been recruited to join the committee, and no one in the family had been told about its existence. The work performed by this group of nonprofits and faith-based groups may have helped some residents, but because there was no oversight or accountability to FEMA or anyone else regarding the reach and impact of this "local" work, it was at best a haphazard effort, poorly equipped to reach out in a systematic way to the full range of parish residents.

It was Sherry's view that FEMA operated from an inflexible set of rules. She laughed and said, "You got to understand, FEMA has its own way of doing things, and the rules they set out are not meant to be adapted locally." FEMA had no strategies to compensate for its lack of local knowledge and awareness, she explained. The agency's written promise to make recovery work through local communities simply bore no relationship to a reality anyone in the family experienced. FEMA's website information seemed to suggest it knew the right thing was to make recovery yield to the needs of local people, but its Long Term Recovery Group didn't do it, the contractors that had been hired didn't do it, and FEMA itself could not shift off-script to respond beyond its own prepackaged template.

Robin is an imposing woman with a good sense of humor and a keen awareness of parish politics. More than others in the family, she expressed the belief that parish politicians and oil-company owners deliberately squashed
job and housing opportunities for blacks in the parish. Perhaps because
she did not hold a single steady job, she had less to lose by making these
claims, but my own research suggested that structural racism, the kind that
is woven into the logic of various institutions and organizations, was a real
problem in this parish.[22]

Amid the unexpected challenges and roadblocks to recovery imposed
from the outside, managing life inside FEMA trailers also presented oppressive everyday problems. In March 2006, Robin had expressed elation about
being back in the parish. In her trailer bursting full of cousins, she had pro-
claimed, "All I need is to be back here in St. Bernard Parish. Home, where
I am comfortable."

Robin was a resourceful and optimistic person. But by that fall, after
seven relentless months of struggle, the relief of being back home where she
felt recognized and understood had shifted into something else. Successive
problems with her trailer and her failed efforts to get FEMA to resolve these
problems brought Robin around to a less forgiving point of view. Living
without a sense of control in her own parish had eroded her optimism. She
worked two jobs to support herself and her daughters. In her mind, she was
doing everything she possibly could to help herself and go with the flow of
the depressingly slow recovery. She didn't need any extra troubles. But her
repeated calls to FEMA went unanswered.

"My trailer is leaking right over the big bed," she said. "I had to put pots
in the middle of the bed. I've called them, but they never come. I have a work
order, they promised to come in seventy-two hours. Nothing."

Robin knew that her problems with FEMA were causing heartache for
others, too. People were getting fed up with waiting.

"It angers me to see nothing getting done here," she said fourteen months
after the storm. Her hair was pulled back tightly, and she sat opposite me
on a dinette-table bench seat bolted to the floor. Her expression looked
stern and her elbows bore the weight of her head, which she had let sink
into her hands. Her FEMA trailer was no way to be home: it was leaky, tiny,
and crowded beyond its smallness by the supplies and the clothes that she
and her two daughters needed and couldn't fit in the closet or small cup-
boards provided.

It was part of Robin's nature to help people in need directly. Years before the storm, she had adopted a three-month-old baby girl who had been abandoned by her drug-addicted mother. She named the baby "Precious," and Precious grew up as a member of the family, baby sister to Trietha. After the storm, Robin rescued a dog she brought to live with them. They named her "Katrina." And one day when I arrived for a visit, I saw her sitting outside her trailer on the steps of her old ruined home. A man was sitting there with her eating a bowl of soup she'd made. She explained to me later that he was a neighbor who had become homeless since Katrina. He had lost everything, had no insurance, and had no way to fix up his home.

"He was living in an abandoned house, and I told him, I said, you don't have to do that, I said, 'I have a porch on my old house that is still okay.' He used to work at the shrimp factory. And sure enough, I remember, right before the holidays, he used to come around bringing shrimp to all the people—little ones that they wasn't using, so everyone would have shrimps and stuff like that, for you to cook. You can't treat nobody like that . . ." For her, it was unacceptable to let someone in Violet live without care.[23] Robin said it was no hardship to feed him and that he had other places to stay—the community was taking care of him.

"When I first came back," she reflected, "and all the trailers arrived, you saw people that you knew, and then you saw they opening the school, it was, like, 'Oh, they doing stuff.' That was happy times. My aunts came back. I felt like nothing really changed, just the way of living for a little while. Okay, that little while turned into a year. And more. And it's still the same! I work in security for the Capital One Bank. It's a job, full time, five days a week, eight hours a day."

Robin's security-guard uniform gave her the look of authority, but her temporary, full-time work to protect Capital One's customers had not earned her the ear of a single recovery agent.

"The holidays are going to be hard this year. You can't put a turkey in those tiny ovens. I'm going to have to cut it in half. For Christmas, you can't put up a tree. For kids, there is no Christmas without a tree. The more you talk about it, the more you try to find a solution, but you can't. No one can figure out how to buy Christmas gifts."

By spring 2007, twenty months after the storm, Robin's exasperation with her trailer had spilled over into her whole life:

"They keep saying everything is getting better," Robin said, giving the thought time to stew. "But it's not true. Half the houses are still not gutted out because the owners don't have trailers to stay in to get the work done. You're working and you still can't do anything."

It wasn't that family members needed special assistance; they needed to feel like they mattered, and that they could retain a sense of control over what was happening. Their own styles of expression—ways of speaking and interacting; ways of sharing information, time, and food; and ways of acting to solve problems—all these variations on bayou communication had been dismissed or ignored or belittled by the recovery culture. FEMA never presented any kind of road map, timetable, or set of guidelines that could explain in clear language how to move along the process. When family members had problems with trailers leaking or needing repairs, they met with unresponsive agents who did not return phone calls and did not assign work in a timely way. No one knew when Road Home money would come. Everything was anybody's guess.

For her part, Robin tried to move forward in spite of FEMA's "nonresponsive response" by making small repairs on her ruined house next door to her trailer, but it was just too hard without the Road Home money.

"I bought one door for my bedroom," she told me. "Now bills is rollin' in. Still have to do floors, kitchen, cabinets. But every time I get a paycheck I have to pay for basics—food, utilities, phone. It's a struggle every day. I think I've cried more now than before because I don't know what to do. To go to a lumber company and beg them to make the cost reasonable. No one can afford this."

The electricians, plumbers, and drywall workers who advertised all over the parish could not be trusted, though many people learned that the hard way. Because demand for their work was so much greater than the supply of available skilled work, fake companies made off with homeowner deposits put down on projects that never materialized. Both Janice and Melanie reported fraud from having lost the money they paid up front to ensure their place in a long line of eager customers, just the kind of vulnerability that predatory companies rely on.[24]

FEMA wasn't responsible for the fraud, or the grossly inflated cost of lumber, or the shrunken supply of rental housing that drove the cost of units up by four times their previous value. FEMA did not cause the widespread price gouging that typified so many commodities needed for rebuilding. But as the government authority responsible for the disaster zone, it could have done more to alert people, to offer support to those cheated, to issue warnings to companies operating illegally.[25] FEMA could have set a more aggressive tone toward those exploiting Katrina's victims. In a disaster zone awash in dollars and unpoliced by the agency in charge, economic greed and political maneuvering left the recovery of ordinary people compromised by dangers of exploitive companies, slowness of Road Home compensation, and the indifference of authorities in charge.

What no one understood two years after Katrina was that at the heart of the family's suffering in their own home environment was not so much their losses as it was the imposing control of outsiders who had taken over their world and did not speak their language. All the forms and paperwork processes, the standard-issue trailers, the language and styles of bureaucratic communication, the indifference of recovery agents, and the reliance on contractors from outside the area conspired to leave family members in a state of chronic frustration.

Communication is the entrée into everything. If you can't bend your ears, you can't bend your mind to get it around what people need. Communication opens doors into the cycle of culture. Delivering comfort must be premised on the will to communicate and to understand. But after Katrina, information did not flow, people were not heard, messages sent to them felt demeaning, and people were left to guess about what was to come.

7

WHOSE ROAD HOME?

One humid summer day in June 2007, nearly two years after the storm, I stepped up into Katie's trailer, the one she had finally gotten from FEMA after months of pleading her clear-cut case. Her prosthetic leg, which she was no longer able to wear, was nowhere to be seen. She was sitting as she often did, sunken down on the end of a narrow institutional beige FEMA couch, her head turned to watch the small TV perched at the top of an étagère standing in the opposite corner. With her new trailer, Katie had a smidgen more room. The dinette table was bolted to the floor, but there were no bench seats on either side. The wheelchair access required space to roll up, so Katie had acquired a set of folding chairs that visitors could arrange as they liked. The bathroom was now large enough to turn around her chair, but still too small to navigate easily between the shower and the toilet. Having the accessible trailer was cold comfort. The original FEMA-issue Cavalier with its flimsy steps had robbed her of the use of her prosthetic leg. Moving around in a wheelchair required more room than walking, so the slight gain in space was still a net loss for Katie. The strain of negotiating such cramped quarters seemed to have nibbled away at the deep reserve of Katie's good cheer. But despite a clear ebb in energy, Katie did not complain.

The TV was tuned to an afternoon game show, but I could tell from her blank face that she had no particular interest in the outcome. The upbeat show was company. Dressed in a wrinkled T-shirt and cut-off gray sweatpants, Katie had the look of a slowly deflating balloon. Or maybe it was just one of those days when her leg hurt a lot or a grandchild hadn't come over.

I moved across her line of sight to grab a metal folding chair with a white padded seat tucked neatly under the table. I ignored the TV but faced the chair that direction to play along with Katie's chosen activity. I knew by then that I would have to ask for the volume to be turned down if I couldn't hear well enough, something we had done countless times during our filming work. But now that the film was finished, I didn't need that accommodation. Just as I had trained my ear to bend to the black dialect and speech rhythms in southeast Louisiana, I had also trained my brain to ignore the voices yakking away in the box. Over time, I had come to realize that in the homes where I visited, the TV just stays on, whatever else might be taking place. The noise was as normal as the up-and-down decibels of children playing or the chatter of women in the kitchen cooking together, erupting periodically into peals of laughter.

I asked Katie how things were going. She shrugged, tilted her head toward me with an arched brow and worn-out eyes; just as quickly, she returned her gaze to the TV and zipped up her mask.

"What do you hear from Road Home?" I asked, knowing full well the answer, having asked the same question every few weeks for months.

"Nothing. I don't hear nothing."

"How long has it been now, Katie?" Maybe if I could get her to talk about it, it would help her realize that things were shifting and that people were finally getting their money.

"Been too long. Look like everybody getting their check but me. And they ain't even called to set up my meeting!"

"So, who has already gotten their money?" I wanted to hear her name the names that meant the most to her sense of being left behind.

"Cynt got hers, Roseana got hers, Nell just waiting on the check, she had her meeting already." So, the two sisters who'd applied, and one of her daughters.

"So have you been calling to see where your case is?"

"Call every week. And every week, they tell me the same thing."

Just then, Gray Eye pushed open the metal door of the trailer, landing him in the middle of our space and conversation. His tall form nearly grazed the low ceiling and his long stride seemed too big for the dimensions of his home. He wore a white ball cap with a gold-and-black Saints logo. The cap set off his smooth dark complexion and new red T-shirt that concealed his bony shoulders. His clean, lean look made him seem younger than a man in his late sixties.

He moved straight for the fridge, muttering something about the overhang outside, greeting me in his enthusiastic way, "Hey, baby, good to see you, baby. Good to see you." He grabbed the fridge door, swung it back, snatched a Budweiser, popped it, and turned to Katie with this latest concern. "What we going to do without the garage top if they go tear it down? We need that out there for having a place to sit."

Katie didn't blink and didn't respond. She took a puff of her cigarette and shook her head. She knew he was a worrier, and every day something or other would preoccupy him—very often related to money. Or it might be about his trouble finding shrimp and crab, or the ache in his shoulder. Could be Katie's health, or the Road Home money. Today, it was about the carport, what Gray Eye called the garage top.

Gray Eye was a slender man, and I came to see his leanness as less a product of his diet than his anxiety. He seldom hung around to talk, but when he did, his hands were always busy, either wrapping circles around themselves or working like flat paddles against his belly as though he needed to iron out the wrinkles. Over the years, I only talked to Gray Eye at length a few times. Each conversation was similar. Though always friendly, he never failed to bring us around to an important worry.

Gray Eye didn't seem comfortable in social settings and rarely visited the inside of a church, save for the funeral of a friend or a family member. At the weekly gatherings in his own yard after church, he would make an appearance to claim his bowl of Katie's gumbo or stuffed bell peppers. Then wraithlike, he would vanish. As he did that day after announcing his concern about letting go of the garage top.

"And what do the Road Home people tell you?" I asked, returning my gaze to Katie.

"They say I'm in some phase"—she searched for the word—"verification."

"Well, what does that mean?"

"I don't know. That just what they say every time. Nobody can explain it."

The game show host sounded louder and more enthusiastic. I glanced up to hear him announce the winner of a final round of something, and there was much hoopla about all the winnings and prizes. Did the dumb luck of a game-show contestant make Katie feel even worse? Maybe she wasn't even thinking about how her struggle to get compensation compared to the easy money thrown around on the show.

"Well, how about you call them right now while I'm here? I want to hear what they say to you." I also wanted to hear what she said to them. She pulled herself out of the depression in the couch and took the crutches I handed her. She was fiercely independent, and even though she could have just pointed me to the folder on the pantry shelf, she stood up slowly, hoisting herself with a crutch, and then hopped past the couch to pull the file off a shelf and up under her arm. After she had settled back into her corner of the couch, she brought the phone that she kept beside her into her lap.

"You know, every time I call, it's a different person. I try to get the name of somebody, and then the next time, nobody heard of that person. You can't get nowhere with these people," she said calmly, "It's frustrating." If Katie called something frustrating, it was truly eating her up.

She dialed the Road Home number she knew by heart and waited for the recorded voice. She held out the phone so I could hear the message, "Remember, Louisiana wants you to come home." In the early months after Road Home got established back in summer 2006, Katie didn't mind the message. It seemed appropriate, almost personal. But it was now a year later and nearly two years since the storm. The same greeting now rang hollow.

Katie prepared herself for the voice on the other end, using her index finger to rehearse a note she had written on the top sheet in her folder. Maybe she would get a real response this time. Surely she had been through enough sorrow in her life—having lost her younger son in a car accident, having lost her leg before that. She faced personal loss by calling on her faith and adopting a practical resignation. She could have chosen to amputate just her dying diabetic toes. But, as she told me, she instructed the doctor to take her leg to the knee.

"I told them I was giving them one time to cut," Katie had said to me. "One cut and that was it. 'Cut up to there,' because I wasn't going to go back for more. You know sometimes they cut a toe and then they cut half of your foot. So I told the doctor, 'Cut up to there.' It healed well. Didn't stop me from cooking. I cook just about every day."

Katie was a woman who wanted some control over her future. Now her home, and everything in it, was destroyed. *Couldn't these people show a little more care? Not really*, I thought, answering my own question. Despite the fact that many FEMA agents tried to be helpful, it seemed to the family that everyone working for FEMA and Road Home knew nothing about them. Agents like the one Katie was waiting for are hired to do a job and read a script. Their offices might as well have been on the moon.

Katie continued to hold the phone out so we could both hear. The recorded voice interrupted the silence, "We are experiencing a high volume of calls. We will answer your call in the order in which it was received. Please be patient."

A minute later, I glanced up to see if Katie's movement was signaling attention from the other end of the phone. It wasn't. She was just getting restless and had reached around for her pack of cigarettes. With her free hand, she tipped back the pack to pull one out and light it up, with a smooth, practiced flow. She inhaled deeply. Then she returned her attention to the pages in the folder on her lap. I could tell that her slow review of these pages had become its own ritual—preparing for the agent by reviewing your papers, then waiting, and more waiting. She continued to puff, right through the indignity.

I passed the time taking in life around the trailer. From my angle in the chair, I could look out the small metal window behind Katie's head to see several people hanging out under the garage top. There was Cynthia, Katie's oldest sister, who could sit anywhere for hours so long as there were people around. There was a teenage granddaughter, Brionna, and her father, Turb (Leroy Jr.). Turb had become Katie and Gray Eye's only son and youngest child now that Leon had died. Neighbor George was there, too. Like Turb, he was a good boiler.

George sat on top of the redwood picnic table, his back to the big field that had never been a homesite. His easy smile exposed a few missing teeth. George was a regular around Katie and Gray Eye's place, a person the family had practically adopted since he had no family of his own. He had lived a troubled life, but at Katie's place, he didn't have to explain himself. He could relax and enjoy the feasts that regularly issued out of the kitchen. Even on a Sunday after service, when congregants spilled out of the sanctuary and walked across the lawn to linger at Katie's place for gumbo, George was there, in T-shirt and jeans, offering no pretense of having spent time inside the church. His attire might have worked in a hip contemporary service in the city, but the black congregation in Verret's First Baptist Church was always dressed up. Never in all the times I had attended service there had I spotted anyone wearing denim, top or bottom. Still, no one would think to question his right to share in the meal. The ethic was bayou born, and hospitality came before rules that excluded.

Besides, often enough, George helped Turb prepare the crab or crawfish boil. He liked to sort the crabs, and he had his own spicy recipe for the marinade they would make together for the boil. He and Turb peeled the potatoes and onions, poured bottles of Louisiana Hot Sauce, added tubs of salt, and squeezed dozens of lemons into the giant metal pot they used for boils.

I stood up, shaking off my reverie; I refocused my attention back outside the metal window: beyond the people, the hodgepodge clutter of picnic tables, plastic chairs, metal shelving, and garbage bins. I noticed a freshly turned row of soil that Katie had staked out for her red geraniums, a two-foot wide border that ran alongside the yard, from the length of the garage top, and then at a right angle down the driveway to the street. Most people on crutches wouldn't consider getting down on their one good leg to undertake the task of planting, but Katie loved flowers.

"Yes, this is Carolyn Williams," said Katie, using her legal name. "My case number is 06HH044398." She gripped the phone tightly while they looked up her file. I leaned in to listen.

"What can we do for you today, Ms. Williams?" I barely heard the agent ask.

"I'm calling to find out where my case is and how much longer I got to wait. Last time I called I talked to Judith. Is she there?"

"No, I'm sorry. She is not here anymore. I can help you. I'll be back in just a minute."

It took the agent several minutes to return to the call.

"I'm showing you are in the verification phase, Ms. Williams."

"Well, how long is it going to take to get out of there? I been waiting all this time to get my check."

It had been more than a year since Katie had submitted the paperwork for the Road Home program. Like everyone else in the family, she and Gray Eye got the forms, filled them out, and mailed them as soon as the program was announced in May 2006. That following November 2006, they had been called to meet with Road Home authorities to review their file. They thought everything was in order. But it was seven months later now, June 2007, and they were still waiting for a call about their closing meeting and final compensation. Without knowing the amount Road Home would compensate them, they couldn't know what kind of home they could buy. Everything was on hold.

"We have no information about that. But it will be as soon as possible. Thank you for calling. Is there anything else I can help you with today?"

"No. Thank you."

Wow, I thought. The Road Home people really know how to clear callers off the phone lines. Polite and completely noncommittal, all in the flow of a single sentence. That could be disarming. But I knew their tricks. I had learned for myself that bureaucracies were full of ordinary people who follow the rules they are given. They don't mean any harm, but there aren't many who can really help you, either. They just don't know enough about what they are handling. They read their scripts and try to do the jobs they are assigned, but they have no reason to bend their ears to the people they are supposed to help. Katie Williams faced a seriously diminished existence. She had flood insurance, and the insurance company had finally paid for structure and contents, but a whopping portion of that check had gone to pay off the mortgage on her destroyed home. Her only hope for replacing the three-bedroom baby-blue home she'd had before the storm was the money she would be awarded from Road Home. The poor clerk she spoke to had no clue about that. She gave her the only answer she had.

"Katie, what if I called them just to see if I could get somebody else who might tell us more?"

"You can't talk to them. Has to be the name on the file. Nobody else."

"So that means you or Gray Eye? What about one of your kids or sisters? Couldn't they be allowed to talk to them if you gave them your permission?"

"Nobody else." Once more, it was clear that neither FEMA nor Road Home had a clue about how a bayou family unit worked.

"All right then, what if I pretend to be you. I'll say I am Carolyn Williams."

She paused. "Okay!" She leaned toward me with a hint of a smile and held out the phone. "You call 'em."

I dialed.

"Louisiana wants you to come home," the recorded voice offered. *Nice but not persuasive*, I thought. I waited, grateful that there was no music, no attempt to distract the needy callers or suggest the wait might be so minimal we would barely have time to hear a favorite song. But silence didn't make the time go faster. I glanced at Katie, who had begun filing methodically through her papers, examining each sheet in turn, licking an index finger to push to the next page. I wondered what it would mean to her if I managed to get someone to explain things. Would she be happy for the help? Would it humiliate her? Was I doing the right thing? I couldn't worry about that. She needed help. I waited at least as long as Katie had to hear a human voice, about eight minutes.

"This is Meredith. How may I help you?"

I identified myself as Carolyn Williams and gave her the case number. "I need to check what's going on with my status, please."

"Just a moment, please."

Okay, I thought. *I've got Meredith*. Katie had talked to someone named Bonnie. And the month before, she told me she had talked with a Judith. She had written Judith's name down and hoped to talk with her again because she was pleasant. But pleasant hadn't gotten Katie an answer. And besides, after all her calls, Katie held little hope that she would be able to talk to Judith again. That didn't keep her from trying. It was one of the only ways she knew to try to get some leverage in a situation involving a bureaucracy. Her daughter in California had coached her: write down the name of the person you talk to, and then ask for that person the next time. But the reality didn't allow for that strategy. Not only was the person on the other end never the same person, but no one at Road Home seemed to be keeping notes of the phone conversations with callers asking about their cases. So no matter how many times you called, you had to start over each time. The system did not set out to demean or frustrate people, but it was not set up to help in any substantive way: survivors were left with all the work of becoming their own advocates.

"Ms. Williams?"

"Yes," I responded, "I'm here. What can you tell me?"

"I see that you are in the verification phase."

"Oh, still? Well, can you explain what that means, exactly?"

"It means your file has to be verified before it can go on to the next phase."

"Well, what is involved in getting my file verified?"

"I don't know that. I just know that's where you are, and until they have finished up that verification, we can't give you any more information."

"Well, I'd like to know what this verification is about. Who has to verify the file? Some kind of third party?"

"I don't know the answer to that, Ms. Williams. This is all I can tell you. We will contact you when you are out of the verification phase."

"Wait. Are you saying you have no idea at all when that will be? I had my meeting for eligibility with your people back in November 2006. It's June 2007. That's seven months I have waited for my closing meeting. Is that normal?"

"Yes, that is normal. I don't know anything else. I'm sorry. Can I help you with anything else today, Ms. Williams?"

"Yes, you can connect me with a supervisor, please."

"Nobody knows anything more about your file than I do. The supervisor can't tell you anything else."

"That's fine, I still want to talk with the supervisor."

"Just a moment."

A glance at the clock above the sink told me it had been twenty minutes since I had placed the call. Katie was still fingering her way slowly through the sheets in her file. It was something to do. I wondered what she thought when she heard my firm tone and when I asked for and then insisted on speaking to a supervisor. I knew she had never heard my professional voice. Over the years, I had sharpened my skills at talking to bureaucrats. I thought back about all my experience—since I had lived on my own as a young adult, I had dealt countless times with new phone companies and their mysterious charges and systems of billing. In my faculty job at the state university, I had learned how to work with administrators whose primary concern was following rules and generating paperwork. I'd also had practice navigating the most authoritative and complicated bureaucracies ever invented during my fifteen years of research in French-colonized areas. The highly centralized and regulated government of France offers those who have to work with it an incomparable training ground for learning how to keep your cool and advance your case.

Absorbing these lessons of communication depended on aspects of my upbringing that seemed invisible until I thought about it now: my upper-middle-class family, home, neighborhoods, and education. My professional livelihood grew out of those privileges. Everything about my life since birth had prepared me to succeed in a world of strangers because I had learned along the way how to speak in different registers, including the one I needed in order to interact effectively with faceless bureaucrats. Realizing how these skills of communication were embedded in my entire life history, I could understand the chasm between Katie's world and mine. Beyond income or occupation, beyond lifestyle—the difference in our worlds began at birth in the way we talked, who we learned to talk with, and what we learned to talk about.[1] Communicating with bureaucrats crystalized it all. And what low-level clerk had any clue that, as part of her job, she had been socialized into a cultural system, one premised on and projecting middle-class values? The thought gripped me. I would spend a good deal more time chewing on this invisible and insidious type of inequality that, among other matters, makes recovering from a disaster all the more frustrating and painful.

There was Katie, working her level best to communicate with Judith/Bonnie/Meredith or someone else whose office had control over her future. Katie's strategy to reconnect to the person who'd helped her before hadn't worked, and once again, for the umpteenth time, she hung up with no answers. Requesting help from outsiders was not something she had practice doing. In her big family, people had relied on each other for generations, and their interdependence liberated them from depending on government for anything. But for family members, the self-reliance of the group meant that, in this circumstance, they had no resources for dealing with government representatives, the very people who had control over how they would live in the future. Nearly all of the family members handling calls to Road Home for their households were in their forties or older. Most had high school diplomas or associate's degrees from community colleges. But because they lacked worldly experience, or an advocate like Connie, they were punished. The stakes of effective communication were very high indeed.

"Hello, this is Victoria. I am a supervisor."

"Hello. I was trying to find out what it means to be in the verification phase. Can you explain that to me?"

"No, ma'am. As Meredith explained, we don't know any more about this. It just means your documents have to be verified, and I don't know when that will be done. I'm sorry."

"Well, can you at least tell me who does the verifying? Is that like a third party that comes in?"

"Maybe so, I don't really know. I'm sorry."

"Well, then, may I please speak to your supervisor?"

"Just a moment."

There was still no recorded music as I waited. Another check of the wall clock: more than thirty minutes had passed since I started the call.

Did Katie imagine this is just how white people talk to each other? Should I tell her that I was pretty sure that Victoria was a black woman? I thought about others in the family and their problems. I had heard more stories than I could count about how impossibly hard it was to work with FEMA and Road Home. Now, I was experiencing this firsthand. Never the same agent. Scripts they repeated over and over, no matter what someone asked. I had gotten to the level of a supervisor and now was trying to reach a third person. The system would wear you down, and maybe that's what they depend on to keep people from rioting. If you never get anywhere, it's easier to just stop calling.

"Ms. Williams? This is Laurie."

"Laurie, I have been on the phone for thirty-five minutes now, trying to get an answer to a really simple question. What does it mean to say my case is in the verification phase?"

"It just means that we need to verify your insurance, that's all."

"You need to verify my insurance. My homeowner's insurance?"

"Yes, your homeowner's—for flood and to be sure everything is correct."

"Well, who has to verify all this? A third party?"

"Yes, the process requires a third-party verification of insurance."

"I see. So what is causing the long delay in getting that done?"

"I don't know what is involved, and I don't know any more about your case."

"Can you tell me how much longer I can expect to wait? Other people seem to be getting their checks, but I am stuck here in this verification phase and haven't even had my meeting yet to close on the amount. It seems like something is wrong."

"Nothing is wrong. It takes time. We have more than one hundred thousand people like you, all waiting, too. We are doing everything we can."

"Can you tell me how much longer I can expect to wait, please?"

"I don't know. I'm sorry"

"May I speak to your supervisor, please?"

Now I was getting somewhere. This third agent, Laurie, was two levels up from the person who answered the phone. She spoke with clarity and authority, and she offered two new pieces of information that the other two agents had not—first, that the verification was all about insurance. And second, that an outside third party had to review these documents and approve them. But it still wasn't clear how an outside party would be able to verify someone's insurance documents. Would they call the insurance company and ask about the record of this policyholder? That sounded weird. I knew there was more to learn.

I also felt myself getting angry. Why couldn't they have trained the initial person to respond to a simple question about what the verification phase meant? Was that so hard? Why did they pretend not to know? Even that first supervisor seemed oblivious. I was looking at the wear and tear on Katie's face, and I knew it didn't have to be like this. I resolved to go as far as I could to figure out what was going on. I imagined Road Home as the Wizard of Oz, and that I was trying to approach this formidable being. Was I on the path to truth? Was I halfway there? Most of the way there? Nowhere near? How much more was there that remained invisible to callers like us? Minutes passed.

"Ms. Williams, this is Laurie again. I'm sorry but there is no one available to take your call. All the supervisors are busy. And there is nothing more anyone can tell you, anyway."

"Thank you, I will wait."

I thought, *Oh, what a smooth tactic that is, and she made it sound so innocent. I'll bet this is where most people give up.*

But I wasn't giving up. Besides, I had committed to continuing my research with the family so long as it was clear that they were not yet on that "road home." I was learning more than I bargained for from Katie's call and mine. It had been nearly two years since the storm, and I had come to care a lot for family members. It was hard to watch the collective wear and tear erode the strength of the rhizome, but how could it be otherwise? They had been assigned these weekender trailers, forced to endure long FEMA delays and inconsistent treatment, denied more than token work for the massive cleanup operation, ripped off by contractor fraud, mystified by Road Home and their way of allocating money. How much more insult could people take from the very "recovery" culture that was supposed to make things easier?

Saying there was no supervisor available might on occasion be true. But it was also a common strategy perfected by call centers. In my Language and Culture class, we talk about real-world problems students notice with language. A female student who worked in a call center shared with us some of the problems that happen with callers. She told the class how they train call-center staff to remain polite and avoid confrontation, to respond with the script provided, and to deter callers from staying on the line. Everyone learns, she said, that longer conversations eat up employee time and can even cost employees their job. So keeping it short means you keep your job.

"Hello, this is Diane. I am a case support specialist. What can I do for you?"

"I guess I need to start over. I have been told by three agents that my case is in the verification phase. I have asked each one of them what this means, and all I found out is that there has to be a third party verifying that my insurance is correct. Right?"

"No. There is no third party involved. We just have to review your documents and make sure everything is there."

"Whoa! There is no third party? But your agent just told me specifically that the verification phase required a third party. So if it doesn't, what is holding things up? You have had all my documents for seven months!"

I felt my throat tighten. What was I doing? My involvement was becoming an intervention that could change the course of Katie's case. I wondered if I had gone too far. There is a professional mantra that many anthropologists repeat: "A good researcher avoids advocacy because there is no way to predict how change in one arena can create unwanted change elsewhere." Ethically, this position never seemed persuasive, and I did reflect on it—briefly—during the wait for the clerk to return. I chose to help, so I pressed on.[2]

After my ethical pause, I did a quick inventory. Three levels up, I had been told by someone who spoke without hesitation just what verification meant. Now, at this fourth level, I was told that the agent I had just spoken to had it wrong. It wasn't about the insurance, and it wasn't a third-party review. I shook my head in astonishment.

"May I put you on hold, please? I will have to locate your file so I can answer your question."

"Yes, of course."

Minutes passed.

"Ms. Williams? I am very sorry, but I can now see the problem. There is nothing in your file."

"What? You can't be serious! Back in November 2006, my husband and I met with your people, and I handed them everything in my file. They made copies of all of it and said we would be hearing from you soon. That was seven months ago. How could they have lost everything?"

Katie was pointing to her inch-thick file folder and looking at me quizzically, realizing from my tone of voice and the look on my face that something was terribly wrong. Could what I was hearing be real?

"I can't say, Ms. Williams. I can only say that they aren't there now."

"Well, doesn't it seem like somebody could have figured that out before now? I have been on the phone with you all for forty-five minutes now, and I have had to push to get up four levels just to learn that there was not anything in my file!"

"I am very sorry, Ms. Williams. What you will need to do is send us copies of your insurance documents and any insurance checks you have received so we can process these. We also need a summary of what these checks were paying for—how much for structural damage, how much for flood, like that."

"Okay, this is unbelievable. Can you imagine being in my shoes right now and hearing after all this time what has been the problem? Do you plan to move me out of verification the instant you get these documents?"

"I'm not the one who can do that, Ms. Williams. Once all the documents are here, we will move you as quickly as possible out of verification so you can get your check."

"No, I'm sorry that is not good enough. I want your assurance that you will move my case along immediately and that someone will call to explain what is happening."

"All right, Ms. Williams, I am sorry for all this. I'm going to turn your case number over to the closing team so they will be ready for you as soon as the documents arrive."

"Good. Thank you. Can I fax you everything? That would be the quickest way to get it."

"Yes, you can fax it. Send it to this number." She read off the number as I jotted it down on Katie's file folder. "And be sure to put your case number on the fax."

"Once you get these, can you tell me who will be handling the case? Who will be calling me or who will I ask for if I have to call back?"

"Just ask for the closing team, and they will route your call to the right people. Once they have gotten your fax, it will take two to three days, and then a manager in the Closing Department assigns your case to a caseworker. The caseworker will call you and begin to finalize all the arrangements for your payment."

"Okay, then. Please be sure to alert the closing manager about this case. I want to be assigned a case manager this week."

"I understand, Ms. Williams. I know they will do everything they can for you."

"Thank you."

I was headed back to Colorado the next day. There was still no place to get copies made anywhere close to Katie's trailer, so I took the file folder all the way "up the road" to Chalmette and made copies of every page, at least seventy-five pages of paper I knew were mostly irrelevant, but I copied them anyway, just in case. Then I drove back down the road to Verret and gave Katie back her folder.

On the plane home the next day, I reviewed all the documents one by one, sorting them into piles of "useful" and "not useful." By the time I had made it through the entire stack, I could see that there were only about five sheets of information that corresponded to what "Diane"—the supervisor I had finally reached four levels up from where I started the conversation—indicated they needed. Once I got home, I went straight to my university office and faxed the documents to Road Home.

That was a Monday. On that Thursday, Katie called me to say her case had been moved out of verification and she had been assigned a caseworker with the closing team.

Katie and I never debriefed this phone odyssey, but in a phone conversation after she had gotten the case agent, I sensed that her relief mingled uneasily with a new awareness of her powerlessness. Her own call had lasted only a few minutes and had left all the trouble unsorted. She had made the effort to call Road Home and check on her status every couple of weeks. But the effort never registered on the other end because she was too polite to escalate the call, too trusting to question vague answers delivered by voices trained to sound emphatic and authoritative. She hadn't pushed because she believed that it would not help her case to get angry. And so she held her tongue and remained polite.

8

ALMOST TO THE GROUND

Something had to give. Eighteen months after the storm, there were no signs of recovery coming. People were feeling worse, not better. Many in the family were anxious, stressed, worried, or angry. Nearly all had gained weight; others took pills to sleep; some developed diabetes, high blood pressure, bad headaches, or stomach disorders. Deep fatigue was chronic. Even though most people found a way to get back to some kind of work, many did not have steady jobs like those they had had before. Some now worked double shifts at lower pay. Decent job opportunities dwindled, and those available became more competitive. Progress to restore their lives was not just slow—it seemed to have sunk into a dead-stop paralysis. A whole series of institutional problems related to FEMA and Road Home had unfairly weighed down the family, and I wanted to understand what I was witnessing.

One obvious source of information was mental health providers. But they had their hands full. There was the literature, but in early 2007, there had not been time to research, analyze, and report the catastrophic failure of the mental health response to Katrina. Only later did journal articles begin to document the "crippled state of mental health care in New Orleans."[1] The surge of mental health needs after the storm had coincided with a drastic shrinkage in the number of primary-care providers and available facilities. Of the 196 psychiatrists registered in the city, only twenty-two had returned by the one-year anniversary.[2] Of the 347 total mental health providers, only 60 percent had returned to the area three years later.[3]

Ironically, one of the chief impediments related to stabilizing mental-health care after Katrina arose from the Stafford Act, the very law that regulates how the government is authorized to manage a federally declared disaster. This act emphasizes the need for short-term crisis counseling, and it only allows the use of public money for that kind of counseling.[4] The rule had created a difficult situation for many local providers whose clients needed financial help to continue their counseling after the storm. But even though those already receiving counseling services might have been especially vulnerable to the trauma of disaster, no compensation was granted for ongoing care. Instead, to meet the letter of the act, the Substance Abuse and Mental Health Services Administration (SAMHSA) paid mental health counselors from other areas to come to the disaster site to provide short-term care to people with mental illnesses and disorders. "Locals would have done a better job," said Harold Ginzburg, a medical doctor and professor of psychiatry at Tulane University and Louisiana State University (LSU) Schools of Medicine.[5] Clearly, the pressure of limited resources and the deficits of outside providers, leashed to short-term rotations and unfamiliar with the local culture, left the mental health infrastructure looking like it, too, had been hammered by a hurricane.

The people charged with managing mental health care delivery in the context of a disaster are located in the Department of Health and Human Services (HHS), the agency that houses both the Centers for Disease Control (CDC) and SAMHSA. These agencies produce publications that distill relevant knowledge for use in training mental health providers who work in post-disaster contexts. In 2003, two years before Katrina, SAMHSA had published a fifty-eight-page guidebook about how to provide culturally meaningful mental health services. Entitled "Developing Cultural Competence in Disaster Mental Health Programs," the publication offered an explicitly cultural approach to understanding the kind of mental health services people needed after a disaster. It was apparent that cultural anthropologists had had a formative hand in shaping it, and the document referenced the work of many disaster sociologists who had made important contributions to the field of disaster studies.[6]

The cultural competency mental health guide presented in clear language the value of cultural knowledge in caring for people impacted by disaster, stating:

> Service providers and funding organizations have become increasingly aware that race, ethnicity, and culture may have a profound effect on the way in which an individual responds to and copes with disaster . . . Service providers must find ways to tailor their services to individuals' and communities' cultural identities, languages, customs, traditions, beliefs, values, and social support systems. This recognition, understanding, respect, and tailoring of services to various cultures is the foundation of cultural competence (2003:5, 8).

So, why hadn't people been out there, in St. Bernard Parish, applying this valuable model of care? What had happened to recognition, understanding, and respect? Had the federal mental health agency decided to ignore these ideas and strategies? I saw nothing at all approximating cultural competence operating on the ground. Had mental health experts actually been trained on these concepts and practical tips, they would have figured out that large black families deeply rooted on the bayou needed a way to be themselves.[7] They needed places to gather and places to cook for large numbers. It would not have been hard to tailor services, but it would have taken an alert observer trained to ask the right questions and pay attention to the sources of comfort among culturally distinct groups. The disparity between the contents of the cultural guide to mental health and the action on the ground precisely paralleled the gulf I had seen between FEMA's words and actions.

In fact, what seemed to have informed mental health practice after Katrina was a slimmed-down version of the "Field Manual for Mental Health and Human Service Workers in Major Disasters."[8] This compact, four-page handout was entitled, "Disaster Mental Health Primer: Key Principles, Issues, and Questions."[9] The primer was issued by the Centers for Disease Control at the Department of Health and Human Services five years after the field manual, two years after the cultural competency guide, and exactly one day after the levees broke and floodwaters drowned the city of New Orleans and rose to rooftops in St. Bernard Parish: August 30, 2005. Its abbreviated contents provided a clue about what might have happened to both the twenty-page field manual and the fifty-eight-page cultural competency guide during the aftermath of Katrina. Briefly, the primer eliminated culture as a guide to recovery. Page two specifies "Factors That Determine the Stressfulness of a Disaster," identifying three categories:

1. Features of the Disaster (such as the suddenness of the onset, whether it was avoidable, its duration and intensity of impact);
2. Community or Societal Factors (such as community resources before and after the event, the nature of damage done, preparedness, whether the community had been impacted by prior events); and
3. Characteristics of the Individuals Involved (actual losses, stress in the person's life, effectiveness of the person's coping skills, prior experience with such events, closeness to the event, and social support).

In the tripartite list of factors, there was no place to situate the devastating losses to the Johnson-Fernandez family, or to any other of the big families so common to the area. The tragic losses for them could be neither captured at the level of the individual nor located at the level of community. There were no people in the "primer's" imaginary community. The message was all about resources, infrastructure, planning. Where was the social tissue that connected the individual to a group? What about the pain of an individual whose loss is not private but rather is shared among everyone grieving together? Nothing explained how cultural life might have fit into the schema. The word *culture* never appeared. Perhaps, in a time of war "over there," in the Middle East, it was simply more expedient, both in terms of dollars and administrative attention, to ignore the research that had inspired the cultural guide that would have served the survivors "over here," on the bayou. The glaring gap between these documents left questions without answers.

As it turned out, and as I detail in this chapter, the cultural needs of the family did not fit into the default mental health approach built into recovery protocols and laid out in the primer. Whereas if the cultural guide had been followed, mental health providers could have been encouraged to pay attention to the relevant coping strategies of black families like the one I had been working with. They could have promoted a therapeutic model in accord with strategies already familiar to the family.

The most valuable insight about the family's predicament and the lack of mental health support came from someone who understood both the cultural patterns of big black families, and how these families cope with trouble. Days of phone calls had led me to Dr. Zarus E. P. Watson, a mental health counseling educator at the University of New Orleans. Finding him in spring 2007 helped illuminate the deteriorating situation. Our first meeting at his academic office at UNO evolved into an ongoing series of meetings we had over the next several years. Dr. Watson quickly recognized the problems I laid out for him, and as an African American, he understood how the stigma of race added a burden to the recovery process. He quickly agreed that the family's chronic difficulties were profoundly tied to the disabled family network that FEMA's recovery program did not address. And there was an additional layer of difficulty for African Americans. On top of the delays and communication problems with FEMA and Road Home that impacted tens of thousands of people in the New Orleans area regardless of racial identity, oppression of one kind or another has "always kept our population under stress," said Dr. Watson. "Katrina is just the latest stressor."[10]

Dr. Watson explained that the wear and tear on the family that I described was predictable, but not only because the big family couldn't act in customary ways. The long delays in the process had also given people time to realize that nothing was happening and that they had no idea when that would change. "When you don't get signals from the larger system that this is what the plan is, it makes it hard to hang on. But we'll still hang in there, we'll still stay here, because that's what we do, we always stay."

The deep roots of the family had made dealing with outsiders all the more difficult. "In this part of the United States," he said, "people just don't move away—not because you fear what's out there—but because what's here is so appealing to you. So when it comes to being rooted to the area and people are attached deeper than in most places, you might say, and with all this tradition, you get cultures that are unlike other cultures anywhere else."

The rhizome nature of family life did not resemble anything else I knew of in the United States. But for the family, there had been no other organizing premise in any generation, ever. People knew from their evacuation time in Dallas or Houston, and some knew from their earlier travels outside the bayou, that their family was different from families in other places. But it wasn't unusual here—both the bayou environment and the entire region of New Orleans had kept its families together and rooted for generations. US Census reports from 2010 show that nearly four of every five residents in Louisiana were born there, the highest proportion for any state.[11]

"Rootedness has an extra significance for us," Dr. Watson added. "With African Americans, you had to fight for what you got, so a home is more than just something that you bought. You have to defend it every generation, you have to defend it and make sure that you do not lose it because there were elements that were trying to take it from you.

"And now to have this happen makes it all the more traumatic. Because now, I'm forcibly out of my home, but I want to make sure that I can take care of that so that all those generations before me did not fight for nothing. You have to go all the way back, to see how things progressed to where they are now. And it's a struggle. It's been a struggle for your family to get where they are right now. So when I think of property that, say, my father owns, it's not just about him. I'm thinking about my grandfathers and what they did to secure the land that he was able to secure. So, you don't want to be the one to lose this part. I don't want to be the one to lose it. To them it is more than just a place, more than just a house. It's a heritage issue."

In the spring and summer of 2007, nearing two years after the storm, frustrations and health problems in the family were peaking. Sitting inside her trailer next to her ruined home in Violet, Robin told me, "We burying four people a week these days." Two elders who had been in good health before the storm were lost in 2006: Lolly, the Peachy Gang's much adored and last living brother of Katie's siblings, had died of a heart attack; and Audrey May (Connie, Deborah, and Robin's mother), had officially died of heart disease. That diagnosis was more correct than the coroner knew. As Robin's daughter put it, "Big Mama died of a broken heart."

In addition to all the physical maladies and mental strains, other sources of discomfort added tonnage to the collective burdens: the problems of "succession" and family land, problems with the church rebuilding, worry among older members for younger ones, and younger adults for their elders, the outrage of being treated like a beggar, and the hurtful stereotypes that constantly circulated in the media.

The power of place as one's "heritage" that Dr. Watson spoke about presented a legal nightmare for many residents because of the informal nature of ownership. Louisiana law is based on the Napoleonic Code, a holdover from the French period that gives the right to family members to pass on their homes to their children without having to file paperwork to change the title. The informal but legally recognized practice of "succession" was not uncommon among bayou residents. But because neither FEMA nor Road Home could understand or respond to this situation appropriately, thousands of people had to slog through the legal process of getting official titles to their homes. Cynthia, the oldest member of the Peachy Gang, had inherited her house without papers. But even though no one else tried to claim it, Road Home would not recognize her title to the property without requiring her to produce a lot of paperwork and testimony from all her children.[12]

Another problem that infuriated many homeowners was the way Road Home refused to recognize their homeowner status if someone happened to be living on land they did not own outright. It was a common local practice to use "family land" as a place to site your own home. Roz and her husband and two sons had lived in a mobile home for twenty-one years before Katrina. They owned the mobile home outright but had situated it on family land. The home had three bedrooms and was lovingly furnished. In Roz's words, "My home was comfortable." It took more than a year and a half for Road Home to finally recognize her "eligible" claim as a homeowner before Katrina.

HOME AND CHURCH:
THE MATERIAL ANCHORS OF FAMILY LIFE

"We go to church—I don't know how many miles it is, but we go every Sunday," Katie said. I sat across from her at the dinette table. It was midafternoon in late spring 2007. "I love it. I enjoy the church, but I mean, it's not like walking across the yard, you know," she said. At this time, Katie was still waiting for word about her Road Home money.

Katie put her finger on the two material sources of comfort her family had always relied on—their homes and their church. "I guess you feel like you're not in your home, you're not in your church. Where else can you go?" she asked, turning her body back around to look at the TV. "Home and church, I mean, that's where we always did go—home and church. You know, Sunday we dare not leave Verret. Everybody come to church and go by they family, you know, and it's a family thing on a Sunday. We're used to one Sunday over here, over there, you know, different places, but not now. Now we got to go by Audrey for every holiday."

Audrey was the only one of her generation to live in Violet before Katrina. Her home had been terribly damaged in the storm, but her brother's son, "little Sherman" wanted to help her out. He knew that his other aunts in Verret—Cynthia, Katie, and Roseana—had no shell of a home to work with, but he could help his Aunt Audrey. So in spring 2006, Sherman Jr., brought his construction crew from Florida to southeast Louisiana to do as much quick and low-cost work as he could. Within a year, they had gutted Audrey's home, re-sheetrocked, installed new electrical lines, plumbing, and floors. She moved back into a functioning, though not completely finished home in early 2007. Audrey's home became the only place people in the family could cook and congregate normally. And it was a lucky thing to have someone's home available for weekend gatherings and holidays.

"Don't get me wrong," Katie said. "We have fun. But you know, we used to moving around," she said, using her hand to make swirls in the air. "And we'd like to be in Verret. Even Audrey would like to be in Verret. But there is nowhere to go on a Saturday morning. Can't fit into that trailer." She paused and took a deep breath. Then she lightened her tone, recalling something that made her smile. "One Saturday morning," she said using her musical storytelling voice, "we was all there at Cynthia's trailer. Half of them couldn't get in." She motioned with her hands, bringing both palms to signal a stop. "We had to take the food to Audrey's house, finish cooking it, and then eat!" Her voice returned to the frustrated one. "You know, when you're used to something big and used to getting around . . ." Katie's words trailed off; she seemed too fatigued to finish her thought.

Katie's sense of being physically constrained by a drastically reduced set of options for family movement mirrored the mental constraints she and others felt, where too little was understood about the landscape of recovery, and too little was happening to indicate that progress was occurring.

As it did with the other parishes impacted by Katrina, FEMA provided funds for St. Bernard Parish to offer mental health counseling services after Katrina. However, these free services did not correspond to the needs of black residents. Individualized mental health counseling made no sense in the context of the family's default coping strategy. People managed trouble together—whether it concerned economic survival, problems at school, disease, illness and death, or clashes with parish police. Good times involved the same collective strategy—organizing leisure-time outings, attending church, sharing meals at weekly gatherings. To cope with their frustrations and anger at FEMA and Road Home, the family expected to depend on each other. With each other, there was no need to edit what was said to an outsider, no need to gauge the trust available, and no need to become self-conscious about one's way of speaking. How family shared their troubles, their fantasies, their plans, all worked as a highly successful kind of talk therapy.

These internal, self-reliant systems of coping among African Americans have proven resilient over 250 years. Even today in the United States, African Americans commit suicide at half the rate of whites.[13] Scholars have proposed a variety of explanations for these dramatically different rates of suicide, including the fact that blacks maintain stronger family connections than whites and that they are generally more religious. Some studies demonstrate greater tendencies of African Americans to feel hope as compared to whites, and to hold more negative views toward suicide because of its incompatibility with the Christian faith so many practice.[14]

The homegrown system of talk therapy provided clear benefits to African Americans. Having a big family rooted in place gave young members a variety of male and female role models and different generations of people to talk to. After returning home from Dallas or other sites of evacuation, the conversation and the porch-sitting ritual that had always nurtured easy conversation shifted, but it did not die. Rather, conversation that glided seamlessly between TV news, news of the bayou parish, and news about the family and the local environment all got squeezed into smaller spaces and fewer occasions when people gathered—under Katie's carport, in Audrey's house, or bunched up inside someone's trailer.

"African Americans are not going to seek that [professional] help," said Dr. Watson. "We're going to still try to look for that social network to buoy us up. That's when you really start to feel isolated, that's when you really start to feel alone. And by alone, you don't have to be physiologically alone, you can just be a group of people and you can still get an isolated feeling, that after a while, even though you're together, it begins to wear members down."

A culturally competent approach to post-disaster mental health provisioning, as suggested by the 2003 SAMHSA document detailed earlier, would begin with the question: How does this population cope with crises? In this case, answering that question would reveal that collectively oriented groups may not find individualized forms of counseling relevant to solving problems, no matter how sensitively the counselors are trained to respond. In the case of the family, when the routine of meeting and talking, bantering and laughing in their self-contained universe could not be replicated back home, the opportunities for talk therapy were diminished. "Little by little," Dr. Watson continued, "if things don't change, the members within the group will begin to show continual signs of stress. And one by one, they will start to fail. Piece by piece, that system will go into dysfunction."

THE ATTEMPT TO LOCATE FRUSTRATION

All the family members had something different that was bothering them, and that in and of itself spoke to the problem of sustaining hope when the "larger system" Dr. Watson referenced was not coming through. Katie stewed about the slow pace of the church's rebuilding. Cynthia fretted about the paperwork for succession; Roseana worried about getting compensation because she did not have current flood insurance. Potchie believed a Small Business Administration loan would allow him to make repairs faster than going through the Road Home system, but he worried after he got no response to his application. Roz struggled to get recognized as a homeowner; Robin worried that her compensation would be too little to repair her home. Everyone was anxious about needing the Road Home money. Many of the cousins, the sons and daughters of the oldest Peachy Gang generation, expressed their feelings of protectiveness toward their elders. In a conversation at Audrey's house in early 2007, Melanie and Roz, daughters of Audrey and Katie, were eager to talk about what was on their minds. They had plenty to say, both about what had not happened with Road Home and how little the public seemed to get what was really going on. They sat at Audrey's dining-room table, in the only home available for conversation.

"My biggest concern," said Melanie, looking at her cousin Roz, "is like Katie, Cynthia, and Roseana. My mama is in her house. I want them to have their own homes, you know. These people were comfortable. You understand what I'm saying? Get them back in something that will make them comfortable. They done worked. They done paid their dues. Give them what's due them." Roz nodded.

"My concern is the older people," Melanie continued. "Why not start with them? Why not give them a place to stay? Why not build them a place to stay? I feel like the state is not doing what they should do for them. They had to get their houses knocked down. It's time for something. Send the Road Home money. Let them find contractors so they can get started. These are older individuals. We're young. We can do it. The Road Home, it's a joke to me."

"Right!" Roz chimed in, while Melanie kept on.

"That's our backbone. That's what we were built on—them. So why not get the older people sixty and up, or whatever age group you decide, make sure they are comfortable."

Roz jumped in, "That's just like them saying, 'Road Home want you back.' To me, it's just a slap in the face."

"Uh-huh," Melanie nodded while Roz continued.

"I owned my home. It may not be a home, per se, to some people, because they downcast it because it was a mobile home, but it was my home. It was clean. I considered it home. I didn't consider it a house, but it was home, and some people degrade people who live in mobile homes, you know." Melanie nodded, sympathizing.

"Yeah," Roz said, "I'm down because as an American citizen, I'm somewhat upset. We hear all about Iraq and everything. You want to spend billions of dollars over there helping those people. What about your people here? We're not asking for nothing that we didn't have." She paused and her voice grew stronger. "I'm not wanting to live in a mansion. We're not asking for millions. We just want a home."

"Roz," I asked, "what is making you feel so emotional right now?"

"I feel as though we fighting a war for no reason at all," she said, pointing with her whole arm to an imaginary place far away. "We going over there, we giving them billions of dollars, but we can't house these people?" She wanted to make clear that this outrage was not just about her. "Take me out of the picture," she said. "I'm going to get back on my feet if I have to rent. What about these people, this eighty-year-old man rebuilding his house by himself?"

Melanie agreed, "Uh-huh."

"He may die before he finish building it, but right now, that's all he thinking about, rebuilding his comfort zone. What about that? This is America, somewhere for Americans to call their own." She looked at Melanie, who was nodding attentively. "We can't live in these FEMA trailers forever," she said, lowering her head and voice, and sounding a lot like her mother.

Melanie picked the energy back up. "We just want the money that's due us. The Road Home," she slapped her hand on the desk, "they don't want you back home! That's what it seems like." Melanie's authoritative voice brought an end to that topic. But the conversation wasn't over, and we will return to their discussion of media impacts later in the chapter.

A BRIEF BUT BEAUTIFUL DIVERSION: TRASHELL'S WEDDING

One thing the dependency on outsiders did not take away was the family's control of their group identity. The rhizome had held on through the steady reenactment of key family practices that reinforced everyone's connection to each other—in Dallas, these practices were easier because the group had access to Connie's large kitchen, and even the apartments of most could handle big pots and lots of dishes in the oven. Back home, the practices that kept the rhizome alive were constrained by space and time, but the life force of the group still depended on participating in church, attending funerals, organizing weddings, celebrating births, and gathering for holidays. The church was miles away, so socializing afterward was not practical since no one had a home nearby. People missed the everyday circulation of family. Yet family members held on to their own cultural vitality as much as they could and did not decline to celebrate the bright spots in their lives.

As astute observers recognize, in a sea of trouble, bright spots twinkle and can offer clues to a way out.[15] Trashell's marriage to, Charles "Dude" Holmes, a handsome young mechanic, glowed in the dark. As the oldest grandchild in the Peachy Gang, and someone Katie helped raise, Trashell would have a special wedding, no matter what.

Nell wanted the very best for her only child, and she and her mother had always imagined Trashell's wedding at the First Baptist Church in Verret. "Nothing is in order with the church," said Nell in March 2007, three months before the wedding. "Which is discouraging." I asked Nell about the provisions and supplies for the event and the reception, knowing that resources were strained.

"I'm working, but I still had to borrow $2,000 for the wedding," Nell said a few weeks before the wedding. "They got to have glasses, cake, gown, cups, handkerchiefs, photographer. We paid for all that. She making her own CDs; she can burn her own. She paid for the favors, boxes from Walmart."

The family managed other costs by doing everything possible them-selves. They made food for all the events, they made the decorations them-selves, and they hired friends from school who had a brass band for the re-ception party afterward. Trashell and her mother planned the bridal shower, the rehearsal dinner, the wedding, and the reception, and family members pitched in to do most of the work. Women took on the most ambitious cooking.

From all reports, Trashell's wedding was the bright spot of 2007. Part of the excitement of a wedding involves all the preparation and planning, and in this family, everyone wanted in on a piece of it. The bridal shower was the first event, held inside a restaurant in Chalmette that allowed the group to rent the space and bring their own food.

"I cooked all day Saturday," Katie said as she sat under the carport, re-flecting on the successful event. She listed everything she had cooked, but she was most pleased with one dish. "Cowan!" she said enthusiastically, using the Creole term for freshwater turtle that lives in bayous and marshes. "This one weighed about fifteen pounds. Gray Eye cut the head, I put it in water, cut off the skin, cleaned it, pickled it in vinegar and salt and pepper and hot peppers, overnight, and then I made the gravy."

The food offerings included Katie's turtle stew, stuffed peppers, and shrimp salad; Turb's jambalaya; Audrey's fried chicken and potato salad; Nell's green salad. Desi, Roseana's daughter, brought lasagna; Janice, meat-balls and punch-bowl cake; Donnatte, tuna salad with crackers; and the groom's mother, sandwiches and cake.

The rehearsal dinner was held at Audrey's house, still the only home functioning in the Peachy Gang. The guests included family and the bridal party of thirteen bridesmaids and thirteen groomsmen. At this event, people ate Cynthia's gumbo; Roseana's red beans and rice and stuffed eggs; Katie's stuffed crabs; Audrey's fried chicken and potato salad; Roz's mac and cheese and muffins; and Janice's miniature meatballs and Ooey Gooey Cake.

Nakia (a great-granddaughter of Davis, Peachy's brother) and her hus-band, Russell Banks, offered their home, with its restored backyard and gar-den, for the wedding reception. The event involved lush displays of food, all kinds of liquor and beer, and a brass band that inspired hours of dancing. The seafood boiled earlier that day got heaped into a wooden canoe known by its French name, *pirogue*. Filling the *pirogue* was a special, ceremonial way to serve seafood. Turb worked on that with Russell and Noel, a long-time friend Turb had grown up with in Verret. For this most festive of all the wedding events, the elders reprised their specialties. Turb fixed jambalaya and Roz made mac and cheese. Relatives and friends added their creations to the meal of the year.

The couple posted twelve hundred pictures on a website.

The hoopla raised everyone's spirits, and it changed the conversation for a few weeks. But in the midst of so much trouble, it seemed like a lot of work. The four sisters had rarely done this much intensive cooking—around the clock, for days on end. Afterward, they talked of exhaustion.

THE PARALYSIS OF PROGRESS

On a sea of trouble, time itself seemed to spread out, as vast as the horizon. By the second anniversary of Katrina, three months after the wedding, there were none of the vestiges of optimism that had held many spirits up at the first anniversary in 2006. That first year, people still talked about figuring things out and solving family problems within the family. Pride had not yet corroded into submission and powerlessness. But another year had passed without any observable progress.

According to Dr. Watson, "As long as we can see the light at the end of the tunnel, we can work our way toward it. And by doing that, you're able to work through a grieving process."

But save for the bright spot of the wedding and the opportunity for group effort it supplied, there was no light. Just the tunnel. The family's normal coping system of talk therapy, integrated into everyday circulation, had been compromised. The chronic sense that the people in the family were not able to take charge of their own lives eroded optimism and the capacity to function. Everything about their predicament matched up perfectly with the mental health literature about the circumstances that produce power-lessness.[16] In the fields of both social psychology and public health, study after study emphasizes how much people's sense of control over the every-day parts of their lives profoundly impacts their health and well-being.[17]

MEDIA STEREOTYPING: PILING ON INDIGNITIES

In addition to the communication problems throughout the FEMA-controlled phase of recovery, there were also many high-profile stories cir-culating in national media and on social-media sites about how Katrina survivors had defrauded FEMA or insurance companies.[18] The impact of these negative portrayals and stereotypes added another source of mis-understanding and made people feel hurt or angry and helpless to change the common perception.[19]

Being made to feel stupid or immoral by a public that didn't have a clue about who they were or what they were going through was especially insulting. "Our American culture has a very short attention span," said Dr. Watson, "and a very adolescent way of looking at real-life issues . . . people just callously saying, for instance, that, well, just move from there, you shouldn't rebuild from there, or why don't they just go out there and get a job, or da-da-da-da. That, in and of itself, is re-traumatizing and it creates a feeling that 'I'm being abandoned, I'm being misunderstood, I'm being sullied by people I don't even know.'"

The conversation in Audrey's dining room that had begun with Melanie and Roz talking about the trouble getting Road Home money turned to this very topic, one that made them furious.

"You know, don't go by [say to] people in Louisiana, 'Well, we not going to give them the money because when they gave them the FEMA money, they were spending it on purses, and they were spending it on entertainment centers, they were buying cars.'" She looked around the room. Melanie laughed with derision and Roz went on, "Every black person in America wasn't going to buy a car."

Melanie agreed, "No. That's right," as Roz kept speaking. "Every black person in America wasn't buying Gucci and Coach purses." She got up and walked into the kitchen to pour herself some water. "I was trying to pay my rent. See what I'm saying?" She took a sip. "You can't base one situation, everybody's situation on one thing that occurred in the media. That's all I'm saying."

I was certain Melanie would have something to add, so I turned to her and asked, "If you could tell the American public something about all this, what would it be?"

She smiled, enjoying the question. She put her hands out, palms touching and straightening up her spine as if she was actually going to speak to an audience. "What I would communicate to them is this. 'Don't believe everything you hear. Know this: We are not all beggars. We are not all looters. We live in respectable neighborhoods, and we live respectable lives. We are not begging for anything. We are asking if the money is there for us, give it to us.'" She relaxed and put her hands on the table. She looked at me. "We want people to know that this disaster is far from over. The economy was so affected. Where are the jobs? Where is the training? We just don't want you all to judge us based upon what you saw when Katrina happened. There are people that live respectable lives. We do have integrity. We do work, and like me, I'm out there picking up trash, and I have two babies, and they're just as tickled as me because I'm working. This is not the end, but it can be a great beginning with the help of other people, and I don't just mean financially. Encouraging one another, being there for one another. If you can help somebody along this way, help somebody along this way, because you never know when it is going to be you, and I guarantee you, the storms just don't come our way, but they come your way, too."

Roz applauded, and I understood why. Melanie had a way with words.

THE NEW CHURCH: MISSING A KEY INGREDIENT

Their own black church was the only institution that embraced the family members for who they were and that could buffer them from the withering attacks on hope.[20] Although all the churches in the parish had been ruined, the rebuilding progress on the church in Verret had been especially slow for reasons that no one understood. After all, the church had received a substantial insurance settlement soon after the storm. Yet it took two full years to rebuild and reopen. And then, the unthinkable became apparent: the church had no kitchen.

One afternoon in October 2007, I met with three of the sisters at Audrey's house. They had seated themselves on the two red couches and recliners of the living room. Roseana, who always dressed smartly, had on white capris and a fitted T-shirt. Audrey wore her denim shorts and striped top with her signature ball cap, and Cynthia had a feminine sheer blouse with a flower pattern and knee-length pinkish pants. They were talking about a funeral service that had taken place at their church in Verret. When the newly rebuilt church had opened in August, the sisters had complained bitterly about the missing kitchen. Roseana now brought it up again, expressing her astonishment, "I can't believe they got rid of our kitchen! We had a big, big kitchen before. They got more money than they need, but they took the kitchen and made offices."

I said, "Well, surely they knew this was where you-all cooked for the Sunday school kids, and where you kept food you brought hot for serving, right?"

Roz had just entered the house looking for her mother. But she caught what Roseana had said and my question. "Thank you," she said, what people often said when they hear something that hits the nail on the head. "We not even allowed to go in there now. They don't care. They appease you by saying we gonna build the kitchen later." She stood in the doorway, not intending to stay, but apparently interested in the conversation.

Roseana responded, "Supposed to start on it right away. What can you do?" she said, shaking her head, looking at the floor.

Roz wanted to make it clear to me. She said, "Quite obvious that with all the things you do, you gotta have a kitchen!" She jangled her keys, indicating she would be walking out any minute.

"Well, what makes a kitchen so important?" I asked. "What can you not do if you don't have a kitchen?" I looked around the room.

"It's important to our culture," said Roseana. I knew she was so fed up it was almost too hard to talk about. "How so?" I asked. "Simply because when there's something going on, like a repast, which is something we have when somebody pass, they feed 'em. But now we can only have cold food." Audrey and Cynthia grunted in agreement. "People come from around the country, and we only have cold food."

"The purpose of the kitchen is this," said Cynthia. "Audrey used to have a van and bring people around to Sunday school and Katie and Nell and them used to cook breakfast because they stay. After Sunday school, they eat, so they stay for church after."

"So, do you feel like a repast is not the same thing now?" I asked, returning to Roseana's point.

"Not at all," Cynthia said emphatically, as others agreed.

I continued to probe. "How long did they say it would take to put in a kitchen again?" Everyone laughed.

"They don't say nothing," said Cynthia, resuming her rocking in the recliner.

"Does the church have the money?" I asked.

"Oh, indeed, yes, plenty money with insurance. Problem is the lack of a church charter," said Roseana, indicating that a board of trustees, which unchartered churches don't have, might have set different priorities.

"Might as well just keep on having a tent," said Cynthia. "Can't bring hot food. No way to keep it hot." Cynthia always mustered a smile when she spoke, even if the topic pained her.

"People from Minnesota sent all that equipment," Roseana said, indicating this was not just about their desires. It involved the investments of others as well. "Walk-in freezer, industrial stuff. They got members out there, and they had their church send us. Minister's niece out there. None of it is getting used."

No one mentioned the possibility that perhaps in planning for rebuilding the church, male leaders had simply forgotten to consider a key domain of sociality that extended from the church: the kitchen. It was from that productive, female-dominated space that an important element of the church's traditions and social cohesion emerged.

THE PARISH AFTER JUNIOR

Now twenty-seven months after the storm, in late fall of 2007, Buffy's job with the parish suffered a blow. Junior got defeated for reelection by Craig Taffaro. Those who had worked for Junior and were loyal to him in the election found themselves out of favor, if not out of work. Buffy's job as road supervisor changed to simply being a crew member.

"But it wasn't a race thing," he said, always careful to avoid using race if it wasn't clearly related. His white boss was also demoted. The change was hard on Buffy. We talked over dinner one evening in 2009. It was a small informal restaurant, another new place to eat opened up by a black couple in Violet. He was enjoying a piece of trout. I had ordered shrimp gumbo.

"I don't want to be biased, but by me and Junior, the relationship we have, to where I was in a position to where Junior pick up the phone and say, 'Buffy, I need you to go such and such and do this shift.' You know, or this person needs, it's, like, I would go over to housing, like, he could have said, 'Buffy, there's a family coming to you, I need you to put them in a house or a trailer,' and that was my job during Katrina, making sure that everybody that go to him with a problem, I was taking care of whatever it was . . . I felt, I was being used for more of my . . . what I know."

The demotion came on the heels of Buffy's heroic work during the storm and his years of unselfish efforts on behalf of the parish and his family. It made everyone mad, but there was nothing to do. He tried not to care. "I don't give a damn, you know," he said, taking a bite of his fish that he was eating slowly. "I tell them, 'I just don't, you know.' I tell them today, my wife's triple my salary." His wife, Aurora, is a registered nurse at Touro Hospital in the city. "I always do things on the side. I hustle, you know."

SILENCING KATIE

In December 2007, Robin confessed something that wasn't easy. I was sitting in her FEMA trailer in Violet. She looked exhausted. "I had a mental meltdown about a week ago. Cried the whole day at work. My house still has no gas. I still can't cook there. I put money aside to try to do something, but it don't get done. We do have somewhere to lay our heads. I know all these volunteers, and I see that things are getting done. I know where they are going. But my aunts and them are wishing and wondering if anybody ever gonna get to them.

"They scared to leave the house in case somebody call and say we going to come and survey your land. They older. Why would they go into debt? Let's make sure she have a decent kitchen. She want to plant her flowers. I want them to hold on and not give up like my mama did."

Her thoughts turned to Katie.

"Katie is very blue right now. I talk to her too much. We know she is feeling it and hurt, but she is still showing good spirit and still laughing. Everybody went by Audrey's for Thanksgiving Day. Katie did the whole Thanksgiving dinner again on Sunday."

Shortly after Thanksgiving, I talked to Katie by phone. "I did a whole turkey dinner on Sunday," she told me, pleased with herself.

"What'd you cook?" I asked, always eager to hear the sound of so much food in my ear.

"I made a turkey, stuffed peppers, crab, gumbo, sweet potatoes, merleton, macaroni, peas. The regular crew came. Cousins, family, friends. I cut up all my seasonings the week before. Boiled squash and froze it, cleaned out peppers. Had all that prepared the week before.[21] The gumbo I did Saturday and the turkey and dressing the night before."

In early December, just a few days after my conversation, I talked to Connie, who had filed an appeal to increase Katie's $22,000 Road Home settlement. Connie said, "They turned her down. I am going to try to get to Brad Pitt.[22] Katie is worried about committing money every month to pay a house note, so I told her to look for something that would cost about $65,000. She needs at least two bedrooms and a big kitchen."

When Katie learned that her Road Home appeal had been turned down, she was heartbroken. No one could get to Brad Pitt, either.

Roz said, "I never seen my Mom cry like that before. She sobbed and sobbed."

I talked to Katie again a couple of weeks into December.

"I don't know what to do," she said. "When Earl get a day off, we going to Mississippi. Need to go about an hour to find some houses." It was there she hoped to find a mobile home she could afford, given the meager Road Home money. "Got to get what your money allow. There are some nice double-wides," she said. She wasn't through believing that somehow, a different reality would emerge for her.

"I ain't even put no decoration up this year, and you know that ain't like me. Just don't have the courage. I'm too blue. I don't see no light on the horizon."

On December 19, 2007, Katie suffered a massive stroke.

From that moment on, Katie would never again feel the sense of control that had been taken from her, back before Katrina, before she fell down the trailer steps.

Katie had never been a retiring person in her own setting. She knew how to make herself visible. She had been socially competent, able to work in a white law-enforcement setting with good results. The recovery landscape was particularly shattering to her because she couldn't get any traction. She knew what to do when she worked for the Sheriff's Office—if there was a social event, she didn't miss it. She had no practice with being almost to the ground. She'd had big blows, but her faith had brought her through them. She had her church. But her church got rebuilt without a kitchen. The contrast of life before the storm and life after the storm could never get righted, and now she could not speak.

Just before her mother's stroke, Roz had been laid off from her bookkeeping job with the parish oil company that was downsizing. After the holidays, she was asked back to work, but by then, she had made a choice: to devote herself full time to her mother's care. She and her father helped move Katie into Audrey's home, where she stayed for more than a year, until her own home was finally ready to move into. Roz handled her bathing, dressing, appointments with nurses and doctors, speech therapists, and occupational and physical therapists. She also cooked, since her mother couldn't.

When I called Connie to talk with her about what had happened, she said, "Katrina was the cause of everything. It has just taken away the spirit of my family. It was just not necessary. My rocks, my foundation is just crumbling before my eyes. This is a ton of bricks. I don't think my thoughts will be back for another five years. It just goes on and on."

III

WAVE OF RECKONING

9

SETTLING

LOOKING INWARD TO FAMILY

Pulling off Esplanade Street in New Orleans and driving into City Park, I smiled. There they were, the mighty live oaks. This quintessential tree of the Deep South, sometimes sporting a ten-foot girth, pushes branches out from its center in lyrical motion, bent and bowed and twisting, as though dancing with the breezes off nearby Lake Pontchartrain. Nowhere in the world do this many mature live oaks congregate in a single stand. Ten varieties of oaks belong to the twenty thousand trees that rise from the grounds of the 1,300-acre park—all survivors of Katrina's blast. The canopy of a single giant old live oak provides relief from the penetrating summer sun. These are trees that offer habitat to resurrection ferns and Spanish moss; almost as often, they shelter large family picnics. In their sheer amplitude and outstretched arms, they seem to invite unhurried leisure.

The origin of City Park dates back nearly 150 years, established about the same time that Emma Fernandez and Victor Johnson, the first generation anyone in the family can remember or knows of, were born near Verret in lower St. Bernard Parish. I came wearing the bright-green family T-shirt printed with a map of Louisiana with the parish location marked on it, and dark blue type that read "Johnson/Fernandez Family Reunion 2008." It was their first reunion since the storm.

People were trickling in and setting up when I arrived with my sister, Becky, a professional videographer I recruited to help me capture some moments from the reunion weekend and my ongoing interviews with family members. The live oaks framed the scene for playing, talking, grilling, and eating, buffering the family members from the struggles they had left back at the trailers where most of them had been living for the past two and a half years.

The day was bright, sunny and hot, with a faint breeze cooled by the shade of the oaks. It would warm up over the hours to come, but by then, no one would notice. A happy vibe prevailed as people carried chairs and tables and baskets with large foil-topped dishes to one of the tents the men had set up earlier that morning. As each car pulled in, there were hollers of recognition, hugs, and laughter. Children bounded out of the cars and dashed away from the adults they had arrived with, beginning endless play with each other. Spending an entire day together with family on a perfectly good Saturday, and then again on Sunday, would have mortified some families, but not this one. Time spent together made life good. The habits of collecting and conversing, attending church together, and eating together developed naturally from shared roots in the bayou and a shared black history of struggle. These habits of coming together regularly still served a central purpose: they laid down grooves of expectation that focused people inward, on the joy of interdependence, and upward, on the grace and healing power of God. At special gatherings like this reunion, young members of the tribe learned to associate family togetherness with maximum fun, good food, and an unalloyed sense of belonging.

Each tent became a home base for one of the family branches—Peachy's Gang, Davis's crew (the Johnson Gang), Tuta's flock, and so on. The tents gave older family members a place to sit in the shade near food and drink. This was a time when teens and curious children could easily learn or relearn who belonged to which branch of the family. For children, learning to cherish family began with knowing where fun lived. Cousins would show up again and again, not just at reunions but at birthday parties and holiday events, at school, and in church. As kids got older, it became a badge of teenage moxie to know the names and faces of family members. No one called this big family an "extended family" because that would have suggested there was some family unit that was not extended. In this family, every relative beyond self was family, and biological closeness did not define importance. Of course, some family members cohered more than others. But Potchie, who had helped organize every family reunion, made the point others agreed with: "Family is family—we don't draw lines because that doesn't make sense. We are one big family, period."

The reunion provided an opportunity for the elders to talk about the family and its deep history. The Peachy Gang sisters had always enjoyed recounting stories about growing up on the bayou. Cynthia, about to turn seventy-six that summer of 2008, was a storehouse of family lore. She loved to reminisce about her father's work in the bayou to pick moss from the swamps and sell it for furniture stuffing. She could recite her mother's recipes for coon and muskrat.

However, family knowledge was not something that could be learned once and committed to memory like a history lesson. That's because so much of what counted as knowledge involved people who were alive, and information about living family needed constant refreshing. People got married and had babies; young adults entered college or a trade school. Others graduated and returned home. There were christenings, baptisms, and funerals. No one ever kept physical notes on all these relationships or the changing details of the group—the knowledge lived strictly in the group's oral culture.

When people think of an "oral" culture, they often think of people who do not read and write. This family helped me understand how literacy and education had nothing to do with keeping up oral traditions. It took curiosity and attention and time to learn about and remember all the changing news of family. That's one reason people liked to spend a lot of time together. It is also a reason that having a regular place to gather would have helped activate this "comfort trigger," thereby adding energy to the weakened cycle of culture. There had always been a lot to catch up on at Saturday and Sunday gatherings and in daily sits on the front porch. At this 2008 reunion, it was easy to spot the tradition of storytelling and relaxed, long conversations. As I observed interactions of all generations of family over the day, I noticed a subtle but important fact: people gravitate toward talking in groups, not one-on-one. It makes sense, given the need to exchange so much and the pleasure people get from sharing their lives with a group.

Knowing the precise placement of each person in their respective family lineage signaled pride and good manners, but annual reunions like this one also pointed up the group's commitment to a shared sense of identity. As philosophers explain, any complex system composed of discrete parts can only achieve meaningful integration after it is clear how the individual parts themselves articulate.[1] The collective, indivisible nature of the family rhizome thus depends on first recognizing the individuality of each member and then how that individuality articulates with the whole. The whole got expressed in many ways, the most striking of which was the Kelly-green T-shirt everyone wore that weekend. The visual impact of a sea of bright green shirts asserted an unmistakably shared identity. The successful turnout made clear to everyone: "We're still here and we still know how to make ourselves happy."

The green-shirted mob of people moved in a generational ebb and flow. The elders and their middle-aged children clumped up for a time and then re-formed in different groupings as people circulated. The children of all branches naturally found each other, and as an adult or two would rotate

Potchie and Roxy

Cynthia and

Cousins:
Spencer and
Leila

Family reunion 2008

In July 2008, several hundred members of
the Johnson-Fernandez family gathered
at City Park in New Orleans for their first
reunion since before Katrina.

Clockwise from
top left: Donnatte,
Melanie, Harmony,
Taelin, Nae

Fig. 26

organizing them for games or photos, the children learned each other's mamas. "Who your Mama?" I heard a child ask another. They all knew their mothers by name, so answering, "Melanie my mama" was no trouble. The adults encouraged this kind of casual inquiry. But the most effective way I saw children learning where each other belonged was when a child brought another into their tent for a bite of food or to sit on a grandmother's lap or talk to an aunt. Since children arrive at such an event already socialized to understand that they belong not just to their parents but to the whole group, there was not the usual "stranger danger," or shyness about approaching other adults. Kids here were free to roam and explore the boundaries of the family universe.

The singular identity of the large group also got reasserted in the everywhich-way flow of information and conversation. There were no groups that remained separate or that did not, in time, splinter off to form new groups. Over the course of the day, people moved around at their own speeds and in their own time, giving a visual form to the abstract notion of circulation.

Although each branch's tent retained a few members like Katie, whose stroke kept her close to the Peachy Gang tent for most of the day, once the sausages and chicken came off the grill and the foil tops off the dishes people brought, the eating spurred movement. Soon, there was no telling who might be where. Like the children and their young mothers, the middle-aged mothers and their aunts circulated broadly—some in the fashion of a slow-moving waltz, others in spurts and dashes.

The only defined group that day was the clustering of men who tended to stick with each other—hovering close to the grills where someone was cooking, playing catch, or relaxing in chairs for card games or conversation; women mixed mostly with each other, too. The pattern of gender segregation at parties is not unusual, but in this family, the separation of women and men goes well beyond party behavior. Women spend a lot of time with each other on a regular basis—shopping, going on outings to the city for festivals, coordinating parties for special birthdays, trading off child care for each other's children, and attending church. Only a few men come to the regular weekend family gatherings, and far fewer men than women attend church. But men are not absent—they come to the larger family events like holiday meals and birthday parties. Sometimes, men will make plans to watch ball games together or fish together, but they rarely run errands or shop together. Just as I learned in Martinique among Afro-Creole couples there, women and men in the family maintain separate social lives, even though they share a home and, typically, parenthood. The arrangement seems to work, as the low incidence of divorce suggests.[2]

Four generations of family lived in close proximity at the time of Katrina. It is worth noting that for family members in St. Bernard Parish, everyone related and in the same generation is automatically considered a "cousin." There are no distinctions between relative degrees of closeness. No one refers to a relative as "my second cousin," for example. The term for a relative or even a close family friend in an older generation who is not your parent or grandparent would be your "aunt" or "uncle," no surprise to Americans. But how many people under age forty or fifty have fifteen or twenty aunts and uncles they know well and who live within a few minutes' drive? The oldest generation of family members had the fewest living cousins and even fewer, if any, aunts and uncles. But those in this oldest group stayed vitally connected to their dozens of nieces and nephews, in addition to their own children and grandchildren.

Although Katie was wheelchair-bound and essentially unable to converse after her stroke, she could still speak a few words, though it took great effort. She positioned herself in a prime spot under the Peachy Gang tent. People would have to walk right by her to get to the food. If they passed without acknowledging her, she belted out a "Hey!" signaling them to turn around and give her a hug or a kiss. Ever since her stroke six months earlier, she had shown plenty of animation, though she had not spoken more than a few words. Except, that is, when she was in church, where she called on an undamaged part of her brain and sang along with everyone else. The occupational therapist at Tulane told the family that Katie's comprehension was fine—the stroke had disabled her ability to speak, but she could understand fully what others said. And she could sing.

I knew for a fact that Katie's cognitive powers were in fine shape. Early that Saturday afternoon at the reunion, I pulled up a chair beside her and showed her a kin map I'd been working on. Her sister, Audrey, was on her other side, so it was a three-way interaction. I told her how much I loved the reunion and how many new people I was meeting. I was eager to incorporate the new names into my kin map, and I rapidly sketched out some connections. Katie already knew my interest in kin relations, and she smiled when I handed her my notebook turned to a page with diagrams of family.

"Have I got TJ's parents right here?" I asked, referring to the charming young man I'd just met in the Davis line.

She shook her head vigorously. No. She signaled with her good hand in the way people indicate that the field goal was no good. I tried to quickly figure out another yes/no sequence that might be correct. "Okay, is he one of Barbara Smith's children?" No again. This time she used her hand to point to another place on the kin map. Audrey chimed in with a possible answer, but I saw her look to Katie for confirmation. Yes, Katie nodded, that was right. From that moment on, I knew that Katie followed the conversation and that it would be up to others to structure things in a way that would give her a chance to weigh in.

By 3:00 p.m., the midday sun bore down with its signature Louisiana-style wet-sauna heat. After five hours tent hopping, eating heaps of homemade food, and conducting informal interviews with members of the family I didn't already know, I suddenly felt exhausted. But I detected no fatigue from anyone else. No one was packing up or mobilizing to leave. Smiles and laughter, games and eating signaled that the day was still in full swing.

Family knowledge, it appeared, needed time to circulate—no one was tired because there hadn't yet been enough time to catch up with everyone. Before Katrina, the weekly gatherings of family had provided the occasion to update family information, to learn what was new, what plans people were making, and to stay in the flow. When half the family had evacuated to Dallas and been marooned for months, it had been possible to circulate information in the familiar ways because of Connie's big home and her desire to share it. It wasn't just that the family re-created familiar rituals of cooking and gathering; they re-created the flow of knowledge.

Once people came back to the parish to live in their "temporary" FEMA trailers, the fact that there was no place to gather and no way to cook for a large group interrupted the flow of knowledge that breathed life into the family system. For the first time in the family's 150-year history, people were cut off from each other, gatherings were hard to organize and execute. There were no resources or skills that could easily be shared because everyone was experiencing the crisis at the same time.

The exuberant Johnson-Fernandez Family Reunion of 2008 made a statement: the family is still potent, a functioning source of strength and belonging. Even if there was no way right now to share physical labor or financial help, there was still something vital to share—moral support, stories and knowledge about each other's struggles and victories, laughter, songs of inspiration, and the mutual recognition that together they could endure this ordeal.

LOOKING UPWARD TO GOD

If gatherings focused the family inward, church focused them upward. The morning after the Saturday picnic in July 2008, nearly a year since the First Baptist Church in Verret had reopened, I showed up on time for the Sunday service. Few people arrived at the stated hour because the official start time was never the actual start time. That was when you could arrive and sit exactly where you wanted to and listen to the organ player. So I beat everyone in the family there except Cynthia and Roseana, who, as was traditional for Peachy Gang women, were serving as ushers and wearing the uniform—white dresses, shoes, caps, and gloves. Katie had served as usher for nearly forty years until her stroke.

Roseana walked me to a pew toward the front, an area where family liked to sit. In time, Roz rolled Katie up beside me in her wheelchair, occupying a small part of the aisle. She and Audrey then sat down to my left. Trashell arrived with several female cousins and Treyvon, called "Trey," one of Roz's sons. Others in the family took their seats. Nell was up front in the choir, along with two of her cousins and Potchie's wife, Darleene. Nell's husband, Earl, was a deacon, and he and other church leaders, including Potchie, sat in the front pew on the opposite side of the church, where only men sat. The young male organist was enthusiastic and gifted, and he was accompanied by other musicians, also male, playing alto sax, a guitar, and drums. The organist both led the female choir and directed the small male band. The quality of the voices and instruments in harmony filled the sanctuary with unexpected vitality and beauty. A congregation in motion, people tapped their feet and swayed their shoulders. They clapped, and as the musicians added volume and variety, rose up, waving hands upward, shouting out an amen or a hallelujah. Even elderly women in two-piece Sunday suits and traditional hats, their "crowns," swayed side to side and pointed their index fingers up to the sky. The whole space was opening up to the spirit, and people did not feel shy about looking and smiling at each other, content in knowing they had all come here for the same rousing inspiration. The celebratory mood moved people into the right heart space for hearing fresh words from the pastor to whom they had remained loyal through the long rebuilding process.

Like attending family gatherings, coming to church was not an obligation (at least for the women); it was a pleasure, a space in the week that people reserved for the renewing of holy love and words that would help them through the next week. The service was part of the family's *habitus*,[3] where the reenactment of spiritual rituals, rooted in the local environment, helped individuals hold themselves up, find comfort in believing in the purpose of their lives, and make sense of the world. Even toddlers knew to follow others in their pew, clapping and swaying to the music. The same lessons that had laid down grooves of familiarity and comfort and belonging in groups of family also got laid down and reinscribed every Sunday in church.

The infectious joy rose up and rendered all the academic studies on faith in black communities one-dimensional. I felt the aliveness of another dimension, the energy of spirit, and I, too, sang out, giving myself to the same brightness I felt around me. The heart, perhaps more than the head, makes sense of suffering. And nothing opens the heart like music in a familiar place. No wonder people needed their own church back. This was where the elders of the family had designated roles and churchwide recognition, where the ancestors had steeped the sanctuary with their own commitment and love.

Pastor Raymond Smith occupied the pulpit. He was an unusual man, only the fifth pastor of this church in its 150-year history. His great-grandfather had founded the church following his service in the Confederate Army during the Civil War. He reported being "called" to create the church. Across the generations, through a mostly unbroken line of succession, the pastor demonstrated leadership far beyond the sanctuary, as black church leaders have often done. Raymond Smith had led the congregation here since 1990. He was a charismatic speaker who used his voice strategically, pitch-perfect, rising from whispers to shouting with unabashed passion. He used stories and scripture to nudge, provoke, enlighten, and inflame.

As the oldest black pastor in the parish, Raymond Smith made known his conservative stances about things like wearing Saints shirts to service or women wearing pants. To some in the family, he ventured too frequently into adversarial politics that alienated whites in the parish. But no one argued about Pastor Smith's outreach toward people in need. And no one questioned his classy personal style of dress. That Sunday, as the music had reached a crescendo and the organ director called for a slow descent of the volume of voices and instruments, Pastor Smith moved on cue into view at the front pulpit, looking sharp and entirely modern. He wore a tailored black suit with red buttonholes, a red square in his breast pocket, and a red silk tie. It was flamboyant, but in a manly, distinguished way.

His sermon opened around the idea of temptation, but near the end, he came to his real point: the role of suffering and how we had to stand up in the face of it. "If you are a child of God," he said pausing for emphasis, "you have been attacked. And you ask yourself, 'Is it worth it?'" Pastor Smith had honed his rhetorical skills over two decades, and his ease with language showed when he used formal phrases that sounded like scripture, "God says, 'You will be tried. You will be persecuted,'" and informal language of everyday conversation, "and you have to hang in there." Slowly, he brought the post-Katrina moment into focus. "Storms come from the inside. When you find yourself being betrayed, don't retaliate. Stand still. Look up."

Using language artfully is part of the "man-of-words" tradition in black culture, and black preachers, like storytellers and rap artists, use "call-and-response" techniques to engage their audiences in that oral tradition.[4] "If you want victory," he said, inspiring cries from the pews, "Yes, Lord!" and "Amen!" "you have to suffer afflictions and hardships," he said. "That's right!" more called out as he continued, "Your friends might be laughing at you." "They laughin', Lord!" a woman yelled out. "There you are," he said, "storm after storm, mountain after mountain, long dark nights in a tunnel of trouble that seems to get longer." "In a tunnel!" someone yelled. "Amen!" other voices added. "I won't give up," he said, and the crowd as one rejoined, "I won't give up!" as he continued, "Till I have a talk with God," punching each word as his voice fell to a whisper, "Amen." "Amen," people echoed. "You wonder why you go through such ordeals," he picked back up, "and you got to stay on. If your home is gonna be repossessed, you got to stay there, stop complaining, rejoice and thank the Lord." Calmer "amens" followed, and he ended his sermon with words he had certainly used before, "If I'd never been sick, I wouldn't know He's a healer. If I'd never been in bondage, I wouldn't know He's a liberator. Just ask and He will help."

"Amen," affirmed many in the pews.

LOOKING OUTWARD TO FEMA AND ROAD HOME

The joy of sharing time with each other at the reunion and Sunday's call to stand tall and look up from the tunnel of darkness embodied the family's two most critical resources: their strength within, and their hope above. Together, these resources helped put a frame around their post-Katrina troubles and gave them a collective way to hold on and seek a different kind of help. Still, new strains pulled at the unmended sense of well-being.

Before the storm, some members of the family had giant-screen TVs and leather furniture, some had double ovens and lots of space. The homes with better furnishings usually belonged to households where men held skilled jobs with higher pay, though sometimes it was the women who earned more. Some had gradually improved their homes, even though none had moved out of the neighborhood.

Cynthia's son, Doozer, and his cousin, Will, both worked at the natural gas plant nearby. Desi, Roseana's daughter and Will's wife, worked at a bank. Anitra, Roseana's other daughter, worked with her husband, Jerry Jr., who had a trucking company. Potchie, too, had been a self-employed big-rig local trucker for sixteen years and his wife, Darleene, had a good job at a bank. Buffy had been road crew supervisor for the parish until he got demoted by the new parish president. Buffy's wife, Aurora, worked as a registered nurse at Touro Hospital. A few other women had semiprofessional jobs. Donnatte worked as a home health nurse. Robin changed jobs frequently but always worked during tax season for H&R Block. She also worked as a security guard and helped out at Camp Hope, a base for volunteers working in the parish. Roseana's son Eugene, (known by his nickname, Pop), worked in trucking along with his brother, Terrance (Mr. T). Nell and Cousin Janice both worked on the janitorial crew in the nearby elementary school. Those with less secure employment and parental responsibilities sometimes, though not always, struggled more: Robin and Melanie were both single mothers who worked part-time jobs, but sometimes two at a time; Adrian, known as "Adra," was a single mother during this time, but she maintained her job at the dollar store and saved on expenses by living with her mother, Audrey. In 2012, Adra got married and the following year was promoted to manager of the store. She and her husband built an addition onto Audrey's house to house them and their three children.

Thus, living standards within the family before Katrina were never identical. Real estate values in the lower parish were lower than other areas of the New Orleans region, and those holding good jobs over many years produced extra, discretionary income that could be used in ways other than meeting everyday needs. Over time, some people were able to take out second mortgages to build onto their homes, or purchase nicer appliances or furnishings, or buy better cars. One couple in the lower-parish neighborhood, Nakia and Russell, both had excellent jobs that earned them enough income to purchase a two-story brick home. They had two children, both of whom Katie had taken care of on a daily basis before and after Katrina, at least before her stroke. By some objective measure, standards of living may have varied, but everyone belonged generally to the same socioeconomic class.

So, while the way people lived inside their homes differed in degree of "niceness" or "comfort," family gatherings acted like leveling events, where other talents and skills got put on display and generated reputations that went well beyond material standards of living. Besides, the variations in homes and house interiors did not create jealousies or wedge people apart because they rose out of differences that people understood—the income differences from different types of education and work, the luck of having inherited a little money or a home. Everyone was used to these relatively small differences in living standards that had evolved over years.

Katrina changed the calculus. Outside money from FEMA, the Red

Cross, insurance companies, nongovernmental and faith-based organizations fluttered into the family's grasp, but unevenly. In Dallas, Connie had helped family members get registered with FEMA, but the checks that came varied dramatically in amounts—some got $2,000, some got $10,000, and some got no money at all. There were no explanations and no answers to questions posed about these differences. Those who had evacuated to Houston or Atlanta also reported getting FEMA checks of wildly different amounts. Connie reassured her family that it would all get sorted out, and she kept them focused on bigger issues—getting temporary housing and provisions for living in Dallas, and getting FEMA trailers back home. With no exceptions, family members survived the financial demands of the initial months thanks to the charity of church groups and private donors. Connie made sure there was no cause to accumulate personal debt. And because the housing situations of family in Dallas varied—some rented apartments, some stayed in hotels, and some bunked up with family—no one was keeping close tabs on the money the others got. Until they got home.

Federal housing assistance got channeled through the Louisiana Road Home program, and from there, the money flowed unevenly to individuals. These awards bore no relationship to any familiar logic, and that made the new discrepancies hard to absorb and hard to dismiss.

By the time of the 2008 summer reunion, nearly three years after the storm, most of the family had finally gotten their Road Home checks; only a few, like Roz and Charles, were still waiting. These disbursements of federal funds to homeowners might have signaled an end to the story of recovery for FEMA, but for survivors of the storm, there was no end in sight. Getting the promised money was just the starting point for getting resettled. People had to figure out how to match up the concrete new reality of a particular sum of money with the dreams that had risen from the suffocating confines of long-term life in a FEMA trailer. Katie's daughter, Nell, reported that before her mother had her stroke, she indicated what she wanted for a home: "My mama going to get a manufactured home," she said, sitting under the carport, fanning her face one day in summer 2007. "We looked at them in Dallas. She want a big kitchen and a big den. The one she liked was $102,000." At the time, before Road Home checks had been issued, Nell was pointing out that her mother had modest taste and did not need as big a home as she had had before the storm—one extra bedroom for grandkids was enough. She had made a choice that reflected realistic expectations. That way, she would not be disappointed. But the reality of Katie's Road Home check came as a shock.

While waiting for Road Home funds, family members had made what progress they could on their own. Some of the cousins, such as Earl, Buffy, Potchie, and Alton, worked with a crew of friends to gut their homes in Violet and take them back to the studs. But because of the massive scale of help most family members needed, the normal system for using lower-cost family labor would not work: it would take real money to hire carpenters, plumbers, and electricians. Once the money had come, people were finally freed to consider options and make choices: How much rehab could be done with X amount of money for an existing home? How much manufactured home could this or that Road Home check buy? What styles of windows, doors, floors, carpet, paint, sinks, toilets, showers, tubs, furniture, wall hangings, fixtures, and appliances should people choose? How did the choices fit the budget? It was a complex set of decisions, actions, and supervisory controls that suddenly became a family preoccupation.

The Louisiana Recovery Authority overseeing the Road Home program publicized its formula for compensation in enough venues that everyone in the family seemed to know how the money would be figured out: the maximum award of $150,000 would be reduced by the amount of insurance a homeowner had collected. The message had the air of clarity and firmness. But the actual variations in awards defied that plain arithmetic time and again.[5] For example, Katie and Gray Eye had flood coverage for their home and after many rounds of work with their insurance company, got a payout of $95,000 to cover damage to the home's structure and its contents, a thin sum for her three-bedroom, two-bath home with a large kitchen, living room, den, porch, all the home's contents, and the backyard shed with all its tools and equipment. By the advertised calculation, the Road Home award should have been $150,000 minus $95,000, or $55,000. But she only got $22,000 and lost her appeal. No one could explain this outcome.

Like others who saw little choice but to pay off their home-loan mortgages, Katie had had to use more than half of her insurance money to pay off her remaining mortgage. That left her with only $45,000 from insurance, and $22,000 from Road Home, a total of $67,000, to start all over—including buying a home and furnishing it completely. The home she wanted cost $102,000, well beyond anything she could afford once the award amount became final. There was no way around the forced mortgage payment that many people faced because their insurance settlements were routed directly to the banks and mortgage companies holding the loans. The money never passed through the hands of the homeowner. This policy was later recognized as an abuse of power, but at the time, no family member thought it was negotiable. One of the FEMA employees working the recovery told me in 2014: "The whole business with people's insurance going to pay off home mortgages was wrong. If someone came directly to us with that situation, we could right that wrong. Of course, we didn't advertise that."[6] So it was settle or nothing.

Generous awards helped quell frustration for those lucky enough to get them, but they were equally baffling to explain. Katie's sister, Cynthia, ended up with more than $200,000 from her combined flood insurance and Road Home settlements, and because she had no mortgage, she was able to use all of this money to purchase a new modular home for $148,000, leaving her with a good sum to buy furnishings and housewares. Roseana had no flood insurance on her Verret home, so she got no insurance compensation. She did get $121,000 from Road Home, and she also got lucky: she was chosen (among applicants that included her sisters) to have a new home built for her by Habitat for Humanity. She accepted Habitat's offer and contributed the required amount to their cost of materials: $35,000. She was thus able to get a new home built and still have money left to help her furnish it.

No logical explanation accounted for the disparities in compensation to homeowners. And no FEMA or Road Home official was prepared to offer one. I was left to try out theories on my own, testing them against the data I had collected from family members. I knew who had gotten awards, the size of many of those awards, and whether or not someone had had homeowner's and/or flood insurance. Based on all my data, there was no way to make the "people got what they had coming" argument. As much as some people want to believe that the "inherent merit" effect explained the differences, I had evidence to the contrary. I had to eliminate the "dedication-and-talent" argument, the "personal-initiative" argument, and the "who-you-know" argument as explanatory models for the caprice of compensation. Any of these possibilities might have been true in a given case, but there was no predicting the outcomes across the family by recourse to any of these models.

Where does this leave us with explaining uneven compensation? We could say the unfairness was a product of chance. To that point, Nobel Prize–winning economist and cognitive psychologist Daniel Kahneman has revolutionized much of our understanding of rationality and human behavior. Based on extensive experiments over decades of work, Kahneman has shown that we are prone to think we know more than the evidence allows and that we underestimate the role of chance. By nature, we want to know that things have turned out for a reason—even if the reason makes us mad or seems unfair. When there are no good explanations that can be reliably attributed to merit, personal initiative, social networks, or class standing, are we then left with the possibility that the Road Home compensations were, to some degree, unavoidable chance outcomes? Perhaps. Or perhaps the institutions charged with recovery provided a void that chance obligingly filled.

This unmitigated arbitrariness of awards created new confusion and discomfort. As Nell said, "People done saw that everybody get something different from FEMA." Those who got more felt reluctant to celebrate; those who got less felt hurt and bewildered. Because the outcomes of compensation did not map onto Road Home's simple formula, the inevitable comparisons created suspicion. Rather than directing their frustration toward the bureaucrats, the hurt got distributed within the group—whoever got too little must have done something wrong, and whoever got too much must have known how to work the system and not shared that information with the group. Shame and blame became everyday enemies of recovery. And as long as people were looking at each other rather than pointing at the system responsible, there would be no accountability for the randomness of these awards.

The very long tunnel of recovery captured and detained an entire cohort of disaster-impacted people and kept them in the dark for three years, unable to help themselves. The recovery machine demanded that the paperwork be completed by its rules, its categories, its deadlines. But there was no corresponding control on the other end for survivors, survivors who endured long stretches of uncertainty with no hope for the machine to be transparent or accountable. In the end, waiting and settling for what they got was their only option.

CALL TO RACE

Geography complicates the nature of race relations in St. Bernard Parish. Historically, the upper and lower areas of the parish developed differently, at different times, for different reasons, and with different cultural influences. Today, race relations divide strongly according to that upper-parish–lower-parish geography.

Communities closer to the Gulf, "lower" in the parish, have always been home to the black population because that's where the largest cluster of sugar plantations was located. But after abolition, many blacks dispersed to areas outside the parish, and the majority of lower-parish residents today are whites of Isleño descent. They were neither slave owners nor owners of plantations, though some did work on the sugar plantations. Over time, a large proportion of these Spanish-speaking settlers relocated to villages closer to the Gulf to establish livelihoods around crabbing, shrimping, harvesting oyster beds, netting crawfish, and trapping in the bayous and coastal marshes of the parish.

With seven to ten generations of ancestors from the same area, blacks and whites have had a long time to get used to each other. Their styles and standards of living and their dependence on the bayou share more in common than either group shares with upper-parish residents in areas like Chalmette or Arabi.

In communities such as Verret, Reggio, Hopedale, Sebastopol, and Violet, blacks and whites live next door to each other. Desegregation was never an issue, and before the storm, schoolchildren from these households had for years attended the same elementary, middle, and high schools. As a result, black and white neighbors and parents of similarly aged children maintained relaxed and familiar relations. Moreover, there is routine interaction around the buying and selling of seafood.

Gilbert King is Roz's brother-in-law. He is well known in the parish for being outspoken at white-dominated council meetings. But like other black men in the parish, Gilbert has longtime ties to white Isleño fishermen. One day, I was eating lunch with Gilbert at a new restaurant in Violet owned by a black couple.

It was early June in 2010, and the shock of a "double dunk" had upset everyone in the region. The explosion and sinking of the BP "Deepwater Horizon" oil rig in the Gulf had, since that April, been pumping oil non-stop into the waters of the Gulf. The gusher was bigger than any previous spill into marine waters in history.[1] Family members had not experienced a direct hit to their livelihoods, but the oil-sullied coastal waters had caused severe shortages in seafood, forcing the cost of family staples like shrimp and crab out of reach and off their plates. In addition, the massive spoilage of their home environment aroused a new round of discontent with the control of outsiders.

On that hot summer day in June, we were both glad to be inside with air-conditioning. Just after we sat down, I asked him whether he liked to crab and shrimp. He immediately brought up his encounter moments earlier with an Isleño friend who crabs for a living and had, despite the oil spill, found some waters he thought were safe. "Right before I come down here just now, I'm leaving the house, and a guy yelled out to me—he a crabber, white guy—he said, 'Hey, King, I got a flounder over here, a big flounder, you want it?' I said, 'Uh, yeah, I guess so.' We do that, that's the kind of thing we do. Matter of fact, the same guy brought me crabs, brought me about four or five dozen crabs last week. You know, it's like this."

Simply put, race relations in the lower parish, "down the road," are built on generations of mutuality—separate social lives, but accommodation and recognition of each other's belonging.

"UP THE ROAD" AND "DOWN THE ROAD"

The upper-parish areas were historically less populated. They were farther from the Gulf, from the rich resources of the bayou, and from the heart of the older parish. But in the late 1950s and 1960s, a massive influx of new white residents fled New Orleans to suburbs like Arabi and Chalmette in upper St. Bernard Parish to avoid the impact of desegregation laws. Almost overnight, a new kind of white majority and power base emerged in the parish. The language blacks use to code their own sense of connection or

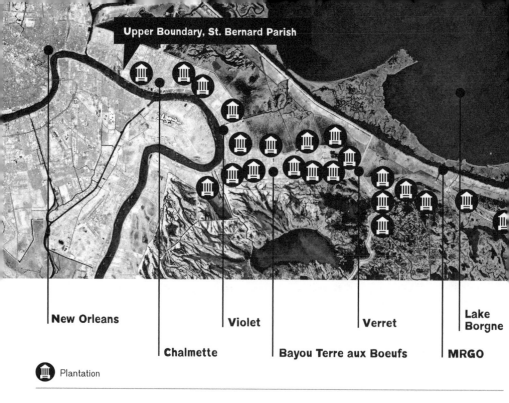

Upper Boundary, St. Bernard Parish

New Orleans | Violet | Verret | Lake Borgne

Chalmette | Bayou Terre aux Boeufs | MRGO

Plantation

Black history in the parish

Across the Bayou Terre aux Boeufs in what was the original St. Bernard Parish, eighteenth- and nineteenth-century colonists established plantations using slave labor to grow sugar cane and harvest cypress timber. But slaves found cracks of opportunity in their environment—the swamps filled with gators and snakes became their allies. They navigated the dangers through interdependent networks, relying on each other and hidden communities of runaways to develop informal economies of trade. These adaptations shaped fundamental aspects of family life.

During slave times, blacks outnumbered whites more than 2:1; by the turn of the twentieth century, white and black populations had evened out. Then, in the 1950s and 1960s, massive numbers of whites fled to the parish from the city of New Orleans and desegregation. This white flight drastically altered the population balance.

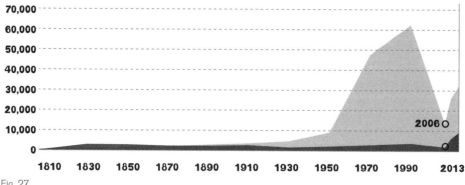

Fig. 27

Data source: US Census for St. Bernard Parish

■ Black ■ White

A changing black presence in the parish

After Katrina, proportionally more blacks than whites returned home to St. Bernard Parish. In addition, blacks from the city also relocated there. These demographic shifts have resulted in a parish with a significantly higher percentage of African Americans than at any other time in recent history.

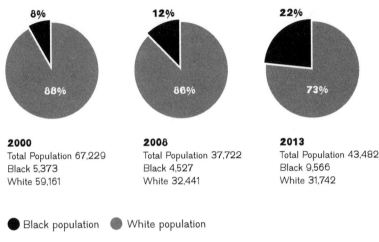

2000
Total Population 67,229
Black 5,373
White 59,161

2008
Total Population 37,722
Black 4,527
White 32,441

2013
Total Population 43,482
Black 9,566
White 31,742

● Black population ● White population

disconnection to areas in the parish says it all: "We from 'down the road,'" but the power in the parish is "up the road," where almost the entire population before Katrina was white, with few ancestral ties to the area.

After 1939, the lower parish began losing political importance when the upper parish, closer to New Orleans, became the new home to the government staff, the parish council, the sheriff's staff, and the school board. The Chalmette Hospital provided health care; major businesses also clustered there, including the port authority, private barges, and the single remaining sugar refinery. Only the oil refineries and the natural-gas plant remain located in or near the lower parish, and only a handful of family members were able to secure jobs with them.

During the first ten months after the storm, as we conducted interviews for our documentary film, I chose not to probe the topic of race. It was one thing to assume (based on a reading of history) that race figured into the equation of bayou life. But as an anthropologist, I preferred to wait for family members to raise the issue. Hard conversations like race arise naturally when people feel the trust they need to speak in an unguarded way.

Before anyone in the bayou family broached the topic of race, Connie had brought it up on a trip back home, wanting to coax Junior to include race-sensitive plans as part of the recovery process for the parish. Her attempt failed. She had become an outsider. But just a few months later, in summer 2006, the subject of race opened up as we filmed a trailer full of women in their forties. We had no agenda other than wanting to hear how people felt about being back in the parish. It quickly became apparent that the honeymoon joy of returning had evaporated.

Five women had crowded into Robin's trailer. Roz had a seat at the dinette table, and three of her cousins sat overlapping each other's shoulders in order to squeeze onto the shallow bench sofa across from her. Another cousin, Debra-Connie (a granddaughter of Peachy's sister, Tuta), stood. Their animated faces and voices told me they were glad to be in each other's company.

From her bolted-down seat, Roz began the conversation about her frustration with job hunting. "I have all the trades you can name," she said, pressing an index finger silently on each of the fingers on her other hand, as if to count what everyone there knew, "and they throw away my application." She paused. "That is pure D racism," she said with irritation as she looked around the tiny room. "They wanted me to be janitorial. If you black, they got a bin under the table where your application goes. Then a white girl comes in, and even if she don't get the job, they at least look at her application," Roz said, raising her voice. Then she dropped her volume to a near whisper and said: "The same thing happened before the storm. Long time ago!"

"So why you obligated to come back here when they treat you this way?" snapped Debra-Connie, looking around the room at the others. "What make you want to come back here? Your child doing better out there. You qualify for a better job. They not giving you a job here. What make you want to come back?"

Roz blurted out, "Well, I'm hoping that they will." Laughs broke the tension, but not because what she said was funny.

"I think it's a bondage we put ourselves in," said Debra-Connie, not ready to leave the topic. "I feel like I being run out of town. This my home." Voices stopped. She had worked up to a tone that was dead serious. Debra-Connie wanted to be here as much as Roz and her other cousins. Before Katrina, virtually every working-age family member had a job. But many weren't the best or most secure jobs. She was under no illusions—coming back to the parish, back to her home, came with costs.

It was my first time to witness family members talking openly about being black in the white-dominated parish. It had taken a year, and now the light turned green to start asking more questions. What did being black mean in the struggle of recovery? Did everyone feel the same about that? The conversation in the trailer that day had begun to circulate among others in the family.

Many parents of school-age children in the family remarked how much less racism they found in Dallas or Houston or Atlanta. When they compared notes, they realized how much each other's children had reported the same thing. Katie helped explain the surprise that life was different elsewhere. "You know," she said from her plastic chair under the carport, "before Katrina, some of these people never been nowhere in their life but in their surroundings. This is the first time that some people ever been away from home. You never go nowhere, you think everybody live like you. If you never go anyplace, right?"

Katie was one of the few who had quietly challenged white assumptions about blacks by demonstrating black competence in a white-parish-office context. Jack Stephens, who lived not far from Verret and who also had deep roots in the lower parish, was sheriff. In 1975, he hired Katie to work as a cook in the jail.

"I had turned down a job offer at Shell because Leroy said you can't be working with all those men," Katie said in that same conversation. "After I got the job with the Sheriff's Office, I thought to myself, he didn't want me working with all those men, but here I am cooking in the jail where the prisoners are." Katie laughed out loud recounting the irony. She went on to describe her philosophy about how to be a single black person surrounded by whites in a system of white power: "Every event they had, I was there," said Katie. "I don't mind staying in the background, but if they got something with the department and it is benefiting me and everybody else is going, then I am going. Look, when I got in there, I got in with the sheriff, the judges, the DA [district attorney], and everybody. Everybody calling me 'Katie.' You got to try and be friendly so people can be friendly to you. I was right there. Only little black spot in the bunch."

For eighteen years as an employee in the Sheriff's Department, Katie supplied a model for other members of the family about how to gently nudge the white establishment into recognizing one's value as a person and as an employee.

Like Katie, most people I talked to felt it was important to avoid exaggerating claims of racial bias. "You can't say that everything is race related, you know," Katie said. "But there is some race, there really is."

In early 1992, Roz's husband, Charles King, became one of the first black police officers on the streets in St. Bernard Parish. He is a tall man with a big frame, an easy smile, and an unexpectedly soft voice. To prepare for his dream of becoming a member of the parish police force, Charles attended LSU, where he got his training. He proudly joined the force, but his white fellow officers turned his dream into a nightmare. The tipping point came on August 28, 1994, when unknown persons killed a squirrel and placed it on Charles' personal car like a hood ornament. He had just had the car painted. Charles reacted and expressed his anger. That was all they needed to fire him.[2]

DISASTER OPPORTUNISM AND EXCLUSION

After the one-year anniversary of the storm, there were clues that disturbing decisions were taking place quietly at the parish level of governance. It was not until several years later, though, that the full weight of parish political maneuvering and racist agendas became clear. FEMA, however inadvertently, was party to these developments.

Ironically, perhaps, the scope of destruction in St. Bernard Parish presented a large canvas of opportunity, a once-in-a-lifetime possibility to enact rapid change or accumulate rapid profit, undeterred by the normal scrutiny of normal times. Private uncertainties and racist fears mixed together in a toxic stew that fed stunning acts of institutional and personal bias and greed. The peculiar breed of greed that operates in the wake of total destruction is known by scholars as "disaster capitalism." Disaster capitalists exploit opportunity-rich sites of disaster in ways that are unethical, largely unmonitored, and immensely profitable.[3]

In the case of St. Bernard Parish, I want to focus attention on a set of actions taken by government officials in the parish. I prefer to call these actions "disaster opportunism" because the nature of opportunism here was designed to benefit power as much as pocket. Identifying a landscape of financial and rebuilding opportunities made possible by the disaster, a small group of parish players seized control and manipulated outcomes. Their actions expanded white privilege in ways that will endure well into the future.

The most public displays of disaster opportunism were institutional. In 2006, parish councilman Craig Taffaro (who would beat Junior Rodriguez to become parish president in 2007) pushed through council an ordinance that made it illegal to rent property to anyone other than a "blood relative." Because few blacks owned rental property in the parish, and some blacks (though few in the family) sought rental housing, this strategy effectively blocked white property owners from renting property to a black person. But Taffaro denied that there was anything discriminatory about the law since it didn't mention race. "This ordinance restricts white people and nonwhite people the same,"[4] he insisted. Two of the seven council members voted against the ordinance, recognizing it for what it was. One of them was Lynn Dean, a seventy-year-old council member and former parish president, who suggested bravely in a *Times-Picayune* interview that the law would give new life to the parish's longtime racism. The council's goal, said Dean, was "to block the blacks from living in these areas. Only we're doing it in a quiet manner . . . I've watched it for years, and I know what they've been trying to do."[5]

The following year, in 2007, the council denied the proposal of a Texas real-estate developer to construct a mixed-income, multifamily affordable housing complex in the upper parish. The developer had the land, the plan, the architect—everything was ready to go. When the council voted down the project proposal, the developer sued and, ultimately, won. In 2012, US district judge Ginger Berrigan found the Taffaro administration and the previous parish council in contempt of court six times in 2009 and 2011, generally stating that their opposition fit discriminatory patterns the parish had exhibited since Katrina.

The racism of multiple institutions interacted and compounded the problems for minority populations. But discrimination and prejudice feed off public attitudes, and I knew after years of experience in the parish that there were plenty of whites who wanted nothing more than to see blacks gone.[6] Many upper-parish residents and shop owners assumed they were safe in revealing their anti-black attitudes to me, a middle-aged white woman. In summer 2010, for example, when I was working to document the impact of spikes in seafood costs after the BP oil spill, I visited several upper-parish shops that sell raw seafood. In one, when I asked if the seafood problem threatened his business, the owner shifted his weight onto the glass counter covering the fish for sale, bringing himself closer to where I stood. "I'll tell you what threatens my business and my life. It's what this hurricane did—and now the parish is going to hell." I asked if he had lost his home, if he was talking about the slow recovery? He replied, "What I'm talking about is the way the parish is changing, the character of people you got coming in now. They are threatening our way of life. We got a culture here, and they are threatening that culture."

"Oh, I see," I said, "you have some people moving here who don't fit in?"

"That's right," he said, standing back up and using his two hands to draw a picture for me. "It's like this," he said. "You take a can of paint," using one hand to cup an imaginary can of paint. "White paint," he specified. "Then you bring in a can of dark paint," he said, using his other hand to show an imaginary can being poured into the can in the first hand. "You see? What you get don't look white anymore. It's dirty."

Black residents of St. Bernard Parish had historically lived in the lower areas, but after the storm, some who had been renters were forced to look for rental property in the upper parish. Some from the destroyed Lower Ninth Ward in adjacent Orleans Parish were also looking for affordable housing in the parish, close to their former neighborhoods. At the same time, many whites from Chalmette were too traumatized by the damage to return to the parish at all. Many moved across Lake Pontchartrain into areas like Covington. The shop owner had expressed discomfort at seeing more black faces in the upper parish than he was used to.

Racist interests did not prevail in these cases. The courts in separate trials ruled that the denial of the affordable housing project and the blood-relative requirement represented illegal, strong-arm tactics to keep blacks out.[7] In May 2013, the Greater New Orleans Fair Housing Action Center (GNOFHAC) and nine individual plaintiffs agreed to settle a federal lawsuit against St. Bernard Parish, alleging that the permissive use permit (PUP) process adopted by the parish in 2007 was racially discriminatory in violation of the federal Fair Housing Act.[8]

Disaster opportunism at the institutional level was not the only display of power grabbing by parish authorities. The sheer dollars that would be flowing into the parish from FEMA created a whirling backstage hustle among people who wanted a piece of the action. As a frame of reference for the power, jobs, and money at stake, by the eighth anniversary of Katrina in August 2013, FEMA had spent more than $1.8 billion to finance repairs and rebuilding work in St. Bernard Parish alone. This staggering amount of money does not include any of the billions spent on individual assistance to homeowners. Stakes on this scale fed ambitions and power-brokering deals that could not have occurred without the disaster. My interest here, however, is not to detail cases of political and corporate corruption, or the many FBI investigations undertaken related to these. The bald-faced greed and fraud on the part of parish leaders and their business partner cronies is well documented. My interest is in identifying the kinds of actions that impacted the family directly.

Traditionally after a disaster, FEMA money is allocated to specific infra-structure repairs. St. Bernard Parish School Board officials launched a campaign to have things work differently after Katrina, and thanks to help from US senator Mary Landrieu, the legislative modification got through Congress. In 2012, FEMA announced its decision to "reassess" the value of St. Bernard Parish public schools. Rather than fund the repairs of individual facilities project by project, it would instead designate one lump sum in the amount of $148.3 million. According to Superintendent Doris Voitier, quoted in the May 2, 2012, *Times-Picayune*, receiving the money as a lump sum allowed the district to "rebuild as we see fit so we can serve the children in our communities." The article elaborated on the value of the lump-sum funding that would "allow the school board to consolidate its Hurricane Katrina rebuilding projects into fewer, but improved, facilities that incorporate the district's reimagined vision for its new community footprint."[9]

The St. Bernard Parish School District pitch to FEMA to "let the local government decide what's best for its own people" seemed reasonable and good.[10] As FEMA's own literature indicated in 2004, recovery authorities agreed that local people should be able to decide what makes sense. But parish authorities twisted this truth. Local control in this case turned out to mean local politicians quietly making decisions with their well-heeled supporters. By working hard to win legislation that would avoid FEMA's "earmarks" for repairs to individual facilities or properties, parish authorities got their hands on enormous, unmarked awards. Then they used their official standing to exercise complete control over decisions about what schools would be repaired, what schools would be demolished or converted to another use, and what schools would be expanded.

With its power to direct money wherever it liked, the parish school board kept it "up the road." They voted to close several schools in the lower parish, including St. Bernard High School, where family members had graduated for decades. Lower-parish residents agonized over the closings and tried to fight back, to no effect. The symbolic import of having no more high school signaled another kind of blow to the old order: the lower parish could no longer hold its own. If young people had to attend the high school in Chalmette, they would (to use Katie's words) become a few "little black spots," unable to feel the strength in numbers and unable to stand with whites from the lower parish as proud members of a distinct community.

Chalmette High School, the athletic archrival of St. Bernard High, had not only been regarded by lower-parish families as "a world away" in the cultural sense, but also in the literal sense. After the storm, the burden of commuting fell solely on the young people of the lower parish: six miles from Violet, fourteen miles from Verret, seventeen miles from Reggio, and twenty miles from the farthest lower-parish town of Yscloskey. With school buses stopping every few blocks, the ride could take two hours each way.

Katie was upset, too, about the name change of the school. One afternoon near the first anniversary after the storm, Katie stood outside her trailer cleaning crabs. She was fuming. "They never let you know what's going on until after. They passed in a meeting that they were renaming it Chalmette. And I didn't know until I went to my granddaughter's Ring Day ceremony. It was Chalmette High School. So I asked her, I said, 'I thought this here was St. Bernard Unified.' 'Oh, they changed it, and nobody knew,' she told me."

Katie looked up to emphasize what she said next. "[At first] they changed the name [of Chalmette High] to St. Bernard Unified because it's St. Bernard Parish. I mean, it's supposed to be unified, right? They renamed it [back to] Chalmette because they want to keep the white reputation."

Even many years later, the loss of the high school in the lower parish still hurt.[11] In spring of 2014, I talked separately to Trashell and her mother, Nell. Trashell told me, "It's not good because they don't want 'St. Bernards' [students who would have gone to St. Bernard High]."

"It's a big deal," she continued, "We were rivals with Chalmette, and to see some of my teachers and coaches there now, it's weird. We were the Eagles. It was the Eagles and the Owls."

Robin and her daughter Tri both had something to say about the school as well. In early 2007, Tri brought it up, transitioning from her discussion of how different life was now. She said, "That's something else that, you know, I miss. There's no high school rivalries. None. You know, it was always St. Bernard against Chalmette, you couldn't wait for that Friday's game, because something was going on, and you couldn't wait." Her mother added, "And now, you have police at Chalmette because the people from the upper part of St. Bernard cannot get together with the people from the lower part of St. Bernard, so it's a big fight at the school constantly."

VIOLET PARK NO. 2

There were other parish-level decisions that involved FEMA funding to restore infrastructure and facilities in the parish. Although these "repairs" carried the air of rational and inevitable work to rebuild streets, schools, and parks, the benefits of the repairs collected around the white upper-parish communities and, interestingly, the lower-parish white Isleño community.

Like churches in the parish, parks are deeply segregated public spaces. Of the twenty parks in St. Bernard Parish operating before Katrina, only one offered black residents a comfortable place to play, and that was limited to baseball: Violet Park No. 2. Violet Park was informally deeded over to black ballplayers back in the late 1960s by a man who owned a large parcel of land that included this field. The uncle of Gilbert and Charles King, Joe Lewis King, had a strong rapport with the white owner of the land who had made the offer. Mr. King told his athletic nephew, Gilbert, and his friends it would be up to them to clear the trees and prepare the ground for a ball field where they could play. Even though the schools had been integrated in the 1960s, there was no place for black athletes to play ball. As he grew up, Gilbert took responsibility for the park, helping recruit players and teams, even from outside the parish, to come to play in Violet Park No. 2. This park became the default park for young black men to enjoy baseball practice and league play, and it drew a few teams from the city's black neighborhoods such as New Orleans East.

By the time Katrina struck in 2005, Gilbert had been at the center of the park's loose structure for some thirty years. The ball field stayed busy with team workouts and practice games, and on Sundays through the season, nine league teams took their turns on the field. Gilbert's brother Charles, who loved to cook, sold his pralines to the Sunday spectators, and he was joined by others who offered their own homemade goods or cool drinks for a little pocket change. Katrina destroyed the park's minimal infrastructure, and by the time there was a review of the parish parks, Craig Taffaro, then parish president, threatened to "decommission" Violet Park No. 2 and absorb the land into parish-controlled property. Then perhaps in response to the outcry from the black community, the president changed his tune, promoting the park in news releases as a historic ballpark. He promised there would be FEMA funds to build it back better. It seemed too good to be true, and it was.

There were improvements made, including a resodded field, new covered spectator stands, and a new small building to house concessions and restrooms. But locals found it hard to understand how the cost of these basic improvements could have totaled $220,000, the rumored amount set aside for the park redo by FEMA. In fact, no one, including the tenacious Gilbert, could get an answer from the parish authorities about how that money had been spent or what exactly FEMA had allotted in the first place. More important, the newly gentrified park got whisked away from Gilbert's voluntary management and assigned to the control of the parish. In 2010, Violet Park No. 2 became an official parish park, operated by the parish's Recreation Department. For the first time in history, the ball field was run by an outsider to the black community, someone President Taffaro assigned to manage it, organize the calendar for league play, and collect fees from all concession sales. According to family reports, that someone had never even played sports. Many blacks in the community were dumbfounded and angered by what took place.

Meanwhile, other parish parks were lavishly endowed with FEMA funds and follow-up monies from Community Development Block Grants. FEMA-supported projects in parish parks totaled $22.6 million (as of 2009). Fully half of this amount ($11.2 million) and another $10 million in CDBG funding was devoted to a massive enhancement of an upper-parish park, an expansion in acreage (by an additional ten acres), facilities, and technology. The new Val Reiss Park in the heart of all-white neighborhoods appears to have been built for white family recreation. Because it is 6.5 miles from the closest lower-parish town of Violet and as much as twenty-one miles from other towns lower in the parish, it is easy to understand the geographic bias that family members and others felt. The website for the Recreation Department of the parish showed the rendering of the new Val Reiss Park (now completed) and included text about the park's purpose.

The park has become a premier location that far exceeds its former purpose and value. Just in the same way that Chalmette High has secured the overwhelming portion of dollars to invest in an entirely new, richly endowed future for education, Val Reiss Park is taking on a similar role in the area of recreation to benefit the same upper-parish population.

The only substantial funding (approximately $1.5 million) for "down-the-road" park projects went to finance important work to rebuild the damaged Isleños Museum complex. The multibuilding complex is devoted to celebrating the heritage of white Isleños and their contribution to the parish. The complex has become a tourist destination, set in the bayou environment of cypress trees and located on the very Bayou Terre aux Boeufs where the Isleños originally settled. In no informational materials on these grounds are blacks ever mentioned, not even as the slaves who were there before the Isleños arrived.

The new Val Reiss Park in upper St. Bernard Parish

VAL REISS PARK
MEYER ENGINEERS, LTD
Engineer & Architect

❝ The Recreation Department strives to design programs that develop fundamentals of the sport, build character, self-esteem, leadership abilities and teach the value of teamwork.

Rendering of the new Val Reiss Park, a 33-acre facility in the heart of Chalmette that promises to be a premier recreational complex when more than $20 million in construction is completed. The work at Val Reiss at the northern end of Palmisano Boulevard in Chalmette—financed by a combination of **FEMA** and Community Development Block Grant funds—is being done in four phases that ultimately will include eight baseball fields, two large concession stands, a **47,000**-square foot massive multi-purpose building and a mini-water park. **❞**

- Website, Recreation Department, St. Bernard Parish

Sometimes, opportunists are merely people who want to rewrite history to better project their preferred view of the past. The current framing of the history of the parish "disappears" blacks from the picture altogether. Promotional brochures and websites were developed to build local pride and draw visitors to the parish. Some of these tourist marketing pitches were prepared by the government, and some by private individuals or "heritage" groups. I reviewed every brochure and website I could locate about the parish, including the government's own website, and quickly recognized that all these digital and printed materials aimed to present the parish as a fascinating and important part of New Orleans lore, primarily because of its quaint "Spanish" history. The alluring, hidden treasures of "Spanish culture" continue to this day, we are told, in the form of annual fiestas, specialty foods, costumes, and a stunning museum complex, fully restored (and much improved) since the storm.

The Spanish heritage, of course, belongs to the lower parish and refers primarily to Isleños—people of the Spanish-colonized Canary Islands. One brochure, in touting the Isleño culture, describes the Canary Islanders as having "flocked to the area, joining the French settlers who arrived in the 1720s." Yet this portrayal omits the fact that by the time the Canary Islanders arrived in the late 1770s and early 1780s, there were already slaves and plantations established in the area. The brochure goes on about how the "natural abundance of wildlife in the marshland was ideal for hunting, fishing, and trapping—the 'mainstay' of those early settlers." Then, we learn that "Italian, German and Irish pioneers later arrived with natives of various other countries." The brochure continues its upbeat tone with a reference to the "impact of these rich cultures."[12]

In 2009, the Louisiana Office of Cultural Development, a division of the Department of Culture, Recreation, and Tourism, issued a two-page color brochure entitled, "A Legacy of Preservation in St. Bernard Parish." The brochure indicates that meticulous attention was taken to restore the Sebastopol Plantation House in the lower parish, now available for touring. Carpenters and current owners are pictured, but there is no mention of slavery or the labor of slaves that the plantation had depended on for its economic success.[13]

On the FEMA-funded Louisiana Recovery Authority website, the following message was posted five years after Katrina:

In lower St. Bernard, a historical community—Los Isleños—exists, preserving and promoting the culture and traditions of the Canary Islanders

who immigrated to Louisiana in the late 1700s. The cultural infrastructure of this community was greatly affected by Hurricane Katrina, with
10 of its facilities, including its main museum and 200-year-old Ducros
Library, incurring storm surges of up to 12 feet. To date, $1.5 million in
FEMA public assistance grants have been obligated for the repair or re-
placement of these facilities.

Two threads weave their way through these promotional materials and
websites. The first thread makes clear that the parish is no mere product of
suburban sprawl. It is home to historically important events and culture.
The second thread concerns the multiple references to the many immigrant
groups and legacies that in one way or another contributed to the parish's
history and culture. Nowhere are any of the following mentioned in any of
these brochures or websites: African slaves, slave labor, slavery, plantation
labor, or free people of color. Native Americans such as the Houma rarely
get a mention. The promotional pitches romanticize the deep history of the
parish by sanitizing it of controversy and omitting the suffering of thousands, who, as slaves, built the wealth of the colony. The only populations
identified are white Americans, Canadians, Canary Islanders, and Euro-
peans. This strategy of whitewashing history for tourist consumption is not
uncommon in post-slave areas in the Caribbean.[14] To encounter such bla-
tant skewing of culture in a region steeped in black history, from slavery to
the present, was breathtaking.

AN UNEXPECTED CALL FOR OUTSIDE HELP

I had planted myself in the parish for much of the summer of 2010. We
were at the five-year anniversary mark, so it was a good time to look back
and try to understand what the post-Katrina trajectory had brought. Nearly
everyone had finally gotten into a new or rebuilt home, and gatherings in
Verret were once again punctuating ordinary weekends as they had before
the storm. There was no getting "back to normal," but people were moving
on with their lives, and Katrina-related conversations no longer dominated
porch-sitting time or after-church exchanges. I believed my work to document the family's struggle was coming to a close, and I expected to start
organizing my book project that fall.

But just as the BP oil spill had become a ghoulish gusher in the Gulf,
something new started happening with blacks in the lower parish: a new
way of engaging race problems. It didn't matter that blacks had historically kept to themselves and relied on each other to get through crises. It

didn't matter that Connie's attempt to address some bigger problems was met with apathy from her family, whose needs at the time were much more basic. Now, in 2010, blacks in the parish were reaching out for help from the National Association for the Advancement of Colored People (NAACP) in an attempt to create a small social movement to end racist practices there.

The development startled and intrigued me. What was motivating this political will and where was the energy to pursue justice coming from? Even though the family's interdependence and self-reliance had been hobbled, until this point there had been no collective calls to reach out for help beyond the family or the community. What problems were so big and so new that recruiting the NAACP seemed to present a solution?

Part of the answer involved timing. By summer 2010, after nearly everyone in the family had gotten resettled, three unexpected problems had converged: (1) the loss of several elders who could hold up the family's old order; (2) the toll of new, race-based affronts that had been occurring more openly in the parish than ever before; and (3) an oil-spill disaster that spoiled the bayou environment and devastated the community of fishermen that the family had long depended upon.

For some of the family's elder members, the sustained cumulative difficulties over years accelerated their physical and mental decline. In the space of just two or three years, the dynamism and leadership of the elder generation had suffered major blows. The sudden defeats of that generation left a void that was not lost on the middle generation. As a result, Buffy, Melanie, Potchie, Alton, Robin, Roz, and others carried new weight on their shoulders. In the years leading up to summer 2010, I saw various signs that the middle generation was becoming emboldened, stepping up to deal with their collective problems in a new way.

In early June 2010, outside the civic center in Chalmette, I stood locked in a long conversation with three men in the family, all cousins, and the male NAACP representative from the state of Louisiana who had co-chaired the public meeting we had all just attended. It was an organizing effort to create a local St. Bernard Parish branch of the NAACP. The attendance was good—well over two hundred people, I estimated.

Afterward, I stayed in hopes of hearing about the priorities a local chapter might develop. It was a beautiful evening, already dark. The sky was brightened with twinkly stars, and the temperature was mild for mid-June. Buffy, Alton, and Mike hung around, too, interested in the same thing. Soon, the NAACP state representative in his handsome, tailored brown suit with peach-colored tie made his way toward us, and over the next hour, our five-way conversation revealed a lot.

"It appears to me that millions of dollars have escaped since Katrina that could have been earmarked to the minority community," said the representative. "Not just to business, but the community at large."

Alton pointed out that it was an issue of not knowing, of being left out of the process. "They go in their closed-door meetings," he said. "That's in parish government, that's in the school board, and in the Sheriff's Department. We don't know what's going on with the Sheriff's Department."

"Executive session," said the representative, holding a notebook with both hands, pressing it to his stomach.

"When the fishing movement was here, you know," said Buffy, "they had a big fallout. They called a meeting and then shut everything down. They went in the back, then they came back out. So that's a closed meeting, because they went in the back and settled whatever they had to settle, amongst theirselves."

Buffy's mention of the "fishing movement" referred to the more than two hundred white fishermen from lower-parish towns who had recently stormed the council meeting, demanding their right to participate in the oil-spill cleanup after having lost their livelihoods because of it. Parish president Taffaro had to call in the police to handle the angry crowd.

The NAACP representative responded quickly, "Yeah, executive session." His shoulders seemed to sway ever so slightly. I wondered if he wanted to leave or if it was just hard for him to not take charge.

"And my point is," said Alton, "that's our tax dollars that you're playing with. But, you know, after the storm, with all this cleaning up, demolition, everything came from out of town. You know, they want you to spend your tax dollars for people from Alabama and Texas and Florida and wherever, is coming here. They be in construction right now!"

The cousins were all truckers, still angry that they had not been considered for hauling jobs despite having followed the exact process they were told to follow to get a contract to pull FEMA trailers or to handle debris cleanup.

The cousins then explained one of the reasons the oil-spill contracts mattered to them, too. Mike had listened without saying anything. He was a slender man like Buffy, but younger than his cousins. As brother to a popular pastor of a black church in Violet, he was well known. He had not only had experience with exposing parish politics, he had also been instrumental in helping recruit the NAACP to look at other issues for blacks in the parish besides oil-spill contracts. His long-sleeved, tucked-in, white oxford shirt seemed to signal his sense of his central role in what was happening with the NAACP.

"The parish government got together, the feds, and FEMA came in and they had contracts to make food, to cook food, prepare food for the people down there," Mike said. He paused, having captured the attention of us all. "So what they did, they got together and got all the restaurant owners—white, not black—got the white restaurant owners together, and then they see who wanted the contracts because you had to cut off your bidders, you had to only cater to that. But the black restaurant owners never got called to the table. Never got called, wasn't never considered."

"You can change the whole community by understanding what monies comes through this parish," said the NAACP representative. "The whole community can change."

"That's right," all agreed.

"As long as they can keep these people who are in poverty in poverty, they get a big check from the federal government. And see, our people don't really understand that, how that works. You stay poor, we get the money through the parish . . . They want you to be poor, they want you to be unemployed, they want you to be uneducated. They want you to be candidates for jail, for prison. Okay? From jail to prison . . . That's the cycle, that's part of that vicious cycle."

The representative's segue made sense, but I wondered how it sounded to the cousins. He had shifted into a more strident, high-toned speech that seemed not to fit into the relaxed dialect of the other men. He held his notebook like a pointer and stabbed the air for emphasis.

I raised a question: "What do you guys think is making all this energy happen? I haven't seen this kind of solidarity and willingness to mobilize in the black community. Is that right?"

"Oh yeah, yes, yes," they all agreed, but before anyone could explain anything, the representative jumped in: "I think it's a level of fear. But the NAACP has the ability to call in the federal troops."

I could not conceive family members wanting to call in federal troops. These were hospitable people who simply wanted respect and decent work. I spotted no indication they were put off, but the conversation ended shortly after that.

Just before the group parted ways, Mike said something important: "You know, one of our things is, we have been going through this for so long, until our people have accepted this as the norm."

And then the representative said something important: "Voter education is not the pastors telling you, you need to vote for someone." That struck a chord. So many people in the family had said that a big part of the problem in making change happen was that the black pastors could not get together, that they were not being real leaders. Some said they took money from the white candidates and then pressed for assurances from their respective congregations that everyone would vote for that person. It was corruption on a small scale, but it kept real change at bay.

I wanted to support this small movement, so at the next meeting, I joined the NAACP. By August that summer, they had passed the threshold of one hundred charter members needed to form a local branch. Many from the family were among the dues-paying members. It seemed like the time had come to try something new—nothing else was working. The newly chartered local branch continued to meet every month. The turnouts were smaller than those early organizing meetings, but the attendance stayed consistent.

But after that first year, the energy had leaked out of the balloon and members who had joined in solidarity with the group did not renew. By 2014, there were no family members with active memberships. As the representative's own language suggested, the NAACP belonged to its own large national organization and as such, it was an outsider, too. Just like Connie and the outsider ethic she had absorbed from Dallas politics, the NAACP seemed to offer a style of confrontation that did not suit local realities or styles.

In 2012, I had a long conversation with Melanie in the living room of her home that St. Bernard Project had helped her complete. We both sat on her small white couch in the room full of toys and children's school materials. I asked her what had happened with the NAACP. She thought about it as she quieted her young teenage son and daughter, asking them to go to the bedroom so we could talk in peace. She put her finger to her mouth and stated the problem from her perspective.

"You've heard of 'bait and switch'?" she asked.

"Um-hmm," I responded.

"You use the kind of bait you think people are going to latch on to."

"Yeah," I nodded, eager to hear what was coming.

"To get in, to get them involved," she elaborated, perhaps not sure if I understood.

"Yeah," I signaled back, "to feel excited, to get the energy going."

"Right. And then when you come and it turns into something else. Okay, everybody's not getting the things that they thought they should have had. Why did it turn into, 'This is what the white people are doing to us'?"

I asked, "Is it because there were old problems that had never been addressed in public?"

"Some of those were personal problems, personal issues," she said.

"Okay. My life against yours?" I asked.

"Exactly!" she said enthusiastically. "And too much of 'This is what happened to me,' and 'This is what needs to be done.' Nobody can agree to say, 'Well, let's start with the government. Let's see what the government is doing.' You understand what I'm saying? 'What's available to us?'"

"So you're saying people just want to, they want to . . ."

" . . . use that platform for their personal . . ."

She paused. "Grudges?" I offered.

"Yes! And that does not make sense to me."

"But," I asked, "isn't it true that a lot of people have been beat up by a system that doesn't care about them?"

"I've been beat up physically, literally, literally. You understand?" Her voice got serious; she wanted me to know that her view of the problems with the local chapter had nothing to do with the lack of race issues she had confronted. Earlier that year, Melanie had described getting pulled over by a parish police car for no reason. Her children were in the back seat, and during the encounter, the police got rough, terrifying the children.

"The police, right?"

"Hm-hmm," she said. "But, you see my grievances, I take it to people who I know."

It occurred to me as she spoke that she was describing the direct-action ethic of the family in how she handled this situation, just as I'd seen with Buffy and Katie and Robin.

"I went to the sheriff and I told him what happened to me," she said softly, "how I felt about it, and how I felt about the fact that they didn't do anything about it."

"Yeah," I said, nodding her on.

"He says to me, 'What are you saying?'" She looked at me and continued in a near whisper. "I told him how my kids felt. Harmony doesn't trust the police. If the police get behind us, that girl will start screaming. And I told him, I need to have a meeting with you. I need to have a meeting with you, but not just you, I need one of your deputies, or three of your deputies there, as well. And I need you to explain to my children that the police are not here to beat up on people, but to protect people. And I need you to act like that. So, when we had the meeting, it was me and my three kids. He gave Harmony a hat, he gave her a tour around the building, you know, he said, 'Whenever you want to bring them back, that's fine. They're always welcome.'"

"Wow," I said, moved by her initiative and how things turned out. Only in a parish where race relations are complicated and historically rich could an exchange like that have happened.

"And he said to my kids," Melanie nodded, "this is what he said, and this is what I needed, ownership. He said, 'What happened to your mom shouldn't have happened.' Ownership," she emphasized. "He knew what happened. He came to get me out of jail the next day. Him. So, he told them, he said, 'Unfortunately, sometimes police have bad days. And they take it out on other people.' And he said, 'And it shouldn't have happened.' And he apologized to them."

"Wow," I repeated.

"I say, that was ownership. I said he would never say it in court. He would never say it in court, but he knew what happened and what was wrong. And that's why I leave it up to God to deal with it. But my point is, if something happens with me, I'm going to handle it with me. I don't need no whole bunch of people . . ."

For reasons like those in Melanie's account, ultimately an outsider system cannot get traction unless there is a more careful attempt to match rhetoric with local ways of doing things, in this case, taking the initiative to solve problems. In a March 2014 conversation with Kevin Gabriel, the new president of the NAACP parish chapter, I learned about his ideas. He has lived in the parish for thirty years and understands it well. His redirection of the local chapter involves his work to transcend the divisions within the black community, and he argues that nothing good can happen until pastors quit fighting and people come together. That is encouraging.

Middle-generation family members like Melanie and Buffy are willing to stand their ground, but they still hold to the local ethic of politeness. The young generation will take new steps that we can't see yet.

The personal and social costs of racism are rarely measured in all the ways they do damage. Our society tends to want direct proof of harm, yet harm comes in ways that might not be direct or visible but are just as real. "Systemic causation,"[15] as cognitive scientist George Lakoff calls it, accounts for a lot of trouble we try to ignore or deny. Lakoff recites examples we all recognize such as smoking, a systemic cause of lung cancer, or driving while drunk, not a direct cause of a car accident but certainly profoundly involved in the outcome. To expand on his point, Lakoff distinguishes "direct causation," which, in the case of the car accident, would be jumping the median and hitting an oncoming car. But the driver's intoxication (like the smoker's damaged lungs) acts as an indirect (and ultimate) cause, a systemic cause, of the accident. Online bullying in schools today acts as a systemic cause of suicide. It doesn't pull the trigger, it just badly corrodes the confidence of young victims at a vulnerable time.

Just because we haven't figured out how to measure the role of systemic causation in producing unwanted outcomes does not mean we should ignore its power. Indeed, there were good reasons for recovery teams to "get" this nuanced experience of race in the parish if they wanted to respond equally to black and white survivors. But without explicit awareness that an area like St. Bernard Parish had a deep history of race-related problems, the recovery culture proceeded as if all people impacted had the same degree of power and opportunity to recover their lives. They did not.

BY AND BY

At last, Katie recovered her wholeness. Her body lay at peace. She looked just like she had six years earlier in Dallas. Her face was plumped and her slightly pouty lips distilled her spunk. I closed my eyes for an instant and saw that smile—the knowing one she wore with her twinkly eyes whenever she teased or joked about something. Smooth, wavy brown hair cupped her brown face at her ear line, and soft strands of bangs swooped across her forehead. The expertly styled short-hair wig fit her character, though no one remembered having seen it before. Her brocade cream suit radiated the lightness of her spirit and complemented the brown skin of her face and hands. Cream piping crossed her chest diagonally and accented the garment's fine quality. It held Katie beautifully—a size twelve, offered by Audrey, who had bought it before losing weight.

The meticulous care of Katie's body had been a collaborative effort of women in the family and the Rhodes Funeral Home, known for its respectful treatment of black bodies. Connie had worked on Katie's makeup early that morning. Everything about her appearance presented classic taste and aesthetic harmony: the cream suit offset Katie's pink lipstick, the pink roses in her clasped hands and on her breast, and her pink nail polish. A small silver cross dangled from one hand. Audrey stood at the head of the casket, and when I paused to pay my respects, she pulled up Katie's sleeve to reveal a watch. "She always watched the time," Audrey whispered without glancing up.

It was a white casket, elegant with cream trim. The tufted inside liner was cushy and satin and had a slightly pink tint that cast a warm glow on the body. I wished for a photo keepsake. After the service, I asked Roz whether anyone had taken a picture of Katie before the viewing. Roz said, "Not that I know of, but I wish somebody had. I would have liked that picture."

Katie's physical decline had been gradual and hard for some to accept.

For the first two years after Katrina, she had been a vision of resilience in the face of horrible loss. But as time went on and she declined, she more nearly became a reflection of the corrosive impact of losing one's agency: losing the ability to make decisions and losing the energy to alter circumstances. Katie's faith and resolve to recover her world could not be easily defeated, but losing her agency presented odds that outmatched her strength. Now in death she seemed triumphant.

The viewing of Katie's body at the Baptist church in Verret had been scheduled for 5:00 to 7:00 p.m., with the wake to follow. The next morning there would be the formal memorial service. Each event would affirm the place of Katie and her family in the black community and the place of grieving and healing in it.

When I entered the church that muggy evening, I bumped into Junior on the front steps as he was leaving. "She was quite a woman," he said, shaking his head. "Everyone thought so," I replied. "Hard to lose her," he said, "she's good people." "The best," I nodded. I later realized that we were the only white people to have come to the viewing. I was the only one at the wake following the viewing, and the only one attending the service that next day.

The sanctuary was brightly lit by an array of pretty chandeliers Reverend Smith had installed as part of the new church's interior. The family had clustered together in the very back pew closest to the entrance. I joined Audrey's four daughters and their children, as well as Nell, Katie's daughter. I wasn't sure about protocol, but after I sat in silence for a few minutes, Nell motioned me with her eyes and face to go up and view the body.

Afterward, I returned to my seat. With a throat full of emotion, I whispered to Melanie what I hoped we all felt, "She is whole, she looks like herself." "Doesn't she?" she replied softly. "She looks beautiful."

The sanctuary was alive with restless children whose bright faces and squirming bodies seemed to lift the weight of the somber tone and dirgelike notes issuing from the organ. They were a welcome distraction. Katie would have been pleased. She loved children enough to raise many more than her own. After her stroke, the hardest adjustment became not having children around her.

The advertised 7:00 p.m. start time for the wake came and passed. At about 7:20, the organist began playing more spirited tunes, signaling a shift in tone from the solemn viewing to the joyous celebration of Katie Williams's life. By then, the Peachy Gang had all arrived, greeted each other, and taken their reserved seats in the first set of pews on the left. I kept my seat at the back: it was a time for the family to be with each other. It was also a good place to observe the whole event. Friends of the family continued to dribble in for the next half hour, squeezing their way without hesitation into already full pews. I had observed over years of attending church in Verret that punctuality was far less important than being present. Every person who entered got a hearty welcome from the ushers and from those they sat beside, whenever they arrived.

It was obvious at a glance that people came dressed in outfits and hairstyles that revealed meticulous care, even beyond the norms of dress that marked the usual Sunday services. A typical Sunday service in black churches is hardly casual—nothing at all like the dress-down affair of many white churches. Black services, at least here, remain weekly opportunities to display the latest look and a sense of style. Yet at this wake, the attire was even more formal. It isn't that black fashion requires more money; it requires the concerted cultivation of style, and that includes hair, nails, accessories, and footwear. It requires caring. Everything visible on a person is part of a canvas, an expression of the artist's imagination.

The young women of the family looked strikingly beautiful. Each had acquired the skill of putting together outfits that look smart and elegant. Each had also learned the latest strategies for making black hair part of their self-presentation. Trashell wore a fitted black dress with netting and a fashionable new haircut. Melanie wore a black dress cut low enough to expose the "Melanie" tattoo script she wore like an ornament above her breast. Her hair, with bangs and curls, complemented her glamorous look. Roz and Nell both wore more traditional hairpieces, invisibly woven into their own hair to double the length, creating a long and flowing look. Katie's sister Audrey, known for her tomboyish athleticism, had chosen fashion-forward curls for her distinctive hairstyle. The other elders of the Johnson-Fernandez family arrived with terrific flair as well: the women wore satin dresses or lovely fitted suits with matching shoes and handbags; the elder men, just like their younger counterparts, wore handsomely tailored suits with colorful shirts and neckties.

As the organist picked up the pace, the congregation began to sway to the rhythm. Some moved forward and back, some moved side to side, a few hummed along. But no one spoke, and no one raised an arm or hand. It takes time to warm up.

Behind the altar, six well-dressed men huddled around Reverend Smith. They were pastors from other black churches in the parish, there to fulfill the tradition of conferring their leadership in the black community to help honor the passing of a special community member. Their presence affirmed the reach of Katie's immense family. Over the evening, each took a turn recognizing the woman Katie was. Interspersed between the presentations of the pastors, Katie's friends, grandchildren, nieces and nephews, and god-children were called forward to offer their own words and songs of praise.

The evening unfolded as a spirited, music-driven memorial to Katie, punctuated with more than a dozen of those spoken tributes. There were musicians playing organ, guitar, and drum. By the end of the first hour of songs and speakers, the heat and energy had gotten so cranked up that the sanctuary seemed to take on a life of its own—alive with spontaneous shout-outs, hand clapping, arm waving, and outbursts of laughter at funny recollections. Some stood almost the entire time; others bobbed up and down, clapping at insightful words or rhythmic songs. Each preacher in his turn aroused responses from the crowd: "Amen!" "That right!" and "Yes, Lord." The pastors at the front encouraged the person speaking with their smiles, clapping, or amens. Many people who spoke then broke into song or used their words to elicit vocal support from the congregation.

In between the collective songs, there were a handful of solos, a few so exquisitely performed that they might have been heard at the Apollo Theater in Harlem. One of the tenderest moments of the evening was the presentation by two young cousins, Katie's grandnieces—Khadaja, age eight, and her cousin, Harmony, age nine. Both girls were Audrey's granddaughters. Together, they wrote a poem for Katie, a prayer that they read together.

Connie's tribute to her nanny was a study in solitary grief. She had stayed up front, to the side of the altar, in a different area from the rest of the family. When it was time for her to speak, she walked to the podium, stunning in her black satin dress with a strand of large beads, wide black belt, and beautiful black straw hat. But before she had uttered a single sentence, she began crying—sobbing, really. Her high-pitched voice cracked at every few words. People supported her with shouts of love, and they made it possible for her to lurch through her loving statement, though it was hard for her to complete a thought. Some family members recognized the poignancy of the moment, since Connie was herself still dealing with cancer and ongoing treatments. We also knew that Connie felt a special bond with Katie, and since leaving for Dallas, she had kept in close contact with her. Katie was Connie's primary link to the parish, her second mother, her beloved aunt and godmother, and her trusted confidante.

Connie's display of emotion contrasted with the more reserved weeping of the closest family. They were sad, too, but seemed to be grieving differently. Connie had been away so long, she no longer had the benefit of the comfort and belonging that gave people a way to be strong together, especially in times of great sorrow. Perhaps Connie's aloneness contributed to her pain. Perhaps, too, the family's everyday experience with Katie's diminished life after her stroke had helped them think of her passing as a letting go, blessedly without struggle or added suffering.

Reverend Smith had the habit of keeping his flock a little longer than they wanted to stay. But on this occasion, even after he had spoken at great length for a wake, about half the congregation stayed put, unready to leave the holy praisefest for Katie. The organist kept playing, and before I knew it, a spontaneous, after-service sing-along broke out, rocking the house for another thirty minutes. When I left at 10:30 p.m., I felt exhausted, but renewed. The service had accomplished its goal.

Katie's wake took me on an emotional passage. During the service, I sang out, I teared up, I sweated rivulets through my pores. By the end, a relief had washed over me that I hadn't expected. I felt a peace I hadn't known, a solidarity with the family and with everyone there. I learned a good deal more that night from what I *felt* than from what I *saw or heard*, which can be a difficult ethnographic experience to relate. I learned what it meant to honor someone's passing in the black community; how spirit, when it is summoned in this collective, wholehearted way, moves through grief to deliver it somewhere new. The revelation offered me a new vantage point from which to recognize the power of faith among slaves and their descendants. The draw of a brutalized people to a supernatural healing force had always made sense. Now I felt it from the inside.

I was to speak in the service of the next day, but now, immersed in the grief and the transcendent solidarity of black community, I felt the prick of my own cultural difference. My words were white, just like my complexion and my attire. I couldn't change any of that. And in that moment, I was reminded how difficult it is to truly merge into another cultural world.

The next morning, at the front door to the church, black-suited ushers with white gloves greeted church members and guests, handing each of us a spiral-bound brochure and a balsa wood fan. I chose to sit at the back again. On this occasion, there would be no need to gradually build toward the momentum of last night's service. We were already there. The bodies, the heat, the buzz of voices could have sparked a flame. No one had expected Katie's death would come this soon after her diagnosis of lung cancer just a few weeks earlier, not even the people closest to her. It almost seemed like she had chosen the time—one last way to reassert her will after having lost so much of her agency after the stroke. Her three sisters had been there at the time of Katie's death, visiting as they often did in the morning. Roz was there, her daily caretaker, and Gray Eye, her husband. She had motioned to Roz that morning to roll her out onto the porch, in and out, several times. Roz wondered why she was so restless. She seemed to be waiting for something. Maybe she knew. On one of her trips back inside, she squeezed Roz's hand tightly. Then she stopped breathing. She was gone.

And now, I was sitting in Katie's church, the small rural Baptist church she had been part of for all of her sixty-nine years. Today, her family and friends, and admirers from all over the parish and the city of New Orleans crammed into every knuckle of space to honor her. Anticipating a packed house, the church leaders had carted in dozens of extra folding chairs they used to fashion extra rows in the back, and extensions of pews, flanking the center aisle, all the way up to the altar, leaving only a wisp of aisle for entering and exiting. People also crowded the space on the wall side of every pew. Shoulder-to-shoulder people stood in these spaces, and dozens of others had found standing room in the chorus area. The front door had been wedged all the way open by a crush of people who couldn't find any space inside.

There were easily four hundred people stuffed into the sanctuary, all of whom knew each other and knew Katie Williams. The organist had been playing all along, but the service was delayed while deacons and ushers scrambled to liberate more standing room for people to move into the church. They had cranked up the air-conditioning to full power, but it was as futile as trying to keep a popsicle frozen in a tropical forest. The July heat was humid and oppressive. Throughout the church, people cooled themselves by opening and flicking the fans they had been handed at the door.

The spiral-bound brochure for the service was large and colorful, with a front-cover photo of Katie's smiling, resilient face. The type above it read, "Celebration of Life for Sister Carolyn James Williams." *I have fought a good fight, I have finished my course, I have kept the faith*—2 Timothy 4:7. Below her photo, it said, "Sunrise: June 6, 1942. Sunset June 29, 2011" and named the church, the pastor, and the address.

The first page laid out the program with the order of service—key speakers, soloists, and the sermon. Next was a page devoted to Katie's obituary, then a page entitled "Bammy," with a poem written by Trashell, the granddaughter she raised, and three pages of photo collages from different eras, with children, grandchildren, nieces, nephews, cousins, and sisters. The inside back cover included the list of "active pallbearers" and "honorary pallbearers." I was surprised to see my name in the paragraph devoted to those she left behind, mentioned as her "loving and committed friend."

People had arrived in their dressiest attire. Women, especially older women, wore hats in the best black tradition of stylish crowns. The variety of straw colors and ribbons, netting, and brim sizes and styles provided a lively contrast to the primary blacks and whites of people's clothing. Many young and middle-aged women wore cloche-style hats.

The wake of the day before, of course, had primarily been a time of grief, but there was also an undercurrent of joy at the plain evidence of a spiritual force in the room. Now, at the funeral service, I felt that same sadness soar into a mysterious collective swirl of emotion. The wholeness of the experience seemed to envelop everyone in a feeling that all of us shared a heartbeat, a synchrony, that we had been whipped into the same upwind of spirit and connection with the divine. And then the feeling would shift back to grief, the knowledge that Katie was gone, that we would never again make her laugh or learn something new from her.

The funeral served a different purpose than the wake. The program was called a celebration of Katie's life, but it was more than that. It was structured like a Sunday service, a time to reflect on God's glory and compassion. In addition to songs and tributes to Katie from church leaders and grandchildren, there were also readings from scripture and a sermon. Reverend Smith's sermons could be eloquent, but he sometimes circled the ending like a hawk that wouldn't land. He had noted the night before that he only had fifteen to twenty minutes of material to present at this service. What he meant, Nell explained, was that he only had a short text of prepared comments, but that no one ever knew what the Holy Spirit might move him to say in the moment. That was, rightfully, out of his control, she indicated. Who could object to the length of a sermon when it was the voice of the Spirit that was speaking through the pastor?

After his final conclusion, the pastor called on me. I faced the all-black crowd and began my comments by noting that people might be wondering just where I fit into the Johnson-Fernandez family. That got a good laugh, and from then on I got my share of shout-outs and kindnesses for a stranger. I noted Katie's warm heart and how she had opened it to me, her love of children and gardening and having a house full of people, her love of St. Bernard Parish—and all the lessons she had taught about keeping humor close, about how big families make life more fun and more bearable when things go wrong, and about how to win people over with good cooking. White as I was, she made me feel like I belonged.

It turned out that I was not the only white person to participate in the service. A dramatic and unexpected moment followed my tribute with the entry of three white deputy sheriffs. They were outfitted in full regalia—blue dress pants with tan stripes, khaki shirts with long sleeves, and colorful bars pinned above their shirt pockets to indicate rank and accomplishments. They wore white gloves and ranger hats and used one hand to grip the rifles at their sides. They entered the narrow center aisle of the sanctuary in single file (the only choice) and rifles on their shoulders, then high-stepped to the front altar where Katie's body lay in the open coffin. The three members of the honor guard lined up alongside each other, standing at attention over the coffin. They raised their rifles in a ritual of honor, and upon lowering them, saluted the body. Sighs and hushed whispers held the pride that swept the crowd. Katie had been a star deputy. She was one of them, and many present knew that she had made history by serving in this role as a black woman. She had also won the admiration of the entire white force, from the sheriff all the way down. That there was a ceremonial ritual by the white officers for Katie spoke more than anyone else could about the respect she had earned beyond the family.

After the service, people formed a single line for one last viewing of the body before the burial. It took a long time because the line moved slowly. Meanwhile, those who had viewed the remains congregated outside, waiting in the wicked heat for the repast to begin. Big white tents supplied by the Sheriff's Office spread out over the large grounds beside the church and provided the only shade. It took forty-five minutes for the viewing line to end, and that was the signal for the pallbearers to heave the coffin up to their shoulders and march it out to the graveyard behind the church where so many members of the Peachy Gang family were buried. After waiting for the body to leave the church, the largest part of the crowd began lining up for plates of food.

On one long table, a spread of home-cooked food covered with foil concealed a great variety of familiar favorites—all contributions from the kitchens of friends and more distant family. Men fried chicken on the spot, and there were dishes of gumbo, red beans and rice, a spicy shrimp-and-noodle concoction, lasagna, mac and cheese, candied yams, sweet-potato casserole, potato salad, cole slaw, and all kinds of desserts. People ate and talked for a long time. Katie was gone and life would go on.

This vivid, two-day rite of passage conveyed the power of culture to make life good, to hold people up and help them feel comfort in the midst of suffering. As scholars make clear, "That deep well of faith from the darkest days of slavery sets the African American experience of religion apart."[1] After the Civil War, black leaders in the United States established their own Christian churches, centered on messages and rituals that corresponded to the needs of African Americans who had endured "the whip, exploitation, and abuse."[2] And as the family made clear, suffering was not a burden to carry alone: black churches nourished faith through a communal context, allowing those who "stand in the need" to reach out individually and find relief collectively.

CODA

Katie's truncated existence after her stroke became an embodiment of the dark side of recovery. She had stood up to the ruin of Katrina, a Category 3 storm that should never have destroyed her home or her parish. But accepting her losses and moving on were not enough to help her recover her life and its delights. Authorities and caseworkers arrived with a template that would define the shape of recovery. Pressed onto the devastated bayou parish, the template indicated how to choose contractors for cleanup and rebuilding, how to issue and process paperwork and define eligibility, how to counsel the stricken, and how to oversee the work of recovery. Together, all these generic, outsider decisions, forms, and actions left family members like Katie no sense of participation in the process and no way to refine the template to match the realities of their lives. Katie fought for her dignity and tried her best to locate a place of comfort, but the system was built neither to renew cultural vitality nor to stanch the loss of zest from the family rhizome. After her stroke, she slowly spiraled into a lonely place. Deep in a space she did not know, she could not heal. Eventually, her body let go.

Two months later, in late August 2011, the region commemorated the six-year anniversary of Katrina. I asked myself: Did Katie's death signal a looming shift in the life of the Peachy Gang? The concern prompted me to commit to one final episode of fieldwork with the family. With six years of serious strain on the health of the family system, the rhizome's capacity to heal remained unclear. Had the trauma of collective disaster and its fragmenting aftermath altered the familiar strategies of the group to endure hard times? Were members of the family, as a result, leaving behind what had once served as "habits of the heart" for a more practical, oak-like individualism? Or were there signs that shared pleasures and obligations had returned, that the integrity of the group had weathered this most challenging of all storms? No. No. Yes. The rhizome sent out new shoots from the muck, its tensile strength measured in the forward movement of weekly group rituals and house-to-house visits, of large group celebrations of birthdays, weddings, holidays. And cooking.

The following update is partial, and of necessity, stops at 2014. But the trend is clear. Near the end of 2011, about six months after Katie had died, the young men in the family announced that they had hatched a plan for a new Christmas tradition: the guys would cook breakfast for the women a day or two before Christmas Day. They would buy all the groceries, arrange the tables, prepare the food, and do the dishes. The new ritual was a great success, bringing together branches of the Peachy Gang and many others in the Johnson-Fernandez family, too. Also in 2011, Katie's older sister, Cynthia, turned eighty without a blink. She continues to cook her weekly gumbo and tend her bountiful vegetable and flower garden; both remain important family attractions. That same year, Audrey celebrated her sixty-fifth birthday at a huge party thrown by her daughters and nieces.

In January 2012, a month after the men inaugurated the new Christmas breakfast ritual, Roz and Charles moved into their new home in Violet. They were among the last in the family to finally get their Road Home money, which they used to purchase a gutted house that St. Bernard Project helped them redo. The organization hosted a big "welcome home" party for the family on Martin Luther King Jr.'s birthday. Gray Eye's health problems led to several hospital visits, and during this time, he moved in with Roz's family. Roseana had to move out of her Habitat-built home because Habitat found that it had been built with toxic drywall from China. She moved temporarily to a home in Violet while the crew dismantled and then re-walled her home. Six months later, she moved back to her new home in Verret.

Three teens left the parish for college in 2012, and more are following suit. The elders praise the new ambitions of their grandchildren, grand-nieces, and grandnephews. They also live in the hope that their babies will come back home, degrees in hand, and raise up their own families.

In July 2012, Katie's granddaughter Trashell and her husband, Dude, had a new baby girl. When I saw her a few months later, her infant eyes startled me (and others) because they are Katie's eyes. Nell's husband, Earl, became a licensed minister. Melanie got admitted that year to Loyola University as a junior and began working toward a bachelor of science degree in psychology. Also that year, Charles and Roz opened up a small shop in Violet called The Praline King, where he makes his famous pralines, bread pudding, and sweet potato pie. Gray Eye recovered his health and moved back to his house in Verret, where he lives alone.

In 2013, years after having taken control of Violet Park No. 2, the parish government offered the low-revenue concession operation of the park to the ball team of the Violet Bulldogs, the team Gilbert King had coached for at least twenty-five years. In that same year, Roseana turned seventy to an elaborate surprise—a family "hullabaloo," themed in red and gold. Dozens of women and men in bright-red clothing make quite an impression. Family birthday parties feature lavish spreads of homemade food, typically brought to a hall rented and decorated for the occasion. Mr. T, one of Roseana's sons, served up the music, and four generations of family danced.

The First Baptist Church in Verret has made no progress toward adding a kitchen, and there are no signs that the omission will be corrected.

In summer 2014, Mr. T threw himself a huge birthday party in his mother's yard in Verret. Hundreds of family members crowded Roseana's lawn and filled tables to near collapse with homemade bayou food. At the Johnson-Fernandez Family Reunion in July, the Peachy Gang once again joined the larger family to eat, laugh, and circulate all the news that was fit to tell.

Three years after Katie's death, it is clear: the rhizome metaphor represents a tenacious cultural reality. The family's rootstock of entangled relationships brings, as it always has, multiple generations into a coherent ritual life punctuated by food and festivity, talk, and sometimes grief and sorrow. Certainly, metaphor is never the same thing as the reality it represents, but a comparison often helps clarify a complex concept. Understanding how the family works and how its culture cycle nourishes family members offers ethnographic value of its own. And as sometimes happens, the light of ethnography also illuminates other vaguely understood places in the human experience. There are general lessons about recovery from disaster that can be drawn from this story. In these final pages, I want to identify a few of them.

The most striking insight I have gained over these past (now) nine years since Katrina is this: family suffering was not primarily about material loss after Katrina; it was about the loss of control, a hardship imposed by outsiders who took charge of a world they intended to help but knew nothing about. These outsiders were ignorant of everything local—the styles of communication, the forms of personal initiative and self-reliance, the types of family, the ways of expressing community. At a time of dire distress for the entire kinship network, the template for recovery left family members feeling invisible, without agency or recourse to their cultural source of strength and without the ear of anyone who would listen. Rather than providing relief, the system imposed new forms of suffering. Recovery institutions and the people representing them surely meant to help, but paving the road to recovery with good intentions did unintended harm.

What went wrong? At the heart of the problems I have documented lies the clash of two cultural systems: the "recovery culture," represented by bureaucratic organizations at all levels—federal, state, and local—and the "wounded culture," those directly impacted by a disaster. Recovery organizations typically share much more in common with each other than they do with those wounded. So for people of the "wounded culture" to heal as quickly and as fully as possible from a disaster, the cultural gaps between them and those charged with helping them must be acknowledged and they must be managed.

The more we learn from direct experience with disaster, the more we can respond with better ideas that produce more life-affirming results. Since Katrina (and, in part, because of Katrina), FEMA has attempted to redirect management of the long-term recovery process. Even before Katrina, in 2004, the federal agency had outlined its plan to deal with the reality that "all disasters are local" by establishing Long Term Recovery Groups in the communities impacted. The LTRGs are envisioned by FEMA to include voluntary organizations, faith-based groups, local governments, and nongovernmental organizations. LTRGs, assumed to have on-the-ground knowledge, are charged with the work of case management, crisis counseling, housing support, and financial aid to individuals. For the large family I worked with in St. Bernard Parish, however, no official arm of the recovery culture—not FEMA, not Road Home, not an LTRG—displayed any such local awareness.

To help a population devastated by disaster requires attention to the ways that people derive comfort and strength. Indeed, the root meaning of *com-fort* comes from Latin and means "with strength." To comfort is thus "to strengthen" or "to console." Research shows us that how people think and how people feel after trauma is significantly shaped by culture.[1] The importance of returning a house to habitable state or getting streets rebuilt and stoplights working is obvious. What remains hidden is that cultural comfort in the aftermath of ruin reduces suffering.[2] Once people feel a little sense of control in an alien context, recovery can move more quickly and more successfully.

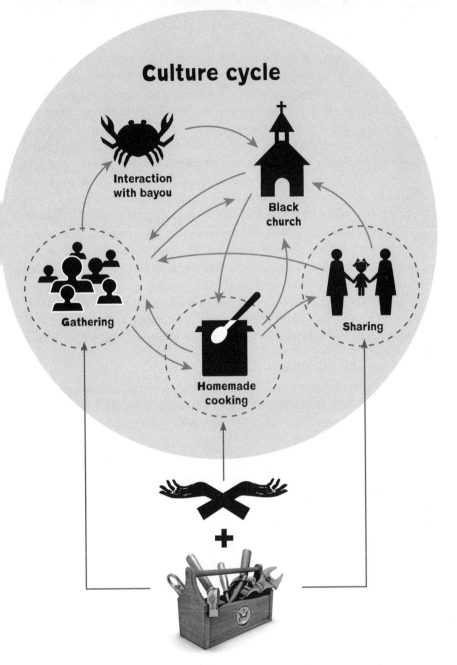

Culture cycle

Interaction with bayou

Black church

Gathering

Homemade cooking

Sharing

Energizing a damaged culture cycle

When disaster strikes a community, recovery agencies can reduce suffering and speed healing by learning about and then supporting meaningful practices of the cultural groups impacted. In this black bayou family's culture cycle, three points of entry would have made good candidates for energizing recovery: providing places to gather, places to cook big meals, and places to care for children. Other cultural groups will have other sources of comfort and different points of entry.

Restoring cultural vitality is no imaginary, dewy-eyed take on disaster recovery. It works and can be generalized, adjusted, and applied. For example, in the 2011 Great East Japan Earthquake that unleashed a tsunami, provoked a nuclear-reactor disaster, and killed nearly sixteen thousand people, recovery authorities recognized a variety of entry points into local culture that could bolster communal confidence and comfort. The cultural need for neighbors and families to gather while other recovery efforts got underway led to the construction of large temporary shelters. Agents of recovery also built temporary public baths to provide comfort and familiarity in the midst of chaos and confusion and despair. Anthropologist Isao Hayashi documented the flurry of folk-art performances that sprang up in devastated coastal communities to honor the dead, a symbolic renewal of "links to a deep conviction in nature and life."[3] Hayashi noted that even in the early weeks after the disaster, when humanitarian relief was still in full swing, there was "enormous interest given to the local culture, especially the folk performing arts. By turning to the familiar folk performances, people were able to experience the continuity of life before the disaster."[4]

By contrast, our recovery agencies seem reluctant to commit to bolstering local culture in the aftermath of a disaster, even if there have been some promising attempts at stating as much in written materials. What is hampering the paradigm nudge that seems so self-evident to a researcher in the field?

First, many recovery authorities may not realize that there is often a major gap between their own ways of talking and doing things and those of the people they are deployed to help.

Second, even when there is recognition of a gap of understanding between recovery and wounded cultures, gathering knowledge at the micro level of community sounds costly and time consuming.

So what is possible? For recovery agents who recognize the gulf and the urgent need to bridge it, the preparation needed for understanding another culture may seem daunting. However, anthropologists have produced treasure troves of research about virtually every society on earth. If we looked to the existing literature for those places we know are at highest risk for earthquakes, tsunamis, hurricanes, and tornadoes, we could compile a working database with targeted information about cultural groups occupying those areas. Additionally, we could identify in advance a set of local scholars and potential culture brokers for each cultural group residing in a disaster-prone area. The point is that agencies and organizations should have readily available the needed cultural information that will let them do their work more swiftly and with a lighter touch.

We can learn what comfort feels like to different groups before they become impacted by a disaster. People of goodwill care about making recovery faster and better, and those standing in the need after Katrina offer their experience as inspiration to this effort.

Women

Women of all generations enjoy gatherin preferably on big porches, and in living rooms. They are the social organizers, th storytellers and the keepers of children and secret family recipes.

Sitting on the steps to Cynthia's new front porch and home: three sisters with a few of their adult children and grandchildren

Cousins are friends for life: Desi, Janice, LaShunn, Melanie

Clockwise from top left: Cynthia, K Roseana, Donnatte

Fig. 31

Cameron, Treyvon, Will, Gregory

Buffy, master cook at work

George and Turb prepping a crawfish boil

Men

Men bond early with their cousins, building lifelong networks of friendship and skill sharing. At family gatherings, they preside over outdoor grills and boils.

Fig. 32

Deshernique, LSU graduate with mother, Donnatte

Turb stirring crawfish boil

Will, high school grad, with parents, Desiree and Wilfred Jr.

Shrimp packing at Shell Beach

Bayou turtle, "Cowan"

Moving forward

When ordinary life takes hold, real recovery begins.

Charles, the Praline King

Fig. 33

Three generations: Trashell, Ameir, and Nell

Leslé with Grandmother Audrey

Roz and son Chuck with grandnephew

Cynthia, left, new "Mother of the Church," with Pastor Smith and her sister-in-law Althea

Anitra and mother, Roseana

2009: the new home for Katie and Gray Eye

IN EVERLASTING MEMORY OF KATRINA
ST. BERNARD, LOUISIANA — AUGUST 2

Memento mori: "Remember death," Shell Beach

Watercolor by Margaret Stone

Iris and its rhizome

Wild red iris (Iris fulva Ker-Gawl) and its rhizome, native to St. Bernard Parish and coastal Louisiana.

Fig. 34

Fig. 35

Appendix

METHODOLOGY

Thanks to the patience of Johnson-Fernandez family members who endured the endless questions of an anthropologist, I was able to continue my research for eight years following Katrina. The comprehensive and long-term nature of the research yielded tremendous insights and taught me how to look into that quiet, terrifying space within disaster and its aftermath. It also helped me nurture lifetime friendships and, in the course of building these relationships, left me with terrible grief from the loss of a special friend.

THE ETHNOGRAPHIC APPROACH

I have worked to understand the cultural universe of black life on the bayou, how the family's sense of belonging fits into this universe, and how its members have fought with everything they had to keep Katrina from destroying their world. To fully grasp another's culture may never be possible, but any attempt to do so requires deep ethnographic work over time, in the place and with the people one wants to understand. In this post-Katrina situation, I had to fit my research interests into my academic responsibilities. Thus, my ethnographic study for the last eight years has taken the form of more than twenty-five highly focused research visits to the bayou. In addition, I have kept in close contact with family members from my home in Colorado through regular and often long phone conversations. With some of the younger members, I also exchange photos and information by text and e-mail.

My study frame encompassed more than three hundred African American relatives whose families have lived for generations in the lower part of St. Bernard Parish. Most of these people consider themselves to be members of the Peachy Gang; a few are descended from Peachy's siblings and part of the broader family known as the Johnson-Fernandez family. My research question focused on how an "extended" African American family copes with the upheaval of disaster and how such a large family manages recovery.

When I was preparing these core questions for submission of a grant proposal to the National Science Foundation, I had no idea that all of the members of the family I would end up studying would be devastated by the flooding or that 155 of them would evacuate together to Dallas. I also did not know that the notion of "extended" family would prove inappropriate because the language itself presumes the primacy of a smaller group, which was not the case. Over eight years of study, my research methods included successive, in-depth interviews with people from six different branches of the Peachy Gang, eight focus groups with family of the same generation—women or men—and hundreds of unstructured interviews and informal observations with family members. My ethnographic data also included participating in and observing a wide variety of small and large family gatherings. The information I collected included everything I could get my hands on that would help me understand life on the bayou and in the community. Very little was irrelevant to my interests. The breadth of holistic data collection creates a massive data set, but it is also the surest way to generate truthful and enduring insights about what is valued, how things work, and how the pieces of life fit together.

In addition to my ethnographic work with family members, I used many techniques to ensure the robustness of the data. I interviewed a wide range of people outside the family—parish government officials, business owners, church leaders, and community leaders, as well as sociologists, anthropologists, historians, and mental health practitioners from New Orleans. I visited at different times during the year so that I could understand better the varying climates, holidays, and seasonality in seafood and outdoor activities. To collect spatial data, I hired my former graduate student, John McGreevy, to map GIS coordinates in order to show the spatial concentration of family homes, their proximity to each other, to churches and schools, and to locate area oil and gas refineries and other employers. I also conducted varieties of archival research, including a search of nineteenth-century slave schedules and census data to identify the earliest generation that the current family could be traced to.

During the first five years of my research, I created four survey questionnaires that I administered to family and other parish residents. I have always used mixed methods, combining a variety of data-gathering techniques as identified above. However, survey instruments did not work well in the bayou setting. I tried varying the form and style of questions, but few were interested in the formality of such questioning. The issue had nothing to do with time, as most people were happy to talk with me as long as I liked. The resistance had more to do with how information flows, which is through conversation. Inadvertently, I had proposed a standard method of collecting information that was as alien as the bureaucratic paperwork people had to complete. I came to realize that what gets understood as true is generally information that gets crystallized through the process of group talk. My revelation about the taken-for-granted survey approach to data gathering speaks to the importance of understanding the cultural gulf that is at the center of this book.

The interconnected-life framework of data collection presents two benefits to the study of disaster generally and to the study of recovery from Katrina specifically. First, this work reflects a holistic mission—a commitment to gathering data about many aspects of family life and a commitment to understanding how these aspects of life interact in the context of disaster. Second, this study takes place over the full trajectory of recovery, with "recovery" defined as the point at which people are not only resettled into homes, but their conversations are no longer dominated by aspects of the disaster or recovery. The benefit of such a long-term, on-the-ground study is that it is possible to document the ebbs and flows and duration of the whole process.

To try to hold on to the richness of ethnographic data yet find a way to systematically organize its vastness took special tools. Fortunately, I had a lot of help from smart and devoted students who made it possible for me to keep up with my accumulating data. As I recorded all my interviews and the majority of informal interviews, students transcribed these. Then, at various intervals, the transcribed interviews were uploaded to a qualitative database software program called MAXQDA. In this program, a few advanced students helped me code the text of each interview according to a variety of general themes so that the codes and subcodes evolved over time. Ultimately, nine major topics emerged from the texts: Cultural Life and History, Economics, Environment, Faith, Family, Gender and Community, Language and Communication, Mental and Physical Health, Race, and Self-Reliance. Each of the major topics also tracked twelve to thirty subtopics.

As any methodologist would agree, powerful software is handy, but it does not do the work of analysis. I read through each transcription many times and made my own notes about key themes. The iterative work back and forth between my reading of transcripts and my review of coding helped me identify the themes most important to the family. I was then able to develop the fullness of each theme by using quotes drawn from coded material from a variety of interviews.

Other data visualization tools I used included a kinship modeling system called Genopro. For maps, I worked with USGS scientists and their Land Satellite mapping systems to generate custom views of coastal Louisiana and St. Bernard Parish at distinct points in time. I created other maps using Google Earth and LandSat to show the approximate distribution of historic plantations, pre- and post-Katrina schools, and parish parks.

In the end, I hope that my approach to this material has done justice to the family. I also hope that the nuance and detail of stories, made possible through long-term ethnographic methodology, will add clarity and inspiration to the struggles many face in the process of recovering from disaster.

NOTES

PREFACE

1. See, for example, Norris et al. (2008:145).
2. Banks and Banks (2010).

CHAPTER 1: WHEN THEY SAY GO

1. *Still Waiting: Life After Katrina* was first broadcast on PBS stations in the United States and Canada beginning in 2007. See Browne and Martin (2007).

2. Carol Stack's *All Our Kin* was a seminal publication about the adaptive nature of large African American families in improving economic stability and survival.

3. We were fortunate to have had a contact in Dallas who attended the same breast-cancer survivor group that Connie did. She connected us.

4. I list nine siblings in the Peachy Gang. However, in accounting for the "full" family, the sisters identify twelve siblings. Because it was not possible or desirable to enumerate all the complications related to different parents and adoption, each kin chart supplied in this book notes that the group identified is "simplified."

5. In 2000, if the St. Bernard Parish population was 67,229, and blacks represented 8 percent of that, then there were 5,373 total blacks in the parish. Violet had 3,317 of them, or 62 percent, so the rest would have been primarily residing in other lower parish towns. See http://en.wikipedia.org/wiki/St._Bernard_Parish,_Louisiana.

6. Published: Saturday, August 27, 2005, 12:00 p.m., *Times-Picayune*.

7. United States Senate (2006:247).

8. Researchers have found that women are more likely than men to evacuate. For an explanation of these patterns, see Bateman and Edwards (2002).

9. Lynn Dean was president of St. Bernard Parish from 1992 to 1996. He served in the Louisiana state legislature from 1996 to 2004, and as a parish council member from 2004 to 2007.

10. Hurricane Betsy galvanized the Army Corps of Engineers to rush through the addition of new safety measures. This "Hurricane Protection Program" improved on the height and strength of flood walls and levees so that another Category 3 storm would not cause the damage Betsy had (Colton 2009).

11. Wolshon (2006).

12. Russell (2005).

13. Geographer David Harvey offered early critiques of the Western assumption regarding the separation of humans and nature (1996). Anthony Oliver-Smith has artfully elaborated on these ideas of separation to show how they do not derive from

any "truth" but rather are a cultural construction that makes our interest in domi-
nating and exploiting nature seem normal (2002). Harvey Molotch first coined the
term "growth machine" in a 1976 article, "The City as a Growth Machine." His ideas
were expanded and applied to New Orleans in Freudenburg et al., *Catastrophe in
the Making* (2009).

14. This area is known as the Mississippi River Delta, and it constitutes one of
the largest coastal wetlands in the United States.

15. Freudenburg et al. (2009:117).

16. The "average" rate of land loss between 1985 and 2010 does not mean that
there is a constant or predictable rate of loss, as these rates vary according to many
factors. For more explanation and detail, see Couvillion et al. (2011).

17. Freudenburg et al. (2009:119).

18. Davis-Wheeler (2000).

19. Rosenthal (2012). Also, the 2006 National Science Foundation independent
investigation team attributed the breaches to design flaws in the levees and flood
walls: https://www.nsf.gov/news/news_summ.jsp?cntn_id=107007. Another independent report issued by the American Society of Civil Engineers (2007) concluded
that the levees and flood walls in the area around New Orleans breached "because
of a combination of unfortunate choices and decisions, made over many years, at
almost all levels of responsibility" (Andersen 2007:v). A separate report was issued
by Ivor van Heerden (2007a), a research professor at Louisiana State University, lead
investigator of a four-year pilot study of hurricane vulnerability in New Orleans, and
head of the independent scientific investigation of the levee failures during Katrina.
His findings concur with others: the levee failures were human-induced failures
attributable to the negligence and faulty science of the Army Corps of Engineers.

20. See http://www.wunderground.com/education/Katrinas_surge_part05.asp?.

CHAPTER 2: THE CULTURE BROKER

1. FEMA has been housed since 2003 under the Department of Homeland
Security.

2. Anthropologists who study cultural constructions are well positioned to
recognize post-disaster cultural divides and the need to bridge them. For example,
Oliver-Smith noted that "many of the benefits and potentials that emerge . . . after
a disaster might not be lost if a culturally knowledgeable mediator were available
to work with communities and agencies" (2010:14). For other studies that deal with
cultural divides in the aftermath of disaster, see Bode (1990); Gill and Picou (1997);
Erikson (2000); Klinenberg (2003); Petryna (2004); and Ritchie, Gill, and Farnham
(2012).

3. In this part of Louisiana, there is a custom borrowed from the eighteenth-
century Spanish tradition of burying people above ground in tombs and vaults. The
wall-vault system of burial makes sense in the context of the area's high water table

and provides a solution to the earlier in-ground burials that proved ineffective when floods unmoored caskets and left them to float away, spreading panic and disease. Since 1789, when St. Louis No. 1 Cemetery was built, the dead have been buried in coffins and placed inside massive concrete walls or tombs with engraved names and headstones.

4. The size of the Peachy Gang is interesting to consider. Evolutionary anthropologist Robin Dunbar developed the "social brain hypothesis," arguing that in the human species, the largest effective and coherent social groups include about 150 members. This number, known as "Dunbar's number," correlates to more than ten thousand possible dyads between any two individuals. The mental requirements of keeping track of these relationships is precisely, he argues, the basis for the growth of the human brain's neocortex. Dunbar's work and the implications of it for understanding our inherently social nature are carefully elaborated in a recent book introducing the new branch of science called "social cognitive neuroscience." See Lieberman (2013).

5. Susanna Hoffman elaborates the complex cascade of emotions that often accompany survivors of a disaster (2013).

6. Mark Granovetter coined the terms "strong ties" and "weak ties" and showed how these distinct types of social connections carry economic implications. Connie's family members had few if any weak ties. Social scientists have used Granovetter's ideas to further investigate patterns of social networks and upward mobility. For the seminal work, see Granovetter's "The Strength of Weak Ties" (1973).

7. In her book about Muslim Americans after 9/11, Lori Peek describes "collective grief" as the pain of a number of people "who simultaneously share the experience" of "large-scale traumatic events" (2011:177).

8. Deleuze and Guattari (1980); Glissant (1981; 1997).

9. Mindy Fullilove coined this term in *Root Shock*, where she explores the displacement of black urban communities during the urban renewal programs of the 1960s and 1970s (2004).

CHAPTER 3: NOT JUST ANY RED BEANS

1. Marshall Sahlins makes the case for the cultural invention of food meanings and thus, taste preferences, in his seminal work, *Culture and Practical Reason* (1976).

2. The term "lifeworld" ("Lebensweld," coined by the German philosopher Edmund Husserl) refers to a world that people experience together.

3. Schoolkids from the New Orleans area who had been displaced to various parts of the country reported the same phenomenon. See Peek (2012:42–43).

4. These studies were conducted by the US Geological Service (USGS), the Environmental Protection Agency (EPA), and the National Oceanic and Atmospheric Administration (NOAA). See http://pubs.usgs.gov/circ/1306/pdf/c1306_ch7_g.pdf.

5. As Wells points out (2008:192), the early return of shrimping required devastated shrimpers to pay to truck in ice and run generators, and to locate markets for the abundant shrimp that the traditional buyers in New Orleans could not use. For an examination of the impact of Katrina on the oyster beds of St. Bernard and Plaquemines Parishes, see McGuire (2006).

6. See http://www.cbn.com/health/naturalhealth/drsears_mindbodydiet.aspx.

7. See Browne (2009).

CHAPTER 4: RUIN AND RELIEF

1. The quotes in this distilled history are fictitious but true to the documented history of south Louisiana. For in-depth treatments about early colonization, slavery, and the Isleños, see the following: Midlo Hall (1992a, 1992b); Hirsch and Logsdon (1992); Din (1988). For a good overview of the social and economic history and geography, see Lewis (2003). For more recent histories of oil and gas and other commercial interests in the parish, see Austin (2006).

2. Sociologist Robert Bellah et al. produced a seminal book by this title, investigating the growing tendency of modern Americans to reject communalism in favor of individualism, and the implications this choice posed for a democratic society (1985).

3. The story in the *Atlantic*, "Struggling to Survive," was written by Jonathan Rauch and was published online on August 15, 2006. See http://www.theatlantic .com/magazine/archive/2006/08/struggling-to-survive/305182/3/.

4. Data from US Census Bureau report, "Special Population Estimates for Impacted Counties in the Gulf Coast Area" (Worldwatch 2006).

5. *A Failure of Initiative: Final Report of the Select Bipartisan Committee to Investigate the Preparation for and Response to Hurricane Katrina.* See US House of Representatives (2006:311).

6. A good deal of media coverage exposed what happened inside the city limits, including the ravaged Lower Ninth Ward. But St. Bernard Parish, bounded on the northwest by the Lower Ninth and on the southeast by the Gulf, was the only one to have been completely inundated. Scientists would later make clear the culpable role of the Army Corps of Engineers. See Van Heerden (2007b); Cobb (2013).

7. Another little-discussed part of the damage from Katrina involved an oil spill originating at the Murphy Oil refinery tank just south of Chalmette in Meraux. The spill unleashed 1.1 million gallons of toxic crude that spread to neighboring communities in the parish. For information about the spill and about the larger history of disaster in the parish, see Button (2010).

8. Freudenburg et al. (2009).

9. Anthony Wallace used this term to describe the desolation after a tornado disaster in Worcester, Massachusetts (1957:127).

10. Some of the Isleño family names, now commonly recognizable to anyone in

the parish, include Alfonso, Campo, Fernandez, Gonzales, Rodriguez, and Nunez (Wells 2008:44).

11. Some intermarried with white Cajuns who had settled to the west of the parish, but among whites, Isleño identity remained dominant in the lower parish. If most Isleños have now lost their Spanish language, they have held onto their heritage in other ways: their Catholic faith; their special foods, such as *caldo*; and traditional festivals, all of which continued to arouse pride and celebration. During the second week of March, an Isleños festival takes place on the grounds of the Isleños Museum complex, located on Bayou Road, on the very Bayou Terre aux Boeufs where Isleños had originally settled in the eighteenth century. The annual event features traditional costumes, dancing, and food, and it has become a "must do" festival for many in the parish and beyond.

12. In the Caribbean context, Creole has a clear meaning: born or "of" the local environment. In the context of southeast Louisiana, the term is more contested, so I have avoided using it, especially since family members don't use the term. Nonetheless, their history belongs to a Creole heritage, in which European and African mixed to form a new Creole language, new kinds of food, and new racial blends.

13. US Department of Health and Human Services, Substance Abuse and Mental Health Services Administration (2000).

14. Disaster scholars have used various terms for the special solidarity of community that develops in the immediate aftermath of a crisis, for example, the "community of sufferers," the "therapeutic community," or the "altruistic community." See Hoffman's review of the actions of Oakland firestorm survivors (1999:138–139); Oliver-Smith's discussion of the unusual gifting that occurred among survivors following the 1970 earthquake and avalanche in Yungay, Peru (1992:77–83); and Peek's demonstration of how Muslim Americans came together after 9/11 (2011:104–105). Erikson's study of the 1972 Buffalo Creek mining disaster documents an interesting exception to these patterns of solidarity among survivors (2000:200–201). Fordham points out that in her case studies of flooded communities, although therapeutic community arose, there was simultaneous competition, conflict, and stress (1999:22).

15. This elegant and economical definition of community was articulated by anthropologist John Watanabe, in relation to his study of the Maya in Guatemala. His work points out how, in the face of radical change and the trauma of war, Maya people restored their sense of community by drawing on collective traditions (1992).

CHAPTER 5: TRIAL BY TRAILER

1. These estimates come from US Department of Housing and Urban Development (2006) and include the damage from Hurricanes Katrina, Rita, and Wilma. See also Plyer (2008).

2. Brodsky (2007). According to Brodsky, "That figure includes a $900 million

purchase of 26,300 mobile and modular homes that FEMA later discovered could not be used in flood zones, where virtually all Katrina victims lived."

3. Stuckey (2005).

4. The Road Home program was put in place and funded by HUD and administered by the state of Louisiana.

5. Straub (2007).

6. Verderber (2008).

7. Erikson describes a similar phenomenon in *Everything in Its Path*, noting that the Buffalo Creek survivors were put in HUD-established trailer communities and that outsiders in charge made them feel like "beggars" and removed them from the sense of community they needed (2000:151). See also Fordham (1999).

8. In their book about change and transformation, Dan Heath and Chip Heath synthesize studies from numerous fields to show how fatigue from loss of control compromises personal motivation and clear reasoning (2010).

9. In 2012, plaintiffs in a class-action lawsuit won $43 million in claims against sixteen FEMA trailer manufacturers and contractors. Plaintiffs represented nearly half of the 114,000 households that had gotten FEMA trailers. Toxic levels of formaldehyde had been found to exist in the particleboard and plywood used in construction, and the chemical is associated with leukemia and nasal cancer (Aziz 2012).

10. In an emerging field, architectural and design professionals are working with psychologists to create cheap, temporary shelters that are also culturally appropriate. See, for example, the work of Japanese architect Shigeru Ban. Ban designs temporary shelters after natural disasters. His work makes use of cardboard, plastic beer crates, and paper tubes (Pogrebin 2014). See also Arslan and Unlu (2008).

11. Wardak, Coffey, and Trigunarsyah (2012:6).

CHAPTER 6: BAYOU SPEECH AND BAYOU STYLE

1. The assumption of effective messaging is critical to the field of study known as "disaster risk communication." Risk communication places central emphasis on making sure that messages work in the specific environment in which they are deployed. Not only must the content of the message be locally adapted, practitioners argue, but the message itself must be put in the hands of those whom community members trust. In this regard, disaster risk messages have evolved much more quickly to recognize the cultural specificity of effective communication. See, for example, Scott (2007); Lachlan and Spence (2007); Reynolds and Seeger (2012).

2. The word was apparently coined in 1944 by Texas congressman Maury Maverick, who expressed disdain for the "gobbledygook language" of his colleagues. "Perhaps I was thinking of the old bearded turkey gobbler back in Texas," he said, "always gobbledy-gobbling and strutting with ludicrous pomposity." See http://grammar.about.com/od/words/a/Doublespeak-Soft_Language-Gobbledygook.htm.

3. For a helpful discussion of the concept of marked and unmarked ways of

communicating, see the work of linguist Robin Lakoff, especially *The Language War* (2001).

4. For example, in an Indian hotel, pronounced HO-tel, one does not sleep. One orders a meal. In Australia, a hotel is a pub.

5. The Ebonics fiasco in Oakland, California, schools in 1996 cast a fascinating light on the fact that black speech, regarded as "bad English" by many in the American public, was fundamentally misunderstood even by black leaders. Ultimately, these leaders, including Jesse Jackson, reversed their positions after linguists made clear that black English is not inherently bad or good, it is a high-functioning, linguistically complex dialect that has roots in plantation Creole. "African American Vernacular English," as it is formally called, is a variation from Standard American English in patterned, regular ways that do not merit stigmatization.

6. There is an entire journalistic industry that has emerged in response to consumer difficulties with large, unresponsive companies. For example, the *New York Times* features a weekly business column called *The Haggler*, to which readers send their unresolved consumer complaints in hopes of assistance.

7. In her epic work about the impact of the 1970 earthquake on communities in the Peruvian Andes, Barbara Bode describes how language disconnects characterized the difference between government recovery agents and impacted residents (1990). Roberto Barrios (2010) has detailed how post-Katrina recovery planning teams organized meetings with residents of different areas of New Orleans and how their technical language brought rebuke from citizens present. Bolin (2006) has shown the need for Spanish-speaking caseworkers where Latinos are concentrated. However, as linguists point out, someone with a second-language capacity may be just as blind to cultural realities as someone who speaks no Spanish whatsoever. It is dangerous to assume that language translators can also solve less-visible problems related to cultural meanings and styles that go well beyond vocabulary.

8. Jacquemet (2011:476). See also Cushman (1998).

9. George Bernard Shaw (1856–1950), Irish author of sixty plays, including *My Fair Lady*, won the Nobel Prize in Literature in 1925.

10. "Sherry" had worked as a FEMA employee in various areas of the New Orleans region, including St. Bernard Parish. The work took place during several years following Katrina. She provided robust answers to my questions and expressed interest in helping me understand the disconnects with local people caused by FEMA's inflexible approach to recovery. She requested anonymity in my publications.

11. "Jonathan" was a FEMA employee who began as a "local hire" and eventually got promoted to a full-time temporary salary as a "CORE" employee and worked in several parishes from 2005 to 2009. He requested anonymity in my publications.

12. A number of disaster scholars have pointed out how tensions emerge between "us" and "them" after a disaster, especially when resources are involved. See Hoffman (1999:146); and Fordham (1999:25). Douglas (1970) provides classic anthropological insight into the functional power of accusation.

13. One example of contrasting conversation styles in black and white speech is

the difference between the standard middle-class "turn-taking" style of interacting as compared to the "voice overlap" style common in black interaction. The significance of this example alone demonstrates how confusion and misunderstanding occur easily when people enter into the other's social group. For a wonderful treatment of differences in black and white styles of storytelling and oral communication, see Shirley Brice Heath's *Ways with Words* (1983).

14. Well before Katrina, a number of engineers and scientists had predicted that a massive hurricane would strike coastal Louisiana and drown the city of New Orleans (Wilson 2001; Fischetti 2001; Mooney 2005; Van Heerden 2007b). FEMA had even conducted its own simulation of a major hurricane in the area the year before, called Hurricane Pam Exercise. The agency's website quotes FEMA's regional director, Ron Castleman, saying, "We made great progress this week in our preparedness efforts . . . These plans are essential for quick response to a hurricane but will also help in other emergencies" (July 2004).

15. See FEMA website for additional information: http://www.fema.gov/disaster-assistance-available-fema.

16. United States Senate (2006:17).

17. One of the billion-dollar multinationals that FEMA hired after Katrina was a Louisiana-based company, the Shaw Group. But their headquarters in Baton Rouge meant nothing to family members in St. Bernard Parish who were not recruited for the work Shaw subcontracted. The multinational scope of work, it appeared, made the close-by headquarters of little importance to residents of the area.

18. See report issued by the US House of Representatives Committee on Government Reform (2006:4–6). FEMA allocated a total of $10.8 billion to recovery, but the bulk of those funds went to nineteen multinationals. The committee's report is based on a review of more than 550 reports from government auditors and investigators. The reports reviewed in this publication were prepared by the Defense Contract Audit Agency and the Government Accountability Office, among others. See also Gotham, who notes that of the $3.2 billion FEMA allocated to Katrina recovery in the area of Individual Assistance (IA) and Technical Assistance (TAC), the majority went to four multinational companies: Fluor, Shaw, Bechtel, and CH2M Hill, which were not held to specific terms or conditions of accountability for their work (2012:637).

To keep their seats on the gravy train, some private contractors working in St. Bernard Parish ended up paying a local "toll." A few of these firms balked at the financial blackmail and their case has since landed in the courts. In December 2013, eight years after the storm, WDSU TV news broke a story about a lawsuit filed by an out-of-state trucking firm that FEMA had contracted with in early fall 2005 to do cleanup work in St. Bernard Parish. The firm was hired right at the time Buffy had been rebuffed by FEMA and made to return his load of trash to his work site. By that spring of 2006, the trucking firm from Mississippi was quietly pressured to pay tens of thousands of dollars in fees to a parish law firm in order to keep earning money as a FEMA contractor to collect trash in the parish. The contractor went to the FBI and pressed his case against the old-boy network in the parish, which was just exercising its power of coercion and intimidation. Read more at: http://www.wdsu.com/investigations/iteam-prominent-st-bernard-parish-figures-accused-of-extorting-katrina-cleanup-businessmen/23402314.

19. FEMA has used "local hires" in its recovery work since Hurricane Andrew in 1992, but these hires have been used primarily as cheap labor rather than advocates for local needs.

20. The 2004 inauguration of the ESF-14 is explained in a variety of FEMA documents, including its 2009 publication, *The Road to Recovery: 2008* (2009:3).

21. Louisiana Speaks is the "public face of the LRA" (the Louisiana Recovery Authority 2014:3–5). Its report notes that "there is no question that LTCR, the CRC, local government, and the general public have been engaged in a dynamic process that is laying the groundwork for recovery and creating a blueprint for long-term development. Local buy-in to the LTCR process is high and will continue to benefit the process and citizens of Saint Bernard Parish" (2014:5).

22. Structural racism offers a better explanation of persistent discrimination because it recognizes that when exclusionary practices are embedded across a variety of institutions and public spheres, the impact is far more powerful and thus more difficult to pinpoint and eradicate. See Bonilla-Silva (1996).

23. Homelessness after Katrina increased to record levels for any metropolitan area in the United States. By 2008, one in twenty-five people were homeless, a total of twelve thousand people. By 2013, those numbers had fallen significantly, and by 2014, there were fewer homeless than before the storm (White 2014).

24. The family's experience with contractor fraud was a well-documented problem. See Sisco (2009).

25. Instead, FEMA seemed much more concerned with ferreting out individuals who might be defrauding the agency. Despite the fact that FEMA contractors were found to have committed staggering amounts of fraud and to have wasted tens of millions of dollars, FEMA worked diligently and in highly public ways to identify fraudulent claims and prosecute individuals who were getting "too much" (Gotham 2012). One thing every FEMA worker was trained to spot was any "duplication of benefits" (interview with "Sherry," FEMA rep, 2014).

CHAPTER 7: WHOSE ROAD HOME?

1. Social theorist Pierre Bourdieu offers brilliant insights about the social values and tastes of people based on their socioeconomic upbringing (1977). For a searing look into the cultural divides of socioeconomic classes in the United States and the implications of these divides on the education of children, see sociologist Annette Lareau's *Unequal Childhoods* (2003).

2. There were many ethical dilemmas I faced in the course of this long-term fieldwork. Colleague Lori Peek and I shared our experiences and together realized

that the human-subjects protocols for doing research of this kind offered no help in anticipating the type of ethical land mines that had arisen for both of us over the years of our post-Katrina research. See Browne and Peek (2014); see also Browne (2009).

CHAPTER 8: ALMOST TO THE GROUND

1. See D'Antonio's "The State of Mental Health Care in Post-Katrina New Orleans" (2009).

2. St. Bernard Project, a volunteer-based rebuilding organization that was founded in 2006 in St. Bernard Parish, opened an auxiliary facility in 2009 devoted to mental health care of the people it was serving.

3. This aggregate number includes adult and child psychiatrists and psychoanalysts. See Lamberg's "Katrina's Mental Health Impact Lingers" (2008).

4. See FEMA website, http://www.fema.gov/additional-assistance#0.

5. Lamberg (2008).

6. In the list of authors of the document, I found anthropologist Elzbieta Gozdziak, PhD, research director for an institute at Georgetown University that studies international migration. The report identifies the special vulnerability of ethnic minorities and migrant communities that are impacted by disaster. Sociologists referenced in the guide included Kai Erikson, Russell Dynes, Ben Wisner, Brenda Phillips, and Elaine Enarson, among others.

7. Other disaster scholars have shown the devastating costs of breaking up social networks that were important to the provisioning of self-care and confidence in the midst of uncertainty (see Morrow 1997; Fussell 2012; Litt 2012).

8. In 2000, SAMHSA published the "Field Manual" as a pocket reference for the 123-page "Training Manual for Mental Health and Human Service Workers in Major Disasters."

9. See US Department of Health and Human Services, CDC (2005); US Department of Health and Human Services, SAMHSA (2000; 2003).

10. Racism can enable some to unfairly secure and hold onto power and wealth, and can cause systematically oppressed people to regard members of dominant groups and institutions with low levels of trust. Thus, like all injustice, the fruits of racism can undermine the basis for genuine democracy.

11. See http://www.census.gov/prod/2011pubs/acsbr10-07.pdf.

12. For a comprehensive look at the problems of succession and heir property in the aftermath of Katrina, and the implications of these problems for African Americans in particular, see Kluckow (2014).

13. Davidson and Wingate (2011).

14. Wang et al. (2013); Bender (2000); Davidson and Wingate (2011); and Borum (2012).

15. Dan Heath and Chip Heath discuss bright spots in their book about change (2010).

16. According to Wilkinson and experts in the nursing and mental health fields, powerlessness is "the perception that one's own action will not significantly affect an outcome; a perceived lack of control over a current situation" (2005:386). The problem, by various names, has also been identified as a problem for people recovering from disaster. See, for example, Erikson (2000); Bode (1990).

17. Classic early studies still remain seminal in identifying the powerful impact of a sense of control on health. See, for example, Langer and Rodin (1976); Lefcourt (1973).

18. As late as 2012, during the aftermath of Superstorm Sandy, politicians used these same insulting tropes of immorality to reference Katrina's primary victims: "Did Katrina Victims Really Spend Their Relief Money on Gucci Bags and Massage Parlors?" (Weissmann 2012).

19. For an analysis of how stereotypes about race permeated media coverage following Katrina, see Tierney, Bevc, and Kuligowski (2006).

20. Scholars of black history and the black church echoed what family members demonstrated. In my interview with Raphael Cassimere, local historian at the University of New Orleans, he pointed out how African Americans become extremely attached to their own home church because that is where a sense of belonging develops, where opportunities for leadership become possible, and where social recognition affirms everyday life. For that reason, churches with a similar doctrine or the same denomination, whether in Dallas or even nearby churches in the parish, do not serve the same role as one's home church. See Floyd-Thomas et al. (2007:101).

21. Limited trailer space had required Katie to adjust her way of preparing ingredients, doing some things in advance.

22. Actor Brad Pitt created a well-publicized housing project focused on innovative designs for the demolished Lower Ninth Ward area. Pitt's "Make it Right" Foundation has built affordable homes that are resistant to battering by storms, and some are even built to float.

CHAPTER 9: SETTLING

1. Philip Shepherd (2010) has elaborated at length on this idea. The philosophy of mereology, the relations of parts to wholes, is an entire field of study, popularized into English by Leonard and Goodman (1940).

2. See Browne (2004, 2010).

3. The term *habitus* refers to Pierre Bourdieu's concept of how people learn what they take for granted: manners, ways of speaking and interacting, values, foods, and ritual practices. *Habitus* is a concept that helps explain how people get attached to ways of seeing and doing that they grew up with (1977).

4. The "man-of-words" tradition in black culture is related to the emphasis on oral culture and finds expression in public oratory, black churches, rap and hip-hop, jive talk, and "sweet talk." The "call-and-response" style of black performance

is standard fare in black churches, and in black performances of all kinds, including gospel concerts and public speeches. Like the "man-of-words" tradition, the "call-and-response" tradition also comes from West Africa (Smitherman 2000).

5. By the end of 2008, nearly three and a half years after the storm, Louisiana's Road Home program had closed 120,155 files of homeowners who had applied for assistance, but 15,334, or nearly 13 percent of everyone who had applied for assistance, were still waiting. In Mississippi, the corresponding number of homeowners with closed files by the end of 2008 was 24,212; and 1,395 people were still waiting (less than 6 percent of total applicants). These numbers are published by the Public Affairs Research Council of Louisiana, a private nonprofit research organization, in the GulfGov Reports (2008).

6. All of the FEMA staff members I spoke to asked me not to use their names when conveying their perspective on what happened during the recovery.

CHAPTER 10: CALL TO RACE

1. British Petroleum (BP) chartered the oil rig and operated it. The sullied Gulf waters were captive to an unstopped flow of oil for eighty-seven days, a spill that ultimately released nearly five million barrels of oil into coastal areas of the Gulf states. See Robertson and Krauss (2010) and Valentine et al. (2014).

2. Charles might have guessed that he would be tested in uncomfortable ways. In 1991, not long before he had begun policing the streets, St. Bernard Parish had voted overwhelmingly in support of the radical right-wing politician and former presidential candidate David Duke, who was running then for governor of Louisiana. By a margin of 56 percent to 44 percent, parish residents had endorsed the well-known segregationist and former grand wizard of the Ku Klux Klan, a man who argued for the rationality of his views in the popular media, stating, "All people have a basic human right to preserve their own heritage." No other parish in the New Orleans region had supported Duke over Edwards, drawing attention to St. Bernard Parish as a conspicuous standout, a parish many from the New Orleans area already regarded as a site of rampant, old-fashioned racism.

3. Naomi Klein coined the term "disaster capitalism" and brilliantly captures the workings of this phenomenon in *The Shock Doctrine: The Rise of Disaster Capitalism* (2008).

4. Lugo (2014:93).

5. Turni Bazile (2006). See also a 2006 press release from Lawyers' Committee for Civil Rights Under Law: "Fair Housing Advocates Seek to Halt Discriminatory Zoning Rule," at http://www.lawyerscommittee.org/admin/fair_housing/documents/files/0009.pdf.

6. Liza Lugo documents startling racial epithets spray-painted at construction sites for affordable housing that the parish council tried to block (2014:93).

7. See http://www.justice.gov/crt/about/hce/documents/stbernardsettle.pdf.

8. Title VIII of the Civil Rights Act of 1968 is commonly referred to as the Fair Housing Act. For more information from the news story, see http://www.gnofair housing.org/programs/enforcement/st-bernard-parish/. See also http://www.nola .com/crime/index.ssf/2012/10/st_bernard_parish_fair_housing.html.

9. See http://www.nola.com/education/index.ssf/2012/05/st_bernard_parish _schools_get.html.

10. Anthropologists understand the value of local decision making. Decades of research drive home the fact that only by keeping local people at the center can change, even radical change, be both positive and sustainable. Work in modernization and international development, for example, where rapid socioeconomic change is introduced from the outside, is closely analogous to post-disaster situations that require massive inputs to rebuild infrastructure and communities. Researchers have shown that the failures of international development projects conducted by the World Bank, USAID, and other nongovernmental organizations involve projects that could not be sustained, precisely because they did not attend to putting the "people first." See Cernea (1991); and Chambers (1997).

11. By 2010, in the key population centers of the parish, blacks had returned at double the proportions of whites, 83 percent compared to 42 percent (US Census Bureau 2010). It was a sad irony that they were the ones to lose the longtime indicators of the strength and cultural independence of their community. Without a high school, a major grocery store, or a bank, the lower parish seemed to have disappeared.

12. This tourist brochure produced by the St. Bernard Parish Tourist Commission promotes the history of the parish by giving visitors a self-guided tour of historical sites, including sites of former plantations in the lower parish. A digital version can be found at http://www.gulf-of-mexico.com/Louisana/St._Bernard_Brochure .pdf. On the website of the St. Bernard Parish Office of Tourism, the visitor learns that the St. Bernard Parish is "New Orleans' Most Historic Neighbor." See http:// www.visitstbernard.com.

13. Daniell DiGiuseppe was the project officer. The brochure was published in *Preservation in Print* by the Louisiana State Historic Preservation Office in December 2008–January 2009.

14. See "Shadowboxing in the Mangrove" (Price 1997).

15. The term "systemic causation" was coined by cognitive scientist and linguist George Lakoff (2012) to explain types of causation that are indirect and even invisible to the observer but nonetheless powerful. See http://www.huffingtonpost .com/george-lakoff/sandy-climate-change_b_2042871.html.

CHAPTER 11: BY AND BY

1. Williams and Dixie (2003:4).

2. Williams and Dixie (2003:5); and Dvorak (1991).

CODA

1. See Henrich, Heine, and Norenzayan (2010) for new cognitive research that demonstrates the role of cultural influences in shaping how we think and feel. One example includes the global phenomenon of post-traumatic stress disorder (PTSD), a mental disorder that is not universal, despite our attempts to treat it as such with a universal template of diagnosis and treatment. Recently, researchers studying PTSD have found that the checklist of symptoms once assumed to be universal does not capture the particular form of stress that crops up in different cultural groups. That's because the feeling of anxiety or stress following a traumatic event is always a "cultural expression," one that the surrounding cultural group recognizes and validates. These findings support a long tradition of research in medical anthropology known as "culture-bound syndromes," in which stress manifests in ways that are particular to the cultural group. For elaboration of these ideas, and a discussion of how PTSD diagnoses in Sri Lanka after the 2004 tsunami completely missed the nature of trauma as it was experienced locally, see Watters (2010:65–126).

2. Psychologists tell us that in the process of difficult change, people do far better when they are able to feel "emotional wins" early and with some frequency. See Heath and Heath (2010).

3. Hayashi (2012:85).

4. Hayashi (2012:78).

BIBLIOGRAPHY

Andersen, C. F., J. A. Battjes, D. E. Daniel, B. Edge, W. Espey, R. B. Gilbert,
T. L. Jackson, D. Kennedy, D. S. Mileti, J. K. Mitchell, P. Nicholson, C. A. Pugh,
G. Tamaro, R. Traver, J. Buhrman, C. V. Dinges, J. E. Durrant, J. Howell, and
L. H. Roth
    2007 The New Orleans Hurricane Protection System: What Went Wrong and
        Why. Report. Reston, Va.: American Society of Civil Engineers, ASC
        Publications.

Arslan, Hakan, and Alper Unlu
    2008 The Role of NGO's in the Context of Post-Disaster Housing in Turkey.
        Paper presented at the 4th International i-Rec Conference, Rotterdam,
        Holland, May.

Austin, Diane E.
    2006 Coastal Exploitation, Land Loss, and Hurricanes: A Recipe for Disaster.
        American Anthropologist 108(4):671–691.

Aziz, Naeesa
    2012 FEMA Trailer Makers Poised to Hand Over $43 Million Settlement. BET
        News. May 31. http://www.bet.com/news/national/2012/05/31/fema-trailer
        -makers-poised-to-hand-over-43-million-settlement.html.

Banks, J. A., and Cherry A. McGee Banks, eds.
    2010 Multicultural Education: Issues and Perspectives. Hoboken, N.J.: Wiley.

Barrios, Roberto
    2010 Budgets, Plans and Politics: Questioning the Role of Expert Knowledge in
        Disaster Reconstruction. Anthropology News 51(7):7–8.

Bateman, Julie M., and Bob Edwards
    2002 Gender and Evacuation: A Closer Look at Why Women Are More Likely
        to Evacuate for Hurricanes. Natural Hazards Review 3(3):107–117.

Bellah, Robert N., Richard Madsen, William M. Sullivan, Ann Swidler, and
Steven M. Tipton
    1985 Habits of the Heart: Individualism and Commitment in American Life.
        Berkeley: University of California Press.

Bender, M.
    2000 Suicide and Older African-American Women. Mortality 5(2):158–170.

Bode, Barbara
    1990 No Bells to Toll: Destruction and Creation in the Andes. New York:
        Charles Scribner's Sons.

Bolin, Bob

2006 Race, Class, Ethnicity, and Disaster Vulnerability. In Handbook of Disaster Research. Havidán Rodríguez, Enrico L. Quarantelli, and Russell R. Dynes, eds. Pp. 113–129. New York: Springer.

Bonilla-Silva, Eduardo

1996 Rethinking Racism: Toward a Structural Interpretation. American Sociological Review 62(3):465–480.

Borum, V.

2012 African American Women's Perceptions of Depression and Suicide Risk and Protection: A Womanist Exploration. Affilia 27(3):316–327.

Bourdieu, Pierre

1977 Outline of a Theory of Practice [original publication 1972]. Cambridge: Cambridge University Press.

Brodsky, Robert

2007 Overcoming Katrina. Government Executive. May 15. http://www.govexec .com/magazine/features/2007/05/overcoming-katrina/24435/.

Browne, Katherine E.

2004 Creole Economics: Caribbean Cunning Under the French Flag. Austin: University of Texas Press.

2009 Economics and Morality: Introduction. Pp. 1–40. In Economics and Morality: Anthropological Approaches. Katherine E. Browne and B. Lynne Milgram, eds. Lanham, Md.: Altamira Press.

2010 Lifting the Weight of History: Women Entrepreneurs in Martinique/ Au Tournant de l'Histoire: les femmes chefs d'entreprise en Martinique. Documentary film. Broadcast on French national and overseas TV, and on the French global satellite channel, TV5.

Browne, Katherine E., and Ginny Martin

2007 Still Waiting: Life After Katrina. Documentary film produced by Ginny Martin and Katherine E. Browne. Broadcast on PBS stations in US and Canada.

Browne, Katherine E., and Lori Peek

2014 Beyond the IRB: An Ethical Toolkit for Long-Term Disaster Research. International Journal of Mass Emergencies and Disasters 32(1): 82–120.

Button, Gregory

2010 Disaster Culture: Knowledge and Uncertainty in the Wake of Human and Environmental Catastrophe. Walnut Creek, Calif.: Left Coast Press.

Caplan, Patricia

1997 Approaches to the Study of Food, Health, and Identity. In Food, Health, and Identity. Patricia Caplan, ed. Pp. 1–31. London: Routledge.

Cernea, M. M., ed.

1991   Putting People First: Sociological Variables in Rural Development. Oxford: Oxford University Press.

Chambers, Robert

1997   Whose Reality Counts: Putting the First Last. London: Intermediate Technology Publications.

Checker, Melissa

2005   Polluted Promises: Environmental Racism and the Search for Justice in a Southern Town. New York: NYU Press.

Cobb, James

2013   Flood of Lies: The St. Rita's Nursing Home Tragedy. Gretna, La.: Pelican Publishing.

Colton, Craig

2009   Perilous Place, Powerful Storms: Hurricane Protection in Coastal Louisiana. Jackson: University of Mississippi Press.

Couvillion, B. R., J. A. Barras, G. D. Steyer, William Sleavin, Michelle Fischer, Holly Beck, Nadine Trahan, Brad Griffin, and David Heckman

2011   Land Area Change in Coastal Louisiana from 1932 to 2010: U. S. Geological Survey Scientific Investigations Map 3164, scale 1:265,000. Pamphlet. 12 pp.

Cushman, Ellen

1998   The Struggle and the Tools: Oral and Literate Strategies in an Inner City Community. Albany: State University of New York Press.

D'Antonio, Heather

2009   The State of Mental Health Care in Post-Katrina New Orleans. Louisiana Law Review 69(3):661–689.

Davidson, C., and L. Wingate

2011   Racial Disparities and Protective Factors for Suicide. Journal of Black Psychology 37:499–516.

Davis-Wheeler, Clare

2000   Louisiana Coastal Land Loss. Tulane University report. http://www.tulane .edu/~bfleury/envirobio/enviroweb/LandLoss/LandLoss.htm.

Deleuze, Gilles, and Félix Guattari

1980   A Thousand Plateaus: Capitalism and Schizophrenia. Brian Massumi, trans. Minneapolis: University of Minnesota Press.

Din, Gilbert

1988   The Canary Islanders of Louisiana. Baton Rouge: Louisiana State University Press.

Douglas, Mary

1970   Witchcraft: Confessions and Accusations. London: Tavistock.

Dvorak, Katherine

1991 An African American Exodus: The Segregation of the Southern Churches. Brooklyn: Carlson Publishing.

Erikson, Kai

2000 Everything in Its Path: Destruction of Community in the Buffalo Creek Flood. [Original publication 1976.] New York: Simon and Schuster.

Federal Emergency Management Agency (FEMA)

2009 The Road to Recovery 2008: Emergency Support Function #14, Long Term Community Recovery. August.

Fischetti, Mark

2001 Drowning New Orleans. Scientific American 285(4):76–85.

Floyd-Thomas, Stacey, Juan Floyd-Thomas, Carol B. Duncan, Stephen G. Ray Jr., and Nancy Lynne Westfield

2007 Black Church Studies: An Introduction. Nashville, Tenn.: Abingdon Press.

Fordham, Maureen

1999 The Intersection of Gender and Social Class in Disaster: Balancing Resilience and Vulnerability. International Journal of Mass Emergencies and Disasters 17(1):15–36.

Freudenburg, William R., Robert Gramling, Kai T. Erikson, and Shirley Laska

2009 Catastrophe in the Making: The Engineering of Katrina and the Disasters of Tomorrow. Washington, D.C.: Island Press.

Fullilove, Mindy

2004 Root Shock: How Tearing Up City Neighborhoods Hurts America and What We Can Do About It. New York: Ballantine Books.

Fussell, Elizabeth

2012 Help from Family, Friends, and Strangers During Hurricane Katrina: Finding the Limits of Social Networks. In Displaced: Life in the Katrina Diaspora. Lynn Weber and Lori Peek, eds. Pp. 150–166. Austin: University of Texas Press.

Gill, Duane A., and J. Steven Picou

1997 The Day the Water Died: Cultural Impacts of the Exxon Valdez Oil Spill. J. Steven Picou, Duane A. Gill, and Maurie J. Cohen, eds. Pp. 167–187. In The Exxon Valdez Disaster: Readings on a Modern Social Problem. Dubuque, Iowa: Kendall Hunt.

Glissant, Edouard

1981 Le Discours Antillais. Paris: Seuil.

1997 Poetics of Relation. Betsy Wing, trans. Ann Arbor: University of Michigan Press.

Gotham, Kevin Fox

2012 Disaster Inc.: Privatization and Post-Katrina Rebuilding in New Orleans. Perspectives on Politics 10(3):633–646.

Granovetter, Mark
  1973 The Strength of Weak Ties. American Journal of Sociology 78(6):1360–1380.
Gulfgov Reports
  2008 Three Years After Katrina and Rita, Challenges Remain. Public Affairs Research Council. http://www.parlouisiana.org.
Harvey, David
  1996 Justice, Nature, and the Geography of Difference. Oxford: Blackwell.
Hayashi, Isao
  2012 Folk Performing Art in the Aftermath of the Great East Japan Earthquake. Asian Anthropology 11:75–88.
Heath, Dan, and Chip Heath
  2010 Switch: How to Change Things When Change Is Hard. New York: Crown Business Publishers.
Heath, Shirley Brice
  1983 Ways with Words. Language, Life and Work in Communities. Cambridge: Cambridge University Press.
Henrich, Joseph, Steven J. Heine, and Ara Norenzayan
  2010 The Weirdest People in the World? Behavioral and Brain Sciences 33: 61–135.
Hirsch, Arnold R., and Joseph Logsdon, eds.
  1992 Creole New Orleans: Race and Americanization. Baton Rouge: Louisiana State University Press.
Hoffman, Susanna M.
  1999 The Worst of Times, the Best of Times: Toward a Model of Cultural Response to Disaster. In The Angry Earth: Disaster in Anthropological Perspective. Anthony Oliver-Smith and Susanna Hoffman, eds. Pp. 134–155. London and New York: Routledge.
  2013 The Oakland Berkeley Firestorm: A Twenty-Year Chronicle of Emotions, Effects, and Their Import. Paper presented at the annual meeting of the American Anthropological Association, November 23.
Hoffman, Susanna M., and Anthony Oliver-Smith, eds.
  2002 Catastrophe and Culture: The Anthropology of Disaster. Santa Fe, N.Mex.: School for Advanced Research Press.
Jacquemet, Marco
  2011 Crosstalk 2.0: Asylum and Communicative Breakdowns. Text and Talk 31(4):475–497.
Klein, Naomi
  2008 The Shock Doctrine: The Rise of Disaster Capitalism. New York: Picador.
Klinenberg, Eric
  2003 Heat Wave: A Social Autopsy of Disaster in Chicago. Chicago: University of Chicago Press.

Kluckow, Rich

2014 The Impact of Heir Property on Post-Katrina Housing Recovery in New Orleans. Master's thesis, Department of Sociology, Colorado State University.

Lachlan, K. A., and P. R. Spence

2007 Audience Responses and Informational Needs: Considering Diversity in Crisis Communication. *In* Diversity and Mass Communication: Evidence of Impact. A. Ferguson and A. R. Narro, eds. Pp. 157–180. Southlake, Tex.: Fountainhead Press.

Lakoff, George

2012 Global Warming Systemically Caused Hurricane Sandy. The Berkeley Blog. November 5. http://blogs.berkeley.edu/2012/11/05/global-warming -systemically-caused-hurricane-sandy/.

Lakoff, Robin Tolmach

2001 The Language War. Berkeley: University of California Press.

Lamberg, L.

2008 Katrina's Mental Health Impact Lingers. Journal of the American Medical Association 300(9):1011–1013.

Langer, E. J., and J. Rodin

1976 The Effects of Choice and Enhanced Personal Responsibility for the Aged: A Field Experiment in an Institutional Setting. Journal of Personality and Social Psychology 34(2):191–198.

Lareau, Annette

2003 Unequal Childhoods: Class, Race and Family Life. Berkeley: University of California Press.

Lefcourt, H. M.

1973 The Function of the Illusions of Control and Freedom. The American Psychologist 28(5):417–425.

Leonard, H. S. and N. Goodman

1940 The Calculus of Individuals and Its Uses. Journal of Symbolic Logic 5:45–55.

Lewis, Pierce F.

2003 New Orleans: The Making of an Urban Landscape. Charlottesville: University of Virginia Press.

Lieberman, Matthew

2013 Social: Why Our Brains Are Wired to Connect. New York: Crown Publishers.

Litt, Jacquelyn

2012 We Need to Get Together with Each Other: Women's Narratives of Help in Katrina's Displacement. *In* Displaced: Life in the Katrina Diaspora.

Lynn Weber and Lori Peek, eds. Pp. 167–182. Austin: University of Texas Press.

Lugo, Liza

2014 How Do Hurricane Katrina's Winds Blow? Racism in 21st Century New Orleans. Santa Barbara, Calif.: Praeger.

McGuire, Tom

2006 Louisiana's Oysters, America's Wetlands, and the Storms of 2005. American Anthropologist 108(4):692–705.

Midlo Hall, Gwendolyn

1992a Africans in Colonial Louisiana. Baton Rouge: Louisiana State University Press.

1992b The Formation of Afro-Creole Culture. In Creole New Orleans: Race and Americanization. Arnold R. Hirsch and Joseph Logsdon, eds. Pp. 58–87. Baton Rouge: Louisiana State University Press.

Molotch, Harvey

1976 The City as a Growth Machine. American Journal of Sociology 82(2): 309–332.

Mooney, Chris

2005 Thinking Big About Hurricanes. The American Prospect. May 23.

Morrow, Betty Hearn

1997 Stretching the Bonds: The Families of Andrew. In Hurricane Andrew: Ethnicity, Gender and the Sociology of Disasters. Walter Gillis Peacock, Betty Hearn Morrow, and Hugh Gladwin, eds. Pp. 141–170. London and New York: Routledge.

Norris, Fran, Susan P. Stevens, Betty Pfefferbaum, Karen F. Wyche, and Rose L. Pfefferbaum

2008 Community Resilience as a Metaphor, Theory, Set of Capacities, and Strategy for Disaster Readiness. American Journal of Community Psychology 41:127–150.

Oliver-Smith, Anthony

1992 The Martyred City: Death and Rebirth in the Andes. Prospect Heights, Ill.: Waveland Press.

2002 Introduction and Theorizing Disaster. In Catastrophe and Culture: The Anthropology of Disaster. Susanna M. Hoffman and Anthony Oliver-Smith, eds. Pp. 1–47. Santa Fe, N.Mex.: School for Advanced Research Press.

2010 Voices in the Storm: Social Relations of Relief and Reconstruction. Anthropology News (October):14–15.

Peek, Lori

2011 Behind the Backlash: Muslim Americans After 9/11. Philadelphia: Temple University Press.

2012 They Call It "Katrina Fatigue": Displaced Families and Discrimination in Colorado. *In* Displaced: Life in the Katrina Diaspora. Lynn Weber and Lori Peek, eds. Pp. 31–46. Austin: University of Texas Press.

Petryna, Adriana

2004 Biological Citizenship: The Science and Politics of Chernobyl-Exposed Populations. Osiris 19:250–265.

Plyer, Allison

2008 Four Years After the Storm: The Road Home Program's Impact on Greater New Orleans. Testimony presented to the House Subcommittee on Housing and Community Opportunity on August 8, 2008, by Deputy Director of the Greater New Orleans Community Data Center.

Pogrebin, Robin

2014 Pritzker Architecture Prize Goes to Shigeru Ban. New York Times. March 24.

Polanyi, Michael

1966 The Tacit Dimension. Chicago: University of Chicago Press.

Price, Richard

1997 Shadowboxing in the Mangrove. Cultural Anthropology 12(1):3–36.

Rauch, Jonathan

2006 Struggling to Survive. The Atlantic. August 15.

Reynolds, Barbara, and Matthew Seeger

2012 Crisis and Emergency Risk Communication. Centers for Disease Control and Prevention. http://emergency.cdc.gov/cerc/.

Ritchie, Liesel Ashley, Duane A. Gill, and Courtney N. Farnham

2012 Recreancy Revisited: Beliefs About Institutional Failure Following the Exxon Valdez Oil Spill. Society and Natural Resources: An International Journal 26:655–671.

Robertson, Campbell, and Clifford Krauss

2010 Gulf Spill Is the Largest of Its Kind, Scientists Say. New York Times. August 2.

Rosenthal, Sandy

2012 The Spectacular Failure of the Outfall Canals in New Orleans During Katrina: How Did It Happen? Research report issued by Levees.org. August 22.

Russell, Gordon

2005 Nagin Orders First-Ever Mandatory Evacuation of New Orleans. Times-Picayune. August 28.

Sahlins, Marshall

1976 Culture and Practical Reason. Chicago: University of Chicago Press.

Scott, John C.

2007 Concept Paper: Importance of Cultural Competency in Disaster Management. Center for Public Service Communications. Consensus Building Meeting for the Cultural Competence for Disaster Preparedness and Crisis Response (CCDPCR) project.

Shepherd, Philip

2010 New Self, New World: Recovering Our Senses in the Twenty-First Century. Berkeley: North Atlantic Books.

Sisco, Annette

2009 Point of View: Justice Elusive in Post-Katrina Contractor Fraud. Times-Picayune. July 31.

Smitherman, Geneva

2000 Black Talk: Words and Phrases from the Hood to the Amen Corner. New York: Mariner Books.

Stack, Carol B.

1983 All Our Kin: Strategies for Survival in a Black Community. New York: Basic Books.

Straub, Richard O.

2007 Health Psychology. New York: Worth Publishing.

Stuckey, Mike

2005 Life in a New FEMA Trailer. MSNBC, October 25, 2005. http://rising fromruin.msnbc.com/2005/10/new_life_in_a_f.html.

Tierney, Kathleen, Christine Bevc, and Erica Kuligowski

2006 Metaphors Matter: Disaster Myths, Media Frames, and Their Consequences in Hurricane Katrina. Annals of the American Academy of Political and Social Science 604(1):57–81.

Turni Bazile, Karen

2006 Bias Lawsuit Puts Council on Defensive: Lawyer Hired to Fight Allegation of Discrimination in St. Bernard Parish. Times-Picayune. November 8.

United States Department of Health and Human Services, Centers for Disease Control.

2005 Disaster Mental Health Primer: Key Principles, Issues and Questions. August 30, 2005.

United States Department of Health and Human Services, Substance Abuse and Mental Health Services Administration

2000 Field Manual for Mental Health and Human Services Workers in Major Disasters. Rockville, Md.

2000 Training Manual for Mental Health and Human Services Workers in Major Disasters. 2d edition. Washington, D.C.

United States Department of Health and Human Services, Substance Abuse and Mental Health Services Administration, Center for Mental Health Services
  2003 Cultural Competence in Disaster Mental Health Programs: Guiding Principles and Recommendations. Rockville, Md.

United States Department of Housing and Urban Development: Office of Policy Development and Research
  2006 Current Housing Unit Damage Estimates: Hurricanes Katrina, Rita and Wilma. February 12, 2006 (revised April 7, 2006).

United States House of Representatives Committee on Government Reform—Minority Staff, Special Investigative Division
  2006 Waste, Fraud, and Abuse in Hurricane Katrina Contracts. Washington D.C.: US Government Printing Office.

United States House of Representatives Select Bipartisan Committee to Investigate the Preparation for and Response to Hurricane Katrina
  2006 A Failure of Initiative: Final Report. Washington D.C.: US Government Printing Office.

United States Senate Committee on Homeland Security and Governmental Affairs
  2006 Hurricane Katrina: A Nation Still Unprepared. Washington D.C.: US Government Printing Office.

Valentine, David L., G. Burch Fisher, Sarah C. Bagby, Robert K. Nelson, Christopher M. Reddy, Sean P. Sylva, and Mary A. Woo
  2014 Fallout Plume of Submerged Oil from Deepwater Horizon. Proceedings of the National Academy of Sciences of the United States of America (PNAS) 111(45):15906–15911.

Van Heerden, Ivor
  2007a The Failure of the New Orleans Levee System Following Hurricane Katrina and the Pathway Forward. Public Administration Review 67(s1):24–35.
  2007b The Storm: What Went Wrong and Why During Hurricane Katrina. New York: Penguin Books.

Verderber, Stephen
  2008 Emergency Housing in the Aftermath of Hurricane Katrina: An Assessment of the FEMA Travel Trailer Program. Journal of Housing and the Built Environment 23(4):367–381.

Wallace, Anthony F. C.
  1957 Tornado in Worcester. Disaster Study Number Three, Committee on Disaster Studies, National Academy of Sciences—National Research Council.

Wang, M., J. Wong, K. Tran, P. Nyutu, and A. Spears
  2013 Reasons for Living, Social Support, and Afrocentric Worldview: Assessing Buffering Factors Related to Black Americans' Suicidal Behavior. Archives of Suicide Research 17:136–147.

Wardak, Zabihullah S., Vaughan Coffey, and Bambang Trigunarsyah
2012   Rebuilding Housing After a Disaster: Factors for Failure. *In* Fumihiko Yamada and Ryuji Kakimoto, eds. Proceedings of 8th Annual International Conference of the International Institute for Infrastructure, Renewal and Reconstruction (IIIRR), Kumamoto University, Kumamoto, Japan, August, pp. 292–300.

Watanabe, John
1992   Maya Saints and Souls in a Changing World. Austin: University of Texas Press.

Watters, Ethan
2010   Crazy Like Us: The Globalization of the American Psyche. New York: Simon and Schuster.

Weissmann, Jordan
2012   Did Katrina Victims Really Spend Their Relief Money on Gucci Bags and Massage Parlors? The Atlantic. October 31.

Wells, Ken
2008   The Good Pirates of the Forgotten Bayous: Fighting to Save a Way of Life in the Wake of Hurricane Katrina. New Haven: Yale University Press.

White, Jaquetta
2014   Fewer Homeless People Living on Streets in Orleans, Jefferson. New Orleans Advocate. May 4. http://www.theneworleansadvocate.com/home/9058786-172/fewer-homeless-people-living-on.

Wilkinson, J. M.
2005   Prentice Hall Nursing Diagnosis Handbook with NIC Interventions and NOC Outcomes. 8th edition. Upper Saddle River, N.J.: Pearson Education.

Williams, Juan, and Quinton Dixie
2003   This Far by Faith. New York: HarperCollins.

Wilson, Jim
2001   New Orleans Is Sinking. Popular Mechanics. September 11.

Wolshon, Brian
2006   Evacuation Plan and Lessons Learned for NOLA. National Academy of Engineering. http://www.nae.edu/Publications/Bridge/TheAftermathof Katrina/EvacuationPlanningandEngineeringforHurricaneKatrina.aspx.

Worldwatch Institute
2006   Louisiana Counties Hit Hardest by Hurricane Katrina Suffer Massive Population Loss. Based on June 2006 data collected by US Census Bureau and reported in Special Population Estimates for Impacted Counties in the Gulf Coast Area, June 2006. http://www.worldwatch.org/node/4397.

African American Vernacular English (AAVE) compared to Standard American English (SAE) Teachers Guide
https://www.sdcity.edu/Portals/0/CollegeServices/StudentServices /LearningCommunities/Af.Amer.crr.pdf

FEMA Disaster Assistance Related to Housing
http://www.fema.gov/disaster-assistance-available-fema

FEMA Disaster Assistance Related to Counseling
http://www.fema.gov/additional-assistance#0

FEMA's Hurricane Pam Exercise (July 2004)
http://www.fema.gov/news-release/2004/07/23/hurricane-pam-exercise -concludes

Louisiana Recovery Authority (2014). Louisiana Recovery Authority Sunsets
http://www.lra.louisiana.gov/index.cfm

Louisiana Speaks. Saint Bernard Parish Plan. (2014)
http://www.louisianaspeaksparishplans.org/IndParishHomepage _CommunityInvolvement.cfm?EntID=13   http://www.louisianaspeaks -parishplans.org/indparishhomepage.cfm?EntID=13

Track of Katrina
http://www.srh.noaa.gov/jan/?n=2005_08_29_hurricane_katrina_outbreak

National Science Foundation. May 22, 2006
"Researchers Release Draft Final Report on New Orleans Levees" https:// www.nsf.gov/news/news_summ.jsp?cntn_id=107007

Hurricane Betsy info
http://www.hurricanescience.org/history/storms/1960s/betsy/

NOAA: Saffir Simpson Hurricane Wind Scale
http://www.nhc.noaa.gov/aboutsshws.php

Wikipedia
http://www.en.wikipedia.org/wiki/St. Bernard Parish, Louisiana. http:// www.wunderground.com/education/Katrinas_surge_part05.asp

CBN
http://www.cbn.com/health/naturalhealth/drsears_mindbodydiet.aspx
http://www.wdsu.com/investigations/iteam-prominent-st-bernard-parish -figures-accused-of-extorting-katrina-cleanup-businessmen/23402314

ABOUT THE AUTHOR AND SERIES EDITOR

KATHERINE E. BROWNE is Professor of Anthropology at Colorado State University in Fort Collins. She has published two previous books and produced two documentary films, including *Still Waiting: Life After Katrina*, which also portrays the family in this book. It has been broadcast on PBS stations in the United States and Canada.

KAI ERIKSON, SERIES EDITOR, is Professor Emeritus of Sociology and American Studies at Yale University. He is a past president of the American Sociological Association, winner of the MacIver and Sorokin Awards from the ASA, author of *A New Species of Trouble: Explorations in Disaster, Trauma, and Community*, and his research and teaching interests include American communities, human disasters, and ethnonational conflict.

INDEX

Family and community members are alphabetized by nickname or first name, with family name and given name, if any, in parentheses. Locators followed by *f* signify illustrations.

coastal land loss, xxxvf, 63–64

collective grief, 36, 209n7

comfort, 150, 192, 193f

communication, 91, 107, 191–192, 212n1, 212–213n3. *See also* culture brokers; language

community: and collective traditions, 211n15; cultural needs of, 87; expression of, 191–192; imaginary versus real, 124–125; and poverty, 176; power of, 72–73; and resilience, 60; and sense of control, 212n7; and solidarity after disaster, 105, 211n14; symbols of, 219n11. *See also* black community; Isleños

Community Development Block Grants, 170

Connie (Tipado): as culture broker, 2, 23–24, 25f, 31–37, 39, 54, 94–95; on culture shock, 43–46; and FEMA applications, 61, 91–92, 154; and Katie's FEMA trailer, 87–88; on Katie's Road Home application, 139; and Katie's viewing and wake, 181, 184–185; on Katrina devastation, 26–27, 140; and Katrina evacuation, 5–6, 11, 13, 16, 22; in kin charts, xxf, xxviif; making contact with, 207n3; and race relations, 162, 174; on racial bias in St. Bernard Parish, 73–75; and weak ties, 209n6. *See also* culture brokers

contractors, 86–87, 215n25. *See also* fraud

cooking: as cultural resource, 53f, 124; and family, 35, 128; and FEMA trailers, 84; and recovery, 193f; as source of comfort, 49; as source of control, 111; and Trashell's wedding celebration, 133–134. *See also* food

corruption, 214–215n18

counseling, 122–123. *See also* mental health providers

Covington, 166

Creole, meaning of, 211n12

cultural competence, 124, 125, 130

cultural resources, 53f

cultural specificity, 212n1

culture brokers, 23, 25f, 31–33, 38f, 194–195. *See also* communication; Connie (Tipado)

culture cycle, 193f

culture shock, 43–46, 50

Cynthia (Winesbury), 9f; and church, 150, 199f; and cooking, 42, 52, 133; in Dallas, 34–35; and family gatherings, 7–8; as family historian, 144; and Hurricane Betsy, 12; at Johnson-Fernandez family reunion, 146f; in kin charts, xxf, xxiiif–xxxif; and kin relationships, 10, 26, 31; on life in FEMA trailers, 82–84, 128; on new Verret church, 136–137; and parish as home, 73; and recovery of mother's photo, 67f; and return to St. Bernard Parish, 60; and Road Home payment, 109, 156; on snakes in FEMA trailers, 81; sociability of, 112; and succession, 127, 130; work of, 59; and work with disabled children, 69

Cynthia's Branch, xxvf

Dallas: and communication, 43, 94, 149; and Connie as culture broker, 24, 25f, 37, 39, 91–92, 154; and cooking, 51–52, 132; and evacuation, 11–13, 14f, 23, 31, 204; and foods different from bayou, 41, 43, 47, 48–50, 62; versus St. Bernard Parish, 72–75, 163

Darleene (Smith), 150, 152–153

Davis (Johnson), xxif, xxiif, 34, 133, 144, 148

Dean, Lynn, 11, 165, 207n9

Deborah (Green): childhood home of, 80; at Connie's home in Dallas, 26; and FEMA trailer, 61; on food traditions, 42–43, 48–49; in kin charts, xxviif

Department of Health and Human Services (HHS), 123–124

Department of Homeland Security, 99, 101, 208n1. *See also* FEMA

Department of Housing and Urban Development (HUD), 79, 92, 212n4, 212n7

desegregation, 158, 159, 160f

Deshernique (Maurice), xxxf, 198f

Desi (Santiago, Desiree), 133, 152, 196f, 198f
disaster capitalism, 164, 218n3
Disaster Relief Act of 1974, 99
disaster studies, 95, 123, 204–205, 213n12, 217n16
Donnatte (Maurice), 96–97, 133, 146f, 153, 196f, 198f
Doozer (Winesbury, Wayne), 27, 48, 152
Dude (Holmes, Charles), xxixf, 81, 132, 190
Duke, David, 218n2
Dunbar's number, 209ch2n4
Duplessis, Ann, 33

Earl (Rosebud): and church, 150, 190; and cooperative rebuilding among friends, 155; and evacuation, 11, 13, 34; and FEMA trailer, 59; in kin charts, xxif, xxixf; and return to St. Bernard Parish, 62, 65, 73; and search for a new mobile home for Katie, 139
Ebonics, 213n5
elders: and church roles, 151; and evacuation, 12; on family history, 144–145; on grandchildren, 190; and graveyard rituals, 27; loss of, 126–127, 174; protectiveness toward, 130; and rituals honoring Katie after death, 183; and socialization of children, 85; specialties of, 134. See also specific elders
Elie, Lolis, xxif, 86–87
emotional ecosystem, 37
Ethel May's Branch, xxviiif
ethnographic work, 185, 191, 203–206
evacuation: during Katrina, 7–8, 10, 13; during past hurricanes, 27; and gender differences, 207n8; and schooling quality, 75; and traffic flow, 12
evacuation route, 14f–15f
extended family, 144, 203–204. See also family

Fair Housing Act, 166, 219n8
faith-based organizations, 103, 153–154, 192. See also Long Term Recovery Groups (LTRGs)

family: and child-care sharing, 85; and coping systems, 129–130, 134; as cultural unit, 30; and culture cycle, 53f; and FEMA trailers, 87; and food traditions, 40–43; and graveyard rituals, 27; interdependence of, 1, 35, 116, 144–145, 147–149; meaning of, 76, 144, 191–192, 204; nuclear versus rhizome, 36–37; and parish race relations, 68; and recovery culture, 23–24, 32–33, 114, 124–126, 157; and response to disaster, 72–73; and succession, 127. See also extended family; nuclear family; specific people; specific traditions
family gatherings: at Audrey's after Katrina, 128; as coping strategy, 129; as cultural resource, 53f; importance of to bayou culture, 124; as important to recovery, 193f; and information circulation, 149; Katie's understanding of importance of, 84–85; as leveling events, 153. See also food
fatigue, 86, 122, 212n8
FEMA (Federal Emergency Management Agency): and bureaucratic norms of communication, 87, 89–90, 91–92, 94, 95–97, 117; and Connie as culture broker, 23–24, 31–32, 35; and contractors, 79, 100–101, 102, 175, 214n18; and disaster preparedness exercises, 214n14; and disaster response, 98; and fraud, 134, 166; inflexibility of, 213n10; institutional problems of, 122; and Isleños, 172–173; Junior Rodriguez on, 60; and Katie's prosthetic leg, 89; and lack of empathy, 111; and long-term recovery from Katrina, 192; and LTRG in St. Bernard Parish, 103; and mental health care, 125, 129; and misunderstanding of bayou culture, 114; and paperwork, 61; and payouts to mortgage banks, 155–156; and post-disaster mandates, 99; and post-Katrina fraud, 215n25; and racist parish policies, 164; and repairs in white communities, 168–169; and rhetoric-action disconnect, 87, 102; and St. Bernard

63; and Murphy Oil refinery spill, 210ch4n7; and St. Bernard High, 167; and Violet Park No. 2, 169. *See also* levees
hurricane season, 7–8, 75

individualism, 189, 210n2
Industrial Canal, 18, 63
informal economies, 160f
insurance, 82, 86–87, 89, 117–118, 134, 153–154, 155
Iraq War, 131
Iris fulva Ker-Gawl, 200f
Isleños, 10, 49, 58, 158, 172, 210ch4n1, 210–211n10. *See also* Canary Islanders; Catholics; community
Isleños Museum complex, 170, 172, 211n11

Jackson, Andrew, 58
jambalaya, 26
Janice (Tambrella), xxf, xxvf, 96–97, 106, 133, 153, 196f
Janie (Johnson), 26, 34
job opportunities: for bayou residents, 59; before and after Katrina, 122, 135–136, 152–153; and child-care sharing, 85; and disaster opportunism, 166; during evacuation, 35; and growth machine, 16; and Katrina cleanup effort, 175; and race, 162; in St. Bernard Parish versus Dallas, 73–74; in upper parish, 10, 161; versus welfare, 96
Johnson-Fernandez family: and English dialects, 93–94; as focus of ethnographic study, 203–204; generations of, 58–59; and new rituals, 190; and rituals honoring Katie after death, 183; and sense of community, 72–73; simplified kin charts of, xxiif; 2008 reunion of, 146f, 149; 2014 reunion of, 191
Johnson-Fernandez family reunions, 143, 146f, 147–148, 149, 191
Johnson Gang, the, xxiif
Junior (Rodriguez, Henry): and Buffy, 19; and Connie as culture broker, 61; on

decision to return home after Katrina, 65; and evacuation, 7; and Katie's viewing, 182; on Katrina devastation, 60; and meeting with Connie on racial bias, 74, 162; as parish president, xxif, 24, 25f; and 2007 election loss, 138, 164

Kahneman, Daniel, 156
Katie (Williams), 9f; and bureaucratic norms of communication, 116–118; as caregiver before her stroke, 153; on church, 127–128, 137; as church usher, 150; at Connie's home in Dallas, 24; on cooking, 48, 51–52; on Dallas living, 40, 43–44; as deputy sheriff, 188; and evacuation, 7–8, 11–13, 16; on experience as sole black person at work, 163; and family gatherings, 85; and FEMA trailer, 59; on FEMA trailer life, 77, 81, 84; and food trips, 47; and goal of manufactured home, 154; on gumbo, 42; and help with kin mapping, 148–149; and her accessible trailer, 108; and her trailer's limited space, 217n21; on home, 72; and home lost to Katrina, 66; and injury on FEMA trailer steps, 87–90; on Katrina devastation, 26–27, 33–34, 71; in kin charts, xxf, xxiiif–xxxif; on language, 45; and loss of sense of control after stroke, 140; and loss of son Leon, 30; and money worries, 139; new home of, 199f; and post-Katrina stress, 130; on racism inherent in school name change, 168; and recovery process, 189; and return to St. Bernard Parish, 62, 68–69; and rituals honoring the dead, 181–188; and Road Home, 109–113, 119–121, 155; and Trashell's wedding celebration, 132–134; work of, 59
Katie's Branch, xxixf
Katie's carport, 84–85, 110, 129, 133, 154, 163
kinship charts, xxiif–xxxif, 30
kinship networks, 5–6, 192, 205
kitchen, 26–27, 33–35, 136–138

nature and humans, inseparability of in family, 41; separation of in Western life, 207–208n13

Nell (Rosebud): and church choir, 150; in Dallas, 26; and evacuation, 10–11, 13; and family gatherings, 8, 34; on FEMA compensation, 157; and FEMA trailer, 59; and Katie's injury, 89; in kin charts, xxf, xxif, xxixf; on language, 44; and return to St. Bernard Parish, 62; and rituals honoring Katie after death, 182, 183, 187; and Road Home payment, 109; on snakes in FEMA trailers, 81; with Trashell and Ameir, 198f; and Trashell's wedding celebration, 132–133; and work at elementary school, 153

New Orleans: and arrival of Katrina, 18; and breaches of levees and flood walls, 208n19; cuisine of, 49–50; and desegregation, 159; and displaced schoolkids, 209n3; and evacuation order, 10; and family size, 5; maps of, xxxiif–xxxiiif; and rituals honoring the dead, 27; versus St. Bernard Parish, 30

New Orleans, Battle of, 58

nongovernmental organizations, 153–154. *See also specific organizations*

nonprofits, 103

nonverbal communication, 96

nuclear family, 36. *See also* family

oil and gas, 17, 58, 59, 104, 161. *See also* canals

oil-spill contracts, 175

oral culture and tradition, 145, 152, 217–218n4

Orleans Parish, 13, 63, 166

parish police, 178–179

parish politicians, 104. *See also specific people*

Peachy (James, Alma Johnson), xxf–xxxif, 8, 30–31, 58–59, 71

Peachy Gang, the, 201f; and absence of weak ties, 209n6; and cemetery be-

hind Verret church, 188; and church traditions, 150; as collective, 36; and Dunbar's social brain hypothesis, 209n4; and family history, 144; as focus of ethnographic study, 30–31, 203–204; and Hurricane Betsy, 12; and Johnson-Fernandez family reunion, 147–148, 191; and Katie's death, 181–189; and lack of cultural comforts in Dallas, 44; and lower parish race relations, 68; and management of kin charts, 207n4; members of, xxf–xxif; and new rituals, 190; oldest generation of, 9f; origins of, 8; and protectiveness toward elders, 130; and sense of community, 72–73; simplified kin charts of, xxiif–xxxif; and succession, 127; and Trashell's wedding celebration, 132–133

Peek, Lori, 215–216n2

Pitt, Brad, 139, 217n22

plantation labor, 173

plantations, 160f

Plaquemines Parish, 10

Pop (Maurice, Eugene), xxxf, 48, 153

porch, as part of parish culture, 69

port authority, 161

post-traumatic stress disorder (PTSD), 220n1

Potchie (Smith): as business owner of trucking company, 100, 152; as church leader, 150; and cooking, 48; and cooperative rebuilding among friends, 155; and Darleene, 150, 152–153; on family ties, 144; at Johnson-Fernandez family reunion, 146f; in kin charts, xxif; and loss of elders after Katrina, 174; and post-Katrina stress, 130

powerlessness, 217n16

Precious (James), xxviif, 13, 26, 75, 105

prison, and structural racism, 176

psychologists, 220n2

PTSD. *See* post-traumatic stress disorder (PTSD)

public health, 134

public spaces, 86

race relations: after Katrina, 219n11; complexity of in St. Bernard Parish, 178–179; and court decisions, 165–166; and job opportunities, 162; and need for trust to spark conversations about, 161; in St. Bernard Parish, 68, 74, 80, 158, 180. *See also* bayou culture; Catholics

racism: lower levels of in cities evacuated to, 163; and oppressed people, 216n10; personal and social costs of, 179; of some parish business owners, 165–166; and St. Bernard Parish schools, 167–168

Raymond (James), xxif, xxiiif–xxxif, 68

Raymond's Branch, xxvif

recovery culture: and anthropology, 194–195; versus bayou culture, 91; and blindness to St. Bernard Parish's history of race-related problems, 180; and bureaucratic norms of communication, 95, 118; and culture brokers, 38f; of institutions, 24; language of, 213n7; and loss of control after Katrina, 192; and need to learn about and support local culture, 193f; and ways it failed bayou people, 189. *See also specific agencies*

Red Cross, 23, 31, 153–154

red iris, 1, 200f

Reggio, 158, 168

religion, 68, 188. *See also* black churches

revisionist history, 172

rhizome, as metaphor for large, interconnected family, 37, 73, 126, 132, 145, 189–190, 191

Rhodes Funeral Home, 181

risk communication, 212n1

Road Home: and automated phone system, 111; and bureaucratic norms of communication, 92, 94; and failure to recognize bayou homeowner status, 127; and formula for compensation, 157; funding and administration of, 212n4; institutional problems of, 122; and lack of continuity, 113, 114; and lack of local awareness, 192; and loss of Katie's file, 119–120; in Louisiana versus Mississippi, 218ch9n5; and mental health during recovery, 125; and post-Katrina stress, 131; and Roz and Charles's new home, 190; and settlement amounts, 139; versus Small Business Administration programs, 130; and uncertainty of payment time, 82, 106, 109; and unequal payment amounts, 154, 155–156; and verification phase, 110, 116–118

Robin (James): and black bayou dialect, 92; and bureaucratic norms of communication, 94; at Connie's home in Dallas, 26; and direct response to racism, 178; and evacuation, 13; generosity of, 105; in kin charts, xxf, xxviif; and life in FEMA trailer, 61, 82; and loss of elders after Katrina, 174; on parish politics, 104; and post-Katrina stress, 106, 130, 138–139; on racism inherent in school changes, 168; on returning home, 74–76, 80; work of, 153

rootedness, importance of, 126

Roseana (Maurice), 9f, 196f, 199f; as church usher, 150; at Connie's home in Dallas, 26, 34; and family gatherings, 7–8; and home lost to Katrina, 66; in kin charts, xxf, xxif, xxiiif; on new Verret church, 136–137; and post-Katrina stress, 130; and Road Home payment, 109, 156; seventieth birthday of, 191; and toxic drywall from China, 190; and Trashell's wedding celebration, 133; work of, 59

Roseana's Branch, xxxf

roux, 51–52

Roz (King), xxf, xxixf; with Chuck, 199f; and church service, 150; on cooking, 54; and homeowner status, 127; on importance of making elders whole, 130–132; as Katie's caretaker, 140, 185; and Katie's viewing and wake, 181, 183; on lack of respect from recovery authorities, 96–97; and loss of elders